Internet Voting Now!

Here's How. Here's Why – So You Can Kiss Citizens United Goodbye!

William J. Kelleher, Ph.D.

The Internet Voting Research and Education Fund

Los Angeles, California

William J. Kelleher, Ph.D.

To the men and women of our Founding Generation, who were willing to sacrifice everything for the Original American Dream –

Liberty through Self-Government

CONTENTS

ACKNOWLEDGMENTS

While no corporate contributions supported the writing of this book, many individuals offered commentary and encouragement, or provided useful information. Among the many are R. Michael Alvarez, Robert Bennett, Gordon Cook, Ed Gerck, Julia Glidden, Thad Hall, Tarvi Martens, Michael Shamos, Ted Selker, Mark Strassman, and Richard Winger. My wife Crista, and Terry Kennedy provided invaluable editorial assistance. The cover art is by Rene. I am solely responsible for all errors and omissions.

Introduction

Here Comes Internet Voting! Are We Prepared?

Like the horseless carriage 100 years ago, Internet voting is coming to the USA.

Successful trials were conducted in the US in 2000, 2004, 2008, and 2010. Congress encouraged online voting in the 2009 MOVE ACT (Military and Overseas Voters Empowerment Act). In the November 2010 elections, 33 states gave some form of Internet voting a try so that their overseas voters, especially those in the military, could vote conveniently. There have been no reports of either technical or security problems. Indeed, West Virginia's secretary of state, Natalie Tennant, tried a small experiment with Internet voting on the state's secure website, and promptly requested that the state legislature allocate funds to expand the practice. Arizona has provided its overseas voters with some form of Internet voting (such as fax or email) since 2003, and there have been no technical or security problems.[1]

Alaska, Arizona, Hawaii, Michigan, and most recently, Washington state, have each conducted Internet voting trials for their citizens to vote from within the state's borders. Each of these experiments has worked out well. More trials of Internet voting within states are likely to begin soon.

The only failed Internet voting trial in the US was in Washington D.C. in October of 2010. No actual vote was held, but when the public was invited to test the system it was hacked. Hopefully, D.C. officials have learned from their mistake of hiring low cost amateur programmers to set up the system.2

As I show in Chapter One, Internet voting is increasing all around the world. Over the last 10 years, several nations in Europe, and provinces in Canada, have been testing Internet voting systems with success. Elections Canada, which manages national elections in Canada, recommended in August 2011 that Parliament consider making online voting the primary means of voting for the nation. The Russian Duma recently began considering plans to try Internet voting for voters in remote locations, such as Siberia. Estonia leads the world in Internet voting, where participation rates among all age groups increases with each election. Indeed, the Estonian model is transferable to every nation in the world. 3

The companies that have successfully built Internet voting systems have been in every state capital in the US, pitching their products to legislators and elections officials. Local elections officials are beginning to realize that voting via the Net is much cheaper to administer than paper-based polling place voting. Over time, convenience for voters, and savings in the costs of election administration, will be too tempting to resist. Of course, no voting technology is greener than paperless Internet voting. This change is inevitable.

Here, too, is an instance where technological change presents a rare opportunity for the progressive reform of US election practices. Now is the time for progressives to plan, not on how to resist the change, but on how to turn it to our advantage. If we do nothing, or if we protest and fail, Internet voting will emerge as the way Americans vote, and our political system will be no better for it. But if we look ahead, and plan well, we can turn Internet voting into a progressive reform of historic proportions.

What sort of progressive reform? Internet voting, rightly organized, can neutralize the power of Big Money in all US elections. The focal point of Big Money's leverage is the cost of campaigns for those who seek public office, and this book shows precisely how that lock on the political system can be broken. Hence, the main aim of this book is to bring some very original thinking into the public discussion over how to undo the pernicious effects of political money in our democracy.

Because I am keenly aware of the opposition to, and mistrust of, e-voting systems, I know that this book has a heavy burden of proof to overcome. I tackle this challenge in two ways.

First, I address the fear and mistrust of the new technology, which is widespread among progressive, and other, election reformers. Internet voting is often thought to be a prescription for a complete corporate takeover of our election system – indeed, a Republican conspiracy! The first chapter confronts that misunderstanding head on. It recounts the short history of Internet voting in the US and around the world, and addresses the specific claims about the supposed vulnerability of the technology to manipulation. I show that Internet voting security technology is as sophisticated and reliable as the security technology used daily by the US military, international e-commerce and finance, as well as online banking and shopping. I revisit the security issue in the fifth chapter, after the reader has seen how truly liberating and democratizing Internet voting can be.

Of course, convincing the reader of Internet voting's liberating and democratizing potential is the second major challenge for the book. Hence, in Chapter Two I use a seemingly incongruous source to support my advocacy of Internet voting. That chapter is entitled "The Original Intentions of the Framers for Presidential Elections." Those among the Founding Generation who actually wrote our Constitution are known as "the Framers." Drawing from documents such as The Federalist Papers, Madison's Notes on the Philadelphia Convention, Washington's Farewell Address, and quotes from the US Constitution, I highlight the procedures that the Framers of the Constitution originally envisioned for the election of our president and vice president. I show that they originally intended these procedures, centered on the Electoral College, to be as orderly and conducive to reason and deliberation as was their convention in Philadelphia.

Surprisingly to us modern Americans, they anticipated that the costs of elections would be *insignificant*, and that candidates for the two executive offices would *not campaign* in public, and hence not spend any money on getting themselves elected. Well, that didn't work as planned. Some readers may also be surprised to learn that the Framers also intended their system to *deter* political parties from coming to dominate the process. Of course, that didn't work out either, and I offer some reasons why.

In Chapter Three I contrast our country's current presidential election practices with the original intentions of the Constitution's Framers, as discussed in Chapter Two. Some readers may be saddened to see how far off track our practices have become. For example, candidate Obama raised and spent over $740,000,000 in his 2008 campaign. He will likely raise and spend over *one billion* dollars for his reelection campaign in 2012.

According to the Federal Election Commission (FEC),[4] total spending by candidates and their political parties exceeded 1.8 billion dollars in 2008. This was nearly twice the amount they spent in the 2004 campaign. On top of that, individuals and organized groups, such as corporations and unions, collectively spent $168.8 million to advocate the election or defeat of presidential candidates during the 2008 campaign. So, the total spent for 2008 is almost two billion dollars. But, because of the *Citizens United* decision, that may be peanuts compared to the amounts to be raised and spent in the 2012 campaign.

In 2010, the Supreme Court issued its decision in the case of *Citizens United v. the FEC*. Five of the nine

Justices agreed, among other things, that federal government regulations of the independent spending by corporations and unions in political campaigns is an unconstitutional infringement on their freedom of speech. The High Court struck down those regulations. So, without these restrictions, the sky is the limit on how much money these giant organizations can spend for and against presidential candidates.

As I said, besides anticipating *cost free* presidential elections, the Framers hoped for a *nonpartisan* process; but, of course, it has become thoroughly partisan. My position is that such costs and partisanship need not be.

Chapter Four shows how the *new* technology of Internet voting, rightly organized, can fully satisfy the *old* hopes of the Framers for a deliberative presidential election process that would cost the candidates nothing. Let *Citizens United* be the rule; in the system I propose, big spending will be allowed, but it will have little or no effect on the decision-making of the American voter. This chapter will show both a) how our elections can become more of an education for the electorate by encouraging deliberation and rational thinking, and b) how the power of Big Money in elections can be neutralized.

In Chapter Five, as I have said, I revisit the security issue, for a final rebuttal of the critics of Internet voting. And in the book's Conclusion, entitled "What is to be done," I suggest how Internet voting can be implemented. That will be done as the people are ready for it, state-by-state. I also outline other ways by which Internet voting can further democratize American politics.

The "Internet Revolution" in the politics of the United States, and around the world, has only just begun. One day, perhaps not far away, e-technology will help to elevate civilization to heights of civic morality now regarded as mere dreaming. Here is our chance to take an important step along that path to a new political reality. Let's get started.

Chapter One

Internet Voting: The Great Security Scare

PART I: UNDERSTANDING SECURITY

SECURITY! Of course, this is what most folks worry about first when the subject of Internet voting comes up. This is a very emotional issue. While everyone can see the convenience offered by Internet voting in all US elections, the fear factor looms large in many minds. Because feelings about this matter are so intense, security must be the first topic addressed in a book that advocates taking such a revolutionary leap forward.

This Chapter will present a social science paradigm for critically evaluating the security concerns most often expressed by opponents of Internet voting. In 2004, these concerns were so effectively expressed that they resulted in the US government ceasing all efforts to even experiment with voting from overseas via the new technology. However, when now examined within a context of social scientific reasoning – that is, testing hypotheses against the known facts of social experience – the arguments that stopped the progress of Internet voting in the US appear as mere appeals to fear, bereft of rationality.

First, the problem of how to think about e-crime in general will be discussed. Secondly, the framework that emerges from that discussion will be applied to the arguments against Internet voting. The conclusion will suggest that Internet voting can be conducted with a degree of security similar to an online purchase, a million dollar bank transfer, or a secret military communication. As this chapter will show, the security technology already exists, and has been honed over many years of use. While there are differences between the military uses of the Internet, e-commerce, and Internet voting, I will argue that the *degree of security* for each need not vary significantly.

E-commerce, E-voting, E-mischief

Internet commerce and Internet voting differ in some significant ways. In an online purchase, for example, you know there was no cheating because what you paid for is delivered to your door. A detailed electronic record of your purchase exists. If your item is not delivered, or the wrong thing is delivered, your purchase can be proven by the e-record. If you transfer funds from one bank account to another, your name and personal information go along with it. That way, the transaction can be traced and proven, if it should ever be questioned. If there is an error on your credit card report, you can show the credit card company your signed receipt, and they will correct the mistake. Even military communications must be from an identified sender, to an identified receiver.

But, as I will discuss further below, with Internet voting the name of the registered voter and how he or she voted must never be linked together. If a voter received a detailed receipt, whether on paper or by e-mail, indicating how he or she voted, such misconduct as large scale vote buying and selling, as well as voter coercion, would be possible.

The advantages of not linking the voter's name and vote are the voter's privacy, and the prevention of the kind of misconduct mentioned. However, there are other forms of cheating possible in e-voting, which are not possible in e-commerce. One example is the stuffed ballot box. If there are more votes than live voters, then election officials and voters can know there was mischief. But since there is no name/vote link, the bad votes cannot be taken out. What remedies are there when a stuffed ballot box has been discovered? Either all the votes must be counted, or a new election held, or votes must be randomly tossed out until the number of votes matches the number of voters. None of these options is a happy one. A good election should have the exact same number of votes as voters. Undervotes, fewer votes than voters, are less worrisome than over votes, more votes than voters.

Stuffed ballot boxes have been a problem for voting administration since the day the first ballot boxes were used. Whether black and white stones are collected, or paper ballots, the temptation to add votes under the cover of anonymity has often been too alluring to resist. When such stuffing can be done electronically, especially by remote means, the very outcome of an election could be determined by a single wrongdoer. The integrity of the 2004 presidential election was marred by allegations and suspicions of e-mischief. That was the first presidential election to use the newly introduced "DREs," or direct recording electronic touch screen voting machines.

DREs were sold to state election officials as a cure for some of the ills seen on TV in the 2000 presidential election. The pictures of Florida poll workers squinting to measure whether a hanging chad was more than half poked out, and thus probably a vote, or less than half poked out, and thus probably indicating that the voter had changed his or her mind and not completed that vote, have become a part of American history. Seeing this, and hearing of other voting technology problems, Congress passed the Help America Vote Act, or HAVA, in 2002. That law made billions of dollars available to the states to buy new voting equipment. Some of the companies that made ATM machines quickly produced the DRE, with the promise that it would operate as flawlessly as the ATMs. Since the states were spending federal money, and not their own, the DREs sold like hotcakes.

Unfortunately, there were some unexpected questions raised about the use of DREs. These machines gave new meaning to the old worry about stuffed ballot boxes. Some voters actually reported seeing their "x" move automatically from the candidate they favored to the candidate they disfavored. Were the machines programmed to do this? In some jurisdictions, exit polls suggested that a majority of voters favored the guy who the machines tallied as losing. Were the machines remotely controlled to stuff the ballot box? If the machines were honest, were they secure? If not secure, did hackers break in and change the vote totals? Why did the machine manufacturers insist on keeping their programming codes a secret?

DREs With Paper Receipts

In response to the disaffection caused by the DREs in 2004, some people have suggested that the machines should be made to produce a paper receipt, like a cash register, or a gas pump. Then the voter could read and verify what the receipt states, or report any errors on it. This "voter verification," they say, would boost public confidence in the technology. Of course, this receipt would not be for taking home, nor would it identify the voter. The voter would check the paper, and then drop it in a box, or only view it under glass and never touch it. Then, if there are suspicions of ballot box stuffing, because the number of votes exceeds the number of voters, or the exit polls contradict the tally, the paper receipts can be taken out and either counted by hand, or by a paper scanning machine.

Whether all the folks who advocate this idea are financed by the DRE manufacturers, or only some of them, cannot be known for sure. In any case, the manufactures think this is a wonderful idea. Then they can continue to sell the voting machines, and also sell the printers and scanners needed to add on to the DREs. They would make more millions on servicing, supplying ink and paper, and selling new machines when the old ones wear out.

But in practice, this "solution" would surely fail to satisfy the public's desire for fair elections. DREs can be programmed to print out one vote on paper, and record another in the e-ballot box. While doing that, the machine can keep the number of votes the same as the number of voters, so that election officials would have no reason to hold an expensive and time consuming hand recount. The margin of victory can be remotely controlled, or programmed, so that it remains within the statistical margin of error that exit polls are known to operate with, such as plus or minus 3%. Here again, since there is no contradiction with exit polls, there would be no reason for a recount. Random hand recounts are expensive, time consuming, frustrate the public because they delay the announcement of results, and are more likely to miss fraud than catch it. Because fraudulent voting occurs far less often than honest voting, random samples are far more likely to pick out an honest count than a dishonest one. Hence, their value is dubious.

Using a so-called paper audit trail has another serious flaw. Carefully checking the receipt requires more time and effort than many voters are willing to give. Many simply vote and leave the polling place without bothering to check the paper audit trail. On the other hand, suppose a voter sees an error in the paper receipt. If he or she reports the error, all privacy and secrecy are surrendered. The voter would have to announce in the polling place, "I wanted to vote for Obama, but the receipt shows McCain," or "I wanted to vote to support same sex marriage, but the receipt is marked against it." For people who put a high value on the privacy of their votes, this would be a tough choice. Some might walk away in disgust rather than have their privacy violated. Thus, paper receipts will often go unverified.

Of course, voters do not face such onerous choices in the commercial world. An error on a paper receipt can be brought to the store manager's attention, and none of the other shoppers will pay any heed to the event. One might even complain on the store floor that this bra, or these boxer shorts, do not fit right, and take no risk of public shame or ridicule. A polling place and a department store are very different environments, in no small part because people have different privacy expectations in them.

Another problem with DREs is that operating them is often more confusing for the voters than reading and marking a paper ballot, or writing a check. Thus, voter privacy is also likely to be compromised if a voter needs the assistance of a poll worker to operate the DRE. Touch screens are designed by technical geeks, some of whom have no idea of the shock that low-tech voters can feel when suddenly confronted by a maze of squares, buttons, lights, and instructions, especially when there is a line of other voters waiting for their turn to vote. A confused voter could be forced to choose between pushing buttons at random, and hoping it comes out right, or calling for help, feeling ashamed, and risk having some poll worker know how the voter voted.

Finally, making the trek to a polling place, either before or after work, on Election Day, searching for a parking space, and then standing in line, all so that you can confront the problems raised by DREs, is a circumstance that is unlikely to invite greater voter participation, even if the machine spits out a paper receipt. All told, then, while a profitable business for their manufactures, DREs do not make the kind of positive contribution to democracy that electronic technology is capable of making.

An event parallel to the rise of voting on DREs, however, is the now daily use of online commerce. The trust in these systems, and the user's self-confidence in his or her ability to operate their own equipment, has built up among consumers after many years of experience with online commerce. This trust and self-confidence can be transferred over to online voting. If folks can pay bills and buy things online, from home or work or any other place, by PC or cell phone, why can't the same be done for voting?

Living in a Hostile Environment

Of course, online security is never a final, stagnant condition. It is a continual learning process. Both the number of Internet users and the ways of using the Internet are rapidly increasing. The market for computer ownership in the US and around the world is very far from saturated. As more people acquire and learn to use computers, fresh thinking will be applied to its uses, for both good and ill. That is why security threats are, and will continue to be, *a constant challenge* in the online environment.

Hacking is an attraction for many a bright and mischievous mind. Getting rich quick is also a powerful motivation for people. Some folks try it through lawful gaming, or risky business endeavors. Others try it through unlawful means. Because banks are where the money is, as Willie Sutton is reputed to have said, they are irresistible targets for unlawful attempts to withdraw other people's funds. Bankers have had to learn from experience how best to protect the money of their depositors. Lock-making and vault-building have evolved into extremely high-tech sciences by a process of *natural selection*. That is, in the free market, only those security systems survive that the crooks cannot break into.

Evolution, then, can be a paradigm for understanding the development of online security. The forces of natural selection are as resourceful and ruthless as any virus, bacteria, or cancer in nature. But the best online security experts are fast learners, and just as resourceful, if not more so, than the heartless hackers who prey upon their inadequately protected victims. Online security practices continue to adapt well to the hostile environment of the World Wide Web. That is why e-commerce flourishes today.

Hackers probe the security of Internet banking systems 24/7. But no bank loses money today simply because some Wizard of Oz-like hacker has found a way to break into its system and transfer gobs of money to his Swiss account. That only happens in the movies. Money, to be sure, does get stolen from banks. But these losses are more due to such causes as armed robbery, embezzlement, check fraud, insider dishonesty, and identity theft, rather than to genius hackers.

Since the beginning of the PC Revolution, torrents of misinformation have been pouring out of the press, broadcast media, and online sources about the mythical powers of hackers to break into supposedly secure websites and steal from them, or engage in various forms of malicious mischief. Consequently, the *reputation* of online security is out of sync with society's actual experience with the technology. If reputation were reflective of facts, then many of today's doubters would feel more confidence in online security. Let us take a moment to consider the actual conditions of online security.

Identity theft has emerged as the dark side of e-commerce. Occasionally true stories appear about huge amounts of data being lost or stolen from big institutions like banks, credit card companies, and credit rating agencies. Sometimes this data is then used to steal the identities of unfortunate folks. With sufficient information, such as name, birth date, social security number, or credit card number, etc. a villainous hacker can wreak havoc in the lives of innocent victims. Charges can be made in dozens of stores, and bank accounts drained. In some cases, years pass before the victims can have all their records straightened out, their identities secured, and their reputations as good credit risks restored.

While the Internet enables companies to amass huge amounts of personal information, and our law permits it, developing a sense of ethical responsibility for protecting that information has lagged behind the rapid emergence of the technology. Companies that profit by the gathering of consumer and customer information are learning both what their responsibility is and how to fulfill that responsibility. Laws, lawsuits, and loss of market share are teaching these firms that their chief responsibility is to protect the privacy of the people whose information they lawfully possess and sell. These companies must adapt or perish.

Experience shows that the reasons for electronically stored data loss can be divided into two general categories. One is the quality of protective services that companies, and PC owners, subscribe to. Since hackers are a natural part of the Internet environment, incompetent or inadequate protective services are a major enabling condition for data loss. The other category of reasons for data loss includes all the sources of data loss that are extraneous to protective software, such as human error and misbehavior.

US law requires that companies which possess personal information on employees, customers, or the public in general report any security breach to those people who might be affected. Letters sent out with these reports usually become news items, and are reported in the press or broadcast media. One example of how the law works is the Choice Point loss of data in February 2005. Nearly 150,000 people were affected by the security breach. Choice Point lawfully gathered personal information on consumers, and sold it largely to marketing companies. But, while the information was collected, stored, and sent to clients electronically, the breach was not due to hacking.

Their system was secure against that. However, company personnel were fooled by information thieves who posed as legitimate businesses, subscribed to the service, and used the information to steal identities. Several hundred people reported monetary loses due to this identity theft. Had the employees followed standard credential checking processes, this loss would not have happened.5

Since the Choice Point incident, some public spirited foundations, and privacy rights groups, have begun to gather these news reports and post the information on their websites so that everyone can see what is happening in the realm of personal information security. A leader in this field is the Open Security Foundation. It provides a continually updated list of events on its website, at www.DataLossDB.org.6 The list shows the date the breach occurred, the company, the cause of the breach, and how many people could be affected by the breach.

This list of historical facts helps to put online security issues in their proper perspective. One of the trends shown is that over the years, and currently, breaches due to hacking occur far less often than breaches due to human mistake or misconduct. A companion trend is *the learning curve* of the companies. For instance, there are three major consumer credit reporting agencies in the US. These are Equifax, Experian, and TransUnion. The Data Loss "blotter" shows that Equifax had six reported security breaches between 2005 and 2007. An employee's lap top, containing 2500 consumer records, was stolen in 2006. There were four instances of "unauthorized access." These involved employees abusing their access privileges, and someone using a customer's access code without the owner's permission. Only one instance of hacking occurred. That was in 2005, in an office in Canada. But no information losses have been reported by Equifax since 2007.

Experian reported five incidents of unauthorized access in branch offices, during the 2006-2007 period, but none after that. No reports of hacking. And, TransUnion has reported only two loss incidents. One was a stolen computer with information on 3600 consumers. That happened in 2005. The other instance of data loss was due to a scam like the one with Choice Point. That was in 2006, and that was the last loss they have had to report.

Identity thieves would love to break into the data bases of these big companies. Personal information on tens of millions of consumers is stored in those files. Hackers are at it everyday. But the security systems of the companies have evolved to such a high level of sophistication that for the past several years they have foiled the efforts of every hacker.

In 2002, an unemployed British computer expert, Gary McKinnon, hacked into several "unclassified," i.e., minimum security, US military computer systems, including one for NASA. No top secret information was compromised. He was not a spy, he was just looking for info on UFOs. Foolishly, he left an e-trail straight to his home, and within the year Scotland Yard nabbed him.

Upon his arrest in England, a US prosecutor crowed, "The success of this investigation serves as a warning to all hackers: You are not invisible. You cannot act anonymously on the Internet ... If you hack us, we will find you and we will prosecute you and we will send you to prison."7 But the wheels of justice grind slowly. In early 2009, McKinnon was on his second appeal to the House of Lords, Britain's highest court, fighting extradition to the US. If we can get him here, he faces 70 years in prison and a $2,000,000 fine.8

Surely the military has learned lessons from this experience, and so have the managers of computer systems in other organizations. Building secure systems is a trial and error process, and the fast learners have fewer problems than the dunces.

One of the biggest sources of data loss by companies, government agencies, and other organizations is due to lost or stolen electronic gadgets. Hard working employees in these institutions that possess personal information often take work home. The information is stored in their lap tops, flash drives, blackberries, and portable hard drives. These things get stolen from their cars, or forgotten on a bus or park bench, or left in a bar or restaurant. Sometimes burglars steal the equipment while the innocent and exhausted employee is at home asleep.

In 2008, according to Data Loss, AT&T reported the theft of an employee's lap top, with an unknown amount of personnel information in the memory. The US Department of Veterans Affairs reported that twice in 2006 VA computers were stolen containing information on millions of veterans.9 A medical clinic in Santa Maria, California had to write letters to 3200 patients telling them that a blackberry, which might have their personal information on it, had been stolen in April, 2009.[10] The year before, T-Mobile had to report that a disk containing records on seventeen million customers was lost.[11] There have been several reports of citizens of Great Britain ironically forgetting where they last laid down a memory stick full of their employer's important info.

Another source of material for identity thieves is trash containers. Despite numerous stories being broadcast over the media and written about in the press, some companies still have not gotten the message. Reports of printed customer records being tossed into unsecured dumpsters by careless employees often surface in the news. In 2006, the Los Angeles County Department of Social Services had to notify 94,000 people that unshredded documents with their info had been thrown into the trash.[12]

That same year, Chase Card Services reported that one of its employees tossed transaction tapes into the trash with information on 2.6 million current and former Circuit City credit card account holders.[13] A company spokesperson said that the tapes were later dumped in a land fill, so harm to customers was unlikely. Threats to the privacy of patients occur when old or duplicate medical records are simply tossed into the trash. Such reports as these will probably stop once all companies go fully digital in their record keeping.[14]

Some things that might never stop are employee error and employee theft. Employee theft has happened in the offices of even the most reputable companies, such as Sprint, UPS, and MySpace. Employees, entrusted with access codes, have stolen customer information and sold it to spammers and identity thieves. This seems to be a crime of impulse by novice wrongdoers, who rarely get away with it.

In 2009, a school district in Tennessee was embarrassed when one of its employees inadvertently posted the names, addresses, and social security numbers of all its students on its web site for visitors to access without a password. Schools and universities seem to specialize in this particular error. However, a Data Loss graph suggests that accidents like this have been on the decline since their height in early 2008.15 It seems that administrators in these institutions also follow a learning curve. In 2007, a Fraternal Order of the Police group donated a computer to charity, not realizing that it contained financial and other personal information of its members.

Early in 2008, a $150,000,000 per year company specializing in the sale of software and computer accessories from its website, which proudly displayed a "Hacker Safe" seal, had to send out security breach notices to its customers. Apparently, an employee turned off the hacker protection while working on the website, and left the system vulnerable.16 Assuming that hackers had been ceaselessly probing for a way in, the good news here is that the protection worked when it was on.

Clearly, with the high level of security sophistication protecting people and firms in e-commerce, the victims of this crime are always going to be those folks with insufficiently protected systems. 60 Minutes reported that early in 2009 the computer department at   CBS was shocked to find that the "Conficker" worm had infested its highly protected system.17 The worm did not do anything worse than slow down some computer functions. It did not cause any damage, or steal any information. But it embarrassed the security guys, was a nuisance to remove, and made everybody wonder how it got there and what else could happen. Otherwise, the CBS security systems have proven to be quit effective.

The same 60 Minutes story had a segment about a fairly typical event. That is, a mom's computer became infected with spyware after her teenage sons used it to download pirated music and movies through file-sharing websites. The spyware cunningly shut down the mom's anti-spyware update program. Thus, even if her security service developed a way to identify and remove the bug, they would be blocked from entering her computer to uninstall it.

Then the spyware sent the bad guys the mom's banking information. With that, they were able to siphon money out of her account. But the bank's security was not itself breached by hackers. Indeed, the bank stopped the losses, and compensated the mom for what was taken. 60 Minutes added to the myth of unmanageable online insecurity when it neglected to say, somewhat irresponsibly, that the mom would not have had this problem but for her security service being unprofessional in failing to protect its update program from hackers. Such protection ought to be standard practice in all security companies.

A group of hackers in Seattle specialized in preying upon the naïve parents of file-sharing teens. They used file-sharing to get into PCs and search for the unprotected, or inadequately protected, identity information of the parents. Soon arrested, the ring leader received a four year sentence in 2008, and one of his protégés was indicted for the same crime in 2009.[18]

This is how natural selection works in the electronic jungle. Protective services fail, and the vulnerable become victims. On the positive side, however, if the protective software companies do not learn and adapt quickly, they will lose business to the more efficient companies. As long as people choose incompetent or inadequate protective services for their PCs, and their commercial websites, they risk becoming the next victim of the ubiquitous hackers. Indeed, ineptly constructed websites of all sorts continue to give joy to mischief makers and thieves. The Data Loss reports for 2009 show that a university's personnel and student records data base was broken into by outsiders. These were probably student pranksters. Another university's library data base was violated. And yet another US Army branch administrative data base was hacked into. As the Web Masters for these organizations are embarrassed by their neglect of proper security, they will learn to be more attentive to security issues.

If the media was as vociferous in broadcasting about the prosecutions of hackers as they are about the temporary successes of the hackers, that might also contribute to both a decline in the number of hackings, and an increase in the public's understanding of the crime. In reality, hackers only succeed against ineptly protected systems, and they are often caught and prosecuted.

31

The real news in this chronicle of data loss is not that some Internet miscreants are still able to find vulnerable systems in poorly protected places, but that the big targets, like banks, money managing firms, stock brokerages, and e-commerce websites are able to protect themselves from an unrelenting barrage of hungry hackers. Nasty hackers are hard at work on their computers in numerous places all over the world. The businesses that beat them set the standard for security that any system of Internet voting must meet, if it is to be worthy of public confidence. Indeed, this standard *has been met* by Internet voting systems in numerous foreign countries, and in trial cases in the US. It is my contention, therefore, that that standard for security set by the best of e-commerce can be met for Internet voting throughout the US.

The Fear Mongers

Public trust is the single greatest obstacle to the implementation of an Internet voting system in the United States. While most people can appreciate the convenience of online voting, from home or any place else, security concerns cause every prudent person to hesitate before plunging into the unknown. To be sure, there are additional concerns, especially among the more socially conscious citizens, about such matters as the "digital divide," digitally challenged seniors, and the disabled. Those folks can be accommodated. For example, The World Wide Web Consortium (W3C) has developed computer hardware and software for the blind and otherwise disabled.[19]

For those who do not own a PC or cell phone, etc., such as the homeless or poor, local election officials can designate computers in their offices for the public to come in and use. They can also offer computers for voting in schools and libraries. Vans can deliver lap tops for the house-bound to vote on. "Digital divide" concerns were more valid in the very early days of the Internet, such as the 1990s, but easy solutions now exist for these problems.

Still, encouraging public trust remains as the most difficult challenge for a proponent of Internet voting, such as I am, because of the vocal opposition to it.

The central rhetorical strategy of Internet voting's opposition is to fuel fear. They do this well. As I will show, their tactics are to employ baseless hyperbole, illogic, and misinformation. Using a willing media and blogospher, the anti-Internet voting propagandists have so far been very successful at creating in the public's mind an exaggerated image of online insecurity.

A cottage industry currently exists in the US, which provides a handful of these image manipulators with a handsome income. Some of them are free lance writers on elections issues who find that fear sells. Others are professional bloggers who sell advertising space on their blog websites. Many of them are computer science professors who hire out part-time as highly paid consultants and lobbyists. A few anti-Internet voting non-profits are doing well with private contributions; among the well-endowed are such nonprofits as ACCURATE, Verified Voting, the Overseas Voting Foundation, and Vote Here.

Despite their efforts to the contrary, since the late 1990s, the use of Internet voting systems has been increasing. Numerous organizations have been trying Internet voting as a way of facilitating decision-making. Corporations, businesses, and universities are using Internet voting to conduct management and personnel decision-making. Political parties have used it to decide which candidates their members want to support. State and local governments, from the New York City School Board to the Honolulu City Council, have also used Internet voting to elect their leadership.20 And, of course, popular TV shows, such as The People's Choice awards, American Idol, and Dancing with the Stars have used Internet voting to let the audience select contest winners. In all instances, security precautions have prevented perverted election results.21

Internet voting service providers have been successful at selling their product, in large part, because they are able to show a track record that convinces their clients of the security of their systems. In fact, there are numerous profit-making Internet voting service providers, which compete with one another for contracts. Currently, they include Accenture, Every One Counts, Intelivote, SafeVote, Scytl, Votenet, and VotingPlace.net. These, and other companies, are easily found on the Web. Their websites provide lists of their success stories. Despite the efforts of the fear mongers to the contrary, the use of Internet voting systems is increasing in both private and public sectors all over the world. Every successful instance is an example of the user's entrepreneurial courage and the system provider's professional skills.

Growth in the public sector, however, has been slowed significantly by the resistance. Anti-Internet voting activists have an array of effective tactics for achieving their goals. For example, when state legislatures and local governments are deliberating over a bill that would allow Internet voting by law, anti-Internet voting special interests, which could include the manufacturers of DREs, printers, paper products, and paper scanning machines, will hire these experts at fear stimulation in an effort to discourage the law makers with some heavy handed lobbying. By threatening to "go public" with scary claims of "insecurity," lack of protection for voter privacy, and vulnerability to hackers and fraud, these propagandists can intimidate timid law makers into backing away from experimenting with Internet voting.22

The career making moment of success came for the anti-Internet voting activists in late 2003. That is when the US Department of Defense (hereafter "DoD," which is their own abbreviation) was developing a program of Internet voting to make voting in US elections easier and more convenient for Americans living overseas, especially our men and women in uniform. Before showing how the good intentions of the DoD were defeated, I will sketch-in some background to explain the problem that the Department was hoping to solve.

PART II: THE RISE AND FALL OF SERVE

Disenfranchised Americans

The US Constitution puts the states in charge of administering all elections in our country. State legislatures not only make the laws for the conduct of their own state and local elections, but for federal elections as well. Article One, Section Four, gives state legislatures the power to regulate the elections of US senators and representatives. Article Two, Section One, gives the states the power to determine who the Electors will be in the Electoral College, which then elects the president and vice president.

Giving the states the responsibility for administering elections has had numerous consequences on American politics. One unanticipated consequence is especially important to the history of Internet voting in the United States.

While each state is given the responsibility for the conduct of all elections within its borders, none of the states is charged by the Constitution with providing a way for Americans overseas to vote. Since the founding of our nation, Americans, such as ambassadors, business people, teachers, students, travelers, workers, and our men and women in uniform, have had no standardized method for exercising their right to vote. Even Thomas Jefferson, once our ambassador to France, had no way to vote in his home state, Virginia, while overseas. Gradually, a few states began to provide ways for "absentee voting."

During the Civil War, some state election officials took ballots for the 1864 presidential election to soldiers from their jurisdictions that were encamped in other states. Then the soldiers marked their votes and handed back the ballots. Some Northern states allowed soldiers to vote absentee by mail. However, Congress did not pass any legislation making registration and voting laws uniform for military personnel at that time. The whole matter was left to the states.

Indeed, Congress did not pass any laws to help armed service personnel to vote until WWII. In 1942 Congress passed The Armed Forces Absentee Voting Act. Soldiers could request a special War Department ballot, which they would mark, and send back to the War Department. That Department would pass the ballot on to the local election officials. Participation was low, and many ballots were lost, or rejected, or otherwise not counted. This law was repealed in 1955, leaving our soldiers in Korea to work it out with their own state officials. Ditto for American personnel in Vietnam.

Starting with the 1968 presidential election, the Democratic and Republican parties made special efforts to help Americans overseas vote by absentee ballots. The parties organized in foreign countries, held meetings, and provided timely registration and voting information to their members. Thanks to the efforts of voting rights advocates, both in and outside of the military, Congress finally faced the problem and in 1986 passed the "Uniformed and Overseas Citizens Absentee Voting Act," which President Reagan signed into law. Its acronym is "UOCAVA" (pronounced U-O-CAVA).

The law supported the right of more than six million overseas military and civilian Americans to vote in federal elections. It required states to provide information, and to enact registration and voting procedures, especially for overseas Americans who claimed residency in their jurisdictions. Still, each state had its own rules and regulations for eligibility and residency. Also, deadlines for registration, to request absentee voting forms, and for having ballots mailed in to the local elections official varied from state to state. Since the law does not make the process uniform across the country, there are many instances of inefficiency and inequity.

One major problem is that the process is mostly based on snail mail. A written request for an absentee ballot has to be mailed by the American in a foreign land to the local voting authority in his or her home state. The US government offers a postage-free federally printed post card that can be used for this purpose. This written request (or post card) first goes through the foreign mail, then through the US mail, before it arrives at the local election official's office. (Out of a desire to avoid any connection with political activity, the military generally does not carry election materials through its mail channels.) When, and if, the request is responded to, a blank ballot is sent to the American via the same route. When, and if, it arrives, the voter marks his or her vote, and sends it back, paying the proper foreign and US postage, of course. By the time it arrives back home, if it ever does, it is usually set aside until the end of the election. Often, absentee ballots are left in a pile on somebody's desk, or stored in a box, and not counted unless they can make a difference in the election.

This chaos in absentee voting has prevailed since our country's founding. One present day example of what happens to UOCAVA ballots is the Minnesota senatorial election of 2008. The vote was so close that the loser,

Republican Norm Coleman, sued for a recount. The winner, Democrat Al Franken, contested the suit. In the course of the trial evidence was revealed that, six months after the election, 4700 absentee ballots had still not been counted. Among the thousands that had been counted, about 12,000 were disqualified and tossed aside, many for picky reasons; for example, the voter had used "Xs" or checks instead of completely filling in the bubbles, or did not sign his or her name exactly as on the voter registration card, etc. These were challenged in court, and a few hundred were reincluded in the final tally, but not enough to change the election.[23]

While well intended, in practice UOCAVA has not worked well. A Pew research survey of men and women serving overseas in the military, and their voting age spouses, found that millions of those who were eligible to vote did not do so. Nearly 60% of them said they did not vote due to problems with the absentee voting process. 30% said they were not able to vote because their ballots never arrived or arrived too late. Another 28% said they did not know how to get a ballot, found the process too complicated, or were unable to register.[24]

The study also found that 16 states, and Washington D.C., routinely responded so slowly to requests for absentee ballots by Americans in the military that the ballots are guaranteed to not be returned in time to be counted. About ten other states have such cumbersome rules that voters are pressed for time or discouraged from voting. Adding insult to injury, some of these states actually require the marked ballot to be *notarized* before it is returned. This, of course, raises privacy issues. Some eligible voters may not vote because they refuse to have their privacy and their dignity violated.

In 2003, some states began to allow ballots to be requested, sent out, voted and returned by fax or email. This solves the time problem, but raises new issues. Soldiers in the field, or on the move, might have access to a cell phone, but not to a computer or fax machine. Perhaps more importantly, with this method, all privacy goes out the window. A marked paper ballot with no name on it can be placed in a security envelop, and that envelop put into the mailing envelope with the voter's name on it. But a fax or an email must be sent with the name and vote shown together. Employees of the local election office will know how each voter by facsimile or email voted. Indeed, email voters in California and some other states must sign a statement waiving their right to voting privacy. Thus, if their vote is publicized, and they are embarrassed, the local election official is protected from a lawsuit.

Under UOCAVA, then, in any given group of soldiers, depending on what state they hail from, some will have ample time to vote by fax or email, but they will have to give up their privacy; some will have time to vote by snail mail, but they will have to hurry and get their vote notarized before they send it in; while others will have no time to vote because of uncaring local officials, or postal problems.

What kind of absentee voting process is this? Don't our men and women in uniform, and all Americans overseas, deserve a secure, private, convenient, reliable, and efficient means of voting? Doesn't this chaos of state practices violate their right to the Equal Protection of the Law? Shouldn't there be a uniform method of voting from overseas, which is fair to all?

Because we Americans like to see ourselves as living in a democratic country, we feel a strong desire to have our political institutions live up to at least some minimal standard of democracy. That is why, for example, another Pew research survey found that 96% of the Americans who were questioned thought it "unfair" for Americans in the military, stationed abroad, to have no, or an inadequate, means of voting in state-side elections. People intuitively recognize the goodness in the intention of UOCAVA to help all Americans abroad to vote. Once they learn about it, most Americans also recognize the unfairness in the way states have failed to live up to that law's good intentions. Another admirable characteristic of Americans is that some of them have not simply "tisk-tisked" about this injustice, they did something about it.

A Short History of VOI

In the late 1990's, some voting rights activists saw the potential of the Internet to provide overseas Americans with a way to vote that would satisfy all the requirements of a good election process. They took their vision to President Clinton, to the Department of Defense, and to Congress. To our government's credit, it acted upon this inspired idea. Congress gave the Secretary of Defense the responsibility to try a small experimental program in which overseas Americans could vote online, and allocated funds to the DoD to pay for the project. The

program was called The Voting Over the Internet Pilot
Project, or "VOI." Using a secure DoD website, overseas
citizens could register and vote regardless of where they
were living. The secure website allowed a select group of
volunteers to log on from any computer, in any location,
enter their secret password, request a ballot, mark it, and
cast their vote.

Election officials in four states, Florida, South Carolina,
Texas, and Utah agreed to participate in the program. The
DoD website provided registration forms and a ballot that
was tailored to each state's regulations, and which enabled
voters to vote in local, state, and federal races. While the
Alaska Republican Party used Internet voting in January
2000 to run a straw poll on presidential candidates, and in
March 2000 Arizona Democrats voted over the Internet in
their presidential primaries, the VOI project provided the
first opportunity in US history for binding votes to be cast
over the Internet in a general election.

The section of DoD that supervised this project is
called the Federal Voting Assistance Program, or "FVAP."
After the 2000 election, FVAP submitted its Assessment
Report to the Secretary of Defense. While the big story on
TV was the unreliable paper-based voting technology used
in Florida, and other states, the FVAP report happily
declared that there were no significant problems with the
VOI system. The technology worked well. The report
acknowledged the security fears that arise with Internet
voting, and stated that the risks of this venture could be,
and were, acceptably mitigated. No challenges to the
integrity of the VOI system were made by any of its

participants. The authors were pleased to report that FVAP personnel worked well with state and local election officials, and that their particular laws and regulations were respected by the VOI ballots and processes. Because the aim of this project was simply to test the idea of Internet voting for UOCAVA citizens, only 84 votes were actually cast using the VOI system. Since the system worked so well, FVAP suggested that a larger scale trial project be undertaken.25

Dunbar v. Wright

There were, of course, critics of the VOI project. John Dunbar, investigative writer with the Center for Public Integrity, a Nader-founded group, published one of the first critical commentaries on the DoD report.26

After explaining the program, Dunbar expressed some general qualms about the security issue, but admitted that he had no evidence of any security breaches or voting misconduct. His article specifically emphasized the $6.2 million dollar cost of the project. He quoted anti-Internet voting activist, Rebecca Mercuri, a professor of computer science, as saying she would rather see the money spent on "sociological problems" than on Internet voting. But Dunbar also cited defenders of the program who emphasized that the aim of the project was not primarily to take votes, but to run a pilot test of Internet voting and intergovernmental cooperation. Then FVAP director, Polli Brunelli, declared that as to these aims, the VOI was an "exemplar" federal program, and a "groundbreaking event."

43

Mercuri, whose website carries Dunbar's essay, expressed strong feelings about the security issue. She insisted that "The Internet itself is not secure." From this premise she concluded, according to Dunbar's essay, "So there is *no way* you can make the product secure" (emphasis added). Dunbar mentions in his article that FVAP hired hackers to try to break into the system, and that in these tests, and in the actual voting, there were no instances of successful hacking. But Mercuri, exercising her privilege of professorial authority, seems to simply dismiss these facts and insist on the insecurity of the Internet.

One long time advocate of Internet voting for overseas Americans, especially those in the military, is a retired navy lawyer, Captain Samuel F. Wright. He also published a commentary about VOI. In a 2001 article, he wholeheartedly approved of the 2000 VOI experiment. It was fast, accurate, convenient, and the DoD "system provides substantially *more security* than is provided in traditional absentee voting, by mail."[27]

Captain Wright was also an enthusiastic supporter of immediately expanding the project to include all overseas Americans. He wrote, "We want to get all 50 states on board in time for the presidential election of 2004. Electronic [Internet] voting is the long-range solution to the overseas voting problem, in my view."

As to those with security qualms, he wrote, "In the military, classified information is routinely transmitted by secure electronic means. In commerce, billions of dollars are transmitted electronically every day. If electronic means are secure enough for our nation's most sensitive secrets and for huge sums of money, why is it not possible to develop and implement a system for deployed service members to vote by secure electronic means?"[28]

In another article, Captain Wright lamented that in most places where uniformed personnel are stationed, "absentee voting is still conducted in much the same way it was during World War II, by shipping pieces of paper across oceans and continents. There are three time-consuming steps in absentee voting. First, the absentee ballot request must travel from the voter to the election official back home. Second, the unmarked absentee ballot must travel from the election official to the voter. Finally, the marked absentee ballot must travel from the voter back to the hometown election official. Each of these steps can take weeks by mail, but only seconds if secure electronic means were authorized."[29]

Clearly, Captain Wright is among those Internet voting enthusiasts who feel that it should have been done yesterday. Congress and the DoD understood the problem, but choose to proceed towards a solution more cautiously than folks like Captain Wright would have preferred. Thus, in the Defense Act of 2002, Congress directed the Secretary of Defense to undertake a program large enough to show whether an Internet voting system would be feasible for all UOCAVA citizens. It also provided the DoD with funds which were about five times that of the VOI budget. Once again, FVAP would conduct the new project. It would be known as The Secure Electronic Registration and Voting Experiment, or "SERVE."

How SERVE Would Work

Much of my information on the history of the SERVE project comes from a 2007 report to Congress written by Under Secretary of Defense David S. C. Chu. Appointed to office in 2001, Chu became the primary supervisor of FVAP. Chu was very proud of FVAP's work on Internet voting. For example, he wrote Congress that in 2003, the "FVAP received the Excellence.Gov award for the VOI project from the Federal Chief Information Officers Council and The Industry Advisory Council."

Beyond that, the computer science experts in the "Caltech/MIT Voting Technology Project rated the VOI voter registration application a best practice for elections."30 The VOI system, then, became the basic model for the SERVE system to build upon.

Seven states volunteered to take part in the experiment. They were Arkansas, Florida, Hawaii, North Carolina, South Carolina, Utah, and Washington. Military personnel from these states could sign up for the program using their military ID. Then they could register to vote in the state of their last residence. After that, they were ready to vote on SERVE in their state's primaries and the 2004 general election.

The voting process would begin with the voter using his or her PC, or any other computer, from any place in the world, at any time of day or night. First, the voter would log on to the secure SERVE website, enter the PIN that was issued at sign up, and request a ballot. Next, his or her name would be automatically checked against the local election authority's registration records. If cleared, a ballot would appear on the voter's computer screen. He or she would mark the vote, and with a click of the mouse, send in the voted ballot. SERVE would automatically separate the voter's name from the ballot. Then the name would be stored on a list of those who voted, so that there could only be one vote per registered voter. This would prevent ballot box stuffing. The system would also store the vote separately. SERVE would periodically send the voting data to the office of the appropriate local election official, where authorized personnel would be able to download the data.

By storing the separate records of votes and voters, SERVE would act as a back up for the local election officials. This back up data could also be used as an auditing resource. That is, the state officials could compare their lists of how many persons had voted, and their vote tallies, with those of SERVE. Any discrepancies would be cause for investigation.

Another type of auditing mechanism was the online voting confirmation list. When a voter sends his or her vote to SERVE, he or she would receive a "thank you" window with a voter confirmation number. Of course, for privacy the confirmation list would not show either the name of the voter or how he or she voted. To show the voter's actual vote, as I mentioned earlier, would enable buying and selling, as well as coercion. The voter could go online sometime after voting, and see if his or her number appears on the list. If it does, that will confirm that the vote has been received and stored. If the number does not appear, the voter can inquire at the SERVE "help desk" to see if a re-vote is needed. Since name and vote had been separated, this inquiry would not threaten the voter's privacy. While most voters would probably not bother with the extra step of going to the check list, if those who did check it found no problems, SERVE's reputation as a reliable process would be enhanced.

The SERVE system was designed to handle far more votes than the tiny 84 cast in the VOI experiment. SERVE was prepared to process the registrations and votes of up to 100,000 participants. Beyond that, the SERVE technicians aimed to create a show piece of a system, which could be expanded to accommodate roughly six million UOCAVA citizens in the future, without compromising accuracy, privacy, or the voter's identity. Although it was not their mission to demonstrate how a secure, accurate, and convenient Internet voting system could be carried on domestically, the SERVE team understood that this possibility was implied in their work.

By the end of 2003, Chu and his teammates in the states and DoD felt that they had produced a technological achievement comparable to NASA's Apollo 11 project. Just as the Saturn V rocket put the first man on the moon, so the SERVE technology would carry the first large scale multi-state Internet vote in an actual US election. SERVE was ready for the November 2004 presidential election.

Indeed, to be sure that they had left no technological stone unturned, and that this was no secret operation done by government insiders but a fully open process, which is as it should be in a democratic country, the FVAP established a SERVE Security Peer Review Group ("SPRG"). This group was comprised of 10 members from academia and industry. Some of these specialists were chosen because they were *known critics* of Internet voting. Nothing was kept secret from them, and everything was open for their inspection.

Of course, this was a very risky move. The SPRG members with a bias against the project did not share the enthusiasm of Chu et al for the vision of all UOCAVA citizens one day voting over the Internet. Chu was aware that a sharp eyed critic could expose any major flaws in the system. Just one vocal dissenter could become a real party pooper.

Apocalypse Now

As it turned out, there was not *just one* vocal dissenter, but four! And they didn't simply add their dissenting opinion to the final report, as Supreme Court Justices do when they write a dissenting opinion. These critics went public with a passion *to kill the project*!

I will discuss their particular objections in a moment. Surprisingly, the dissenters admitted that they could not find any technical fault with the SERVE system; indeed, five, *a majority*, of the peers gave the project the go-ahead. One of them declined to state an opinion. Although Rebecca Mercuri was not among the SPRG members, like her, the few vocal dissenters objected to *the very idea* of voting via the Internet. No Internet voting system, they said, could be secure against the scenarios they could imagine; therefore, the whole idea behind the SERVE project was, in their opinion, ill-conceived, unworkable, and could have results which would be "catastrophic."[31]

They could *imagine* all sorts of horrible scenarios occurring in the voter's environment, outside of the secure SERVE system. Hacker attacks with viruses, worms, and Trojan horses *might* infiltrate the PCs of many voters. The malware could change or destroy their votes, and *might never be detected.* In their imagination, "Such attacks could occur on a large-scale, and could be launched by anyone from a disaffected lone individual to a well financed enemy agency outside the reach of U.S. law. These attacks could result in large-scale, selective voter disenfranchisement, and/or privacy violation, and/or vote buying and selling, and/or vote switching even to the extent of reversing the outcome of many elections at once, including the presidential election."[32]

This is scary stuff! Their stories of what "could" happen are especially ominous because they come from four professors of computer science. Of course, the press loved the sensational charges, and the professors have received a great deal of coverage in print and online. (My search on their report's title turned up about 25,000 references.)

Chu's immediate supervisor at the time the dissenting report came out was Paul Wolfowitz, a Deputy Secretary of Defense. Coincidentally, he was then on President Bush's short list for nominees to the fabulous job of President of the World Bank. This job carried far more power and prestige than a Deputy Secretary of anything would ever know. Not only was the pay more than twice his current salary, but the perks included world travel on a private jet, with status like that of a head of state. If he were to courageously defend Chu, the SPRG majority, and the SERVE project team, which included a score of experts from the military and private business, he could become embroiled in a public controversy. Then the officials with the final word for hiring at the World Bank might question his judgment. They would wonder whether he was the sort of guy who was attracted to public controversy, or not prudent enough to avoid it. Either way, they might not want to hire him and risk someday putting their institution into a disfavorable light.

Perhaps taking these personal considerations into account, after receiving the dissenting opinion written by four of the ten SPRG peers, Wolfowitz ordered a halt to the implementation of the SERVE project in a memo dated January 30, 2004. As the reason given to the public for this order, a spokesperson for Mr. Wolfowitz expressed concerns that SERVE personnel would be unable to ensure the legitimacy of the votes, "thereby bringing into doubt the integrity of the election results." [33]

In other words, Wolfowitz feared a widespread public disturbance based on a distrust of the tally of votes cast over the Internet. Thus, despite all the expert scientific opinion and the success of the VOI to the contrary, self-interest and the fear of controversy appear to have carried the day. SERVE would be shelved indefinitely; or, until such time as the fantastic objections of the dissenters could be disproved.

Consequently, 100,000 overseas voters, many in the US military, were deprived of the opportunity to vote conveniently, and all further work on Internet voting by the US government was brought to a halt. Soon thereafter, in one of history's sweet ironies, some would say "poetic justice," Wolfowitz became the very nightmare at the World Bank that the Board of Governors thought they would avoid by hiring him. He broke all the rules by giving his girlfriend, who worked at the Bank, a promotion and a fat raise. The press found out about it, and flew into yet another feeding frenzy. In no time Wolfowitz and friend were unhappily unemployed. The man who stopped the progress of Internet voting in the US got his comeupings.34

The Three Components of the Internet Voting Process

Because the four dissenters are professors of computer science, their arguments against the SERVE project merit serious consideration. To that end, I will discuss both their objections and the defenses against those objections.

There are three components in the design for an Internet voting process based on the SERVE system. These are: first, all the voters use their own equipment to vote in the online environment; second, they vote on the secure server upon which the SERVE website is based, with its hardware, software, and personnel; and, third, the role of the local election officials and their personnel and computer systems.

Each of these components performs a distinct function within the Internet voting process. The local election officials are responsible for the registration of the voters within their jurisdictions. These officials are also responsible for providing SERVE with accurate lists of registered voters, as well as providing SERVE with complete and accurate ballots for the voters to vote on when they use the SERVE website. The primary function of SERVE is to provide a secure and accurate medium for the communication of votes from voters to their local election officials. Those officials tally the votes, and after each state's Secretary of State certifies the tally, the election results are reported to the public and to Congress.

Internet voting increases both the convenience and the *responsibility* of the people. Voting is made more convenient because the voter can use his or her own equipment to vote. Currently, in most of the US, the voter must take the trek to a polling station and use the government's equipment to vote. If there was an equipment problem or failure, the government election officials were responsible for it. But with people voting on their own computers, cell phones, blackberries, etc. they have more responsibility for the maintenance of their equipment. This includes contracting with a competent security software provider.

A complete security analysis of this voting process, then, would include an examination of each of these three components for its strengths and weaknesses. Thus, one area of inquiry would be the voter and his or her PC, cell phone, or other voting hardware. The security of SERVE itself would be a second point of examination. And, the local election officials and their procedures and equipment would be the third subject of analysis. Although the report of the dissenters is 34 pages long (including appendices and biographies of each of the four dissenters), and offers numerous reasons as to why they call for the shutting down of the SERVE project; the last two subjects receive little or no discussion.

While their report has very little to say about the security of the SERVE system itself – indeed, they *praise* that system – they argue that the security problems in the first component, the voter's equipment and environment, cannot be overcome. For that reason, they urged ending the SERVE project. Perhaps because they thought the first component was so flawed, they also did not examine the third component; that is, the security aspects of the election officials in the states and localities.

The voter's environment includes several factors. Among these are the voters and the hardware the voters use, including the software in that hardware; the presence of hostile forces, such as hackers and others who want to disrupt or corrupt the democratic process; and, of course, law enforcement officials who want to protect the integrity of the democratic process. All of these factors operate outside of the SERVE system, which only comes into play when a voter logs on to the SERVE website.

The dissenters are primarily concerned with the drama that is acted out on the pre-SERVE stage. Here is where they find almost all of the fatal flaws of Internet voting. To fairly present their point of view, I will start with their praise of SERVE. With this praise, they distinguish the SERVE component of the Internet voting process from the voter's treacherous environment.

They write,

> We want to make clear that in recommending that SERVE be shut down, we mean no criticism of the FVAP, or of [the private contractor] Accenture, or any of its personnel or subcontractors. They have been completely aware all along of the security problems we describe here, and we have been impressed with the engineering sophistication and skill they have devoted to attempts to ameliorate or eliminate them. We do not believe that a differently constituted project could do any better job than the current team. The real barrier to success is not a lack of vision, skill, resources, or dedication; it is the fact that, given the current Internet and PC security technology, and the goal of a secure, all-electronic remote voting system, the FVAP has taken on an essentially impossible task. There really is no good way to build such a voting system without a radical change in overall architecture of the Internet and the PC, or some unforeseen security breakthrough. The SERVE project is thus too far ahead of its time, and should not be reconsidered until there is a much improved security infrastructure to build upon.35

They go on to discuss how they see that "security infrastructure," warts and all. They recognize, as I have previously mentioned, that, as life in nature, the Internet exists in an environment with hostile elements. In discussing e-commerce, I showed that numerous businesses have learned to adapt to, and thrive in, this environment. That is why millions of people can bank, or buy a book, refrigerator, car, or even a house online. But the dissenters refuse to accept that the security of Internet voting can ever rise to the level of security in the world of Internet commerce. Those, they say, are two different systems.

Suppose, for example, a department store deliberately has its clerks overcharge several customers on their credit card purchases. Once the crime is exposed, each customer can check his or her receipts against their credit card reports. Where discrepancies are found, refunds can be obtained. But suppose that somehow numerous fraudulent votes are cast in an election. Because votes are cast anonymously there will be no "paper trail" to show who voted more than once, or whether automated votes stuffed the ballot boxes. Nor is there any opportunity after an election to re-vote, like there is a chance to get a refund, or exchange an item, in e-commerce. "For these reasons the existence of technology to provide adequate security for Internet commerce does not imply that Internet voting can be made safe."[36]

Everyone knows that large scale financial scandals occur periodically, such as the Savings and Loan scandal of the 1980s, Enron in 2001, and the recent scandal based on bad mortgage loans. These financial events can happen without raising a threat to the existence of the *political* system. But if there were a succession of elections with deep and widespread voter suspicion, such as that in the

2000 election, that suspicion could eventually explode into outrage, and the very existence of the political system could be challenged. Because the legitimacy of our political system depends so heavily upon public confidence in the elections process, the dissenters emphatically insist that "*e-commerce grade security is not good enough for public elections*."37

I, of course, disagree with these two conclusions. In my view, the existence of e-commerce security *does* imply that Internet voting can be done securely. Also, e-commerce grade security, when properly understood, can be good enough for Internet voting. As I present the rest of their arguments, I will state some of my reasons for rejecting their positions. I will also give the reasons why the SERVE project team and its leaders have rejected the points made by the dissenters. Finally, I will discuss some of the known techniques for beefing up security that were not mentioned by the four dissenters.

There are reasons why these four dissenters were not joined by the other six SPRG members. However, these six did not submit their own report to Wolfowitz, or to the press, in response to the analysis of the dissenters; indeed, for reasons unknown to me, *no one* on the SERVE project team made a public defense against the charges of the four dissenters. But, as I will show, some of their later writings suggest why the six, as well as the other technical experts, did not join those four.

First, as the dissenters point out, the American people have always been able to tolerate misdeeds in elections *on a small scale*. Thus, the dissenters understood that a government's aim in administering an election is not to achieve Absolute Moral Perfection, but only an election of publicly acceptable integrity.

Few American voters expect flawless elections. Just as most business people expect some losses in the course of their operations, such as those due to shop-lifting or accounting errors, most voters realize that some imperfections in the vote count, or loss of votes due to human error or shenanigans, is to be expected. For example, suppose that in a state gubernatorial election a politically zealous postal clerk throws into a river a box of mail-in ballots, which all came from the wealthy side of town. That clerk will have successfully deprived those folks of the right to vote in this particular election. However, few people are going to call for a new election, or insist that this election be invalidated just because a small percentage of the voters were disenfranchised. The public would not approve of such conduct, but as long as the misdeeds are on a small scale, the legitimacy of the election itself will not be undermined.

Of course, whether in e-commerce or e-voting, huge losses would not be tolerable. As the four dissenters write, "What we must avoid at all costs is any system in which it is possible for a successful large-scale or automated (computerized) attack to compromise many votes."[38] Everyone can agree on that point, so the dissenters have the burden of showing how large scale vote manipulations can be done in a system of Internet voting.

The dissenters recognized that SERVE itself was well protected against the most blatant form of automated voting. They understood that no one could simply fire a series of votes into the secure servers, or computers, upon which SERVE was based, to inflate the count for some candidate or issue. Only one vote per registered voter would be allowed by SERVE.

However, in the voter's environment they see several types of large scale attacks on personal computers that would make wholesale vote changing possible. Each of these attacks depends upon installing some form of malware in many machines. True enough, there are ways by which that can be done.

"Botnets," or networks of robot computers, are an example of a large scale malicious operation. When users go on the Internet, they establish an electronic connection to that world, and in doing so they create an electronic pathway back into their machine. There are devious super-hackers who search these connections to the Internet for vulnerable PCs online, and, when found, install malware that can give them control over other people's machines, making them their "robot," or slave, computers. Some spammers can use hundreds, even thousands, of other people's PCs to send e-mails, and go undetected by the owners. Thus, the capacity to break into poorly protected or unprotected computers does exist in the Internet environment.

In addition, *spyware* can enable a wrongdoer to observe how a voter is voting. This could have several consequences. If unauthorized, it would be a violation of the voter's right to privacy. However, a voter might allow such spyware into his PC. For example, in a vote buying

59

and selling scheme, the seller of his vote could allow the spyware to be installed in his computer so that the buyer could confirm that the seller had voted as agreed. Or, in a coercion case, the victim could be forced to allow the spyware so that the coercer could verify that the victim had complied. In theory, all of these things *could* be done on a large scale.

The dissenters provide many examples of scenarios which they claim to be possible. But in considering what is possible, *all* the elements of the voter's environment must be factored into the equations. Unfortunately, for the sake of veracity, our four experts are quite remiss in their scientific obligation to avoid selecting only those facts and assumptions that will support their theory, while disregarding the realities which seem too inconvenient to include.

For instance, to allege that after certain malware has been installed, voters may be "blocked" from voting is not a complete representation of the situation. The voter would know that his or her vote was blocked, either because the voter could not log on to the SERVE website, or because a warning message would show on the SERVE window. Then the voter could take remedial action. For example, he or she could run a virus removal program, or use a different computer.

The dissenters suggest that a voter's vote may be surreptitiously changed in the moment just before he or she sends the marked ballot to SERVE. But the *whole* story includes other factors. For example, if the SERVE system detected a so-called "man in the middle," it would direct the voter to get the virus removed, or to use a different computer.

Also, after the voter marks his or her ballot, SERVE would present a confirmation message for the voter to confirm. If no such message came back to the voter, or a message with the wrong information on it, he or she would alert the help desk. If a phony confirmation number came back to the voter, and he or she checked it on the list and saw it was not listed, an investigation would be launched. The so-called "man in the middle" would soon be tracked down and arrested.

The dissenters allege that votes may be cast using the misappropriated identity of the voter. Of course, identity theft is a serious problem. A thief could conceivably obtain a voter's registration information and PIN. But this could not result in *large scale* voter fraud. Suppose a crooked employee in the office of some Registrar of Voters stole the registration info for several, even 100 or more, voters in that jurisdiction. Before each vote could be cast, the malicious voter would have to log on and go through the process of voting, which would include entering the PIN, requesting the ballot, voting, confirming the vote on the confirmation window, and waiting for the confirmation number. If this took a few minutes for each vote, how many votes could a frantically working fraudster actually cast? Surely not enough to swing an election.

Besides that, the longer the miscreant spends online casting fraudulent votes, the higher the odds become of his being detected, caught, and prosecuted. How many government workers would think that game worth the candle? There would have to be hundreds of crooked government workers to make a difference in an online election. They would have to conspire among each other, and agree on what candidates and issues to favor. But these assumptions are silly. Just because some large scale unlawful act can be imagined, does not mean that it can be done; especially when all the required conditions are thought through.

Also, most of their fantasy examples assume inactive law enforcement in the voter's environment. Thus, they can *imagine* large scale criminal activity being openly conducted with the perpetrators undeterred by worries of being caught and punished by the law. In reality, however, law enforcement agents would soon become aware of any criminal conspiracy, whether for fraud or the buying and selling of votes, on the Internet. The villains would be apprehended and promptly land in the hoosegow.

The dissenters also assume a landscape of personal voting equipment, such as PCs, cell phones, and black-berries operating with incompetent security software, or none at all. But commercial software is readily available to anyone who is willing to pay for protection.

Finally, the horror stories the dissenters tell presuppose a cynical confidence in the ignorance and gullibility of the electorate. The SERVE project anticipated an effort at educating its users about the safety precautions they should take to protect themselves. With well-protected PCs, few voters would fall victim to invaders from the Web.

Given this faulty methodology, based on fantasy assumptions, and disregarding inconvenient facts, our detractors from SERVE are able to present themselves as a set of Super Sleuths, snooping about the Internet voter's environment and uncovering one crime waiting to happen after another. But their cries of potential "catastrophe" are only as solid as their assumptions.

As we have seen, to be effective, election corrupting malware and spyware must be installed in the voter's equipment. Unlike viruses in nature, computer viruses cannot fly through the air, as projected by a sneeze, and randomly infect any machine it lands on. Some specific opening must first be given to the virus by the user.

There are several ways by which this installation can take place. As we have seen, it can be done from the Internet once an unprotected computer goes online. A common way that computers are infected is when the user opens a loaded email which has been disguised to look innocent. Downloading something purchased or offered for free on the Net can allow bugs into a person's computer.

So can visiting an infected website. Malware can conceivably be installed by a malicious computer manufacturer, before the equipment is offered for sale. The dissenters warn about each of these hazards, but without also advising that security software, law enforcement, and human intelligence can protect against these hazards.

Manufacturing Malware

In one imaginary scenario, the dissenters hypothesize that large scale election crimes could be committed by software manufactures. They write, "Today's computers come loaded with software developed by many different entities; any employee at any of those companies could conceivably leave a backdoor that attacks SERVE [users]. … Backdoors, placed in software and activated when a user tries to vote, can invisibly monitor or subvert the voting process. Every time someone downloads new software, the risk is increased."[39]

This statement suggests that a company favoring Republicans could program all the computers with its software to vote Republican, even if the voter thinks he or she is voting for a Democrat or an Independent. A Socialist-favoring company could adjust the vote its way, etc.

Here, the Super Sleuths think they have uncovered the potential for a massive conspiracy by software makers to control US elections by selling people loaded software. But, what would be necessary to carry out such a scheme, and what risks would the perpetrators be taking? First, such a scheme could only affect an Internet-based election in our country if the company sells tens of thousands of loaded product. But, the more they sell, the greater the risk of being caught. Someone who is wary of just such a scheme, whether a citizen computer scientist, or a law enforcement official, is going to examine the code in every type of voting-related product and discover the trick.

Furthermore, security technology is so sophisticated that a voting website server can screen a voter's computer once it has logged on, and if malware is found, or automated voting detected, the server can deny access to that computer. The server can send a message to the voter to have the machine cleaned, or use a different machine to log on and vote. Users who learn that their purchased software is infected will still be able to vote, but they will never buy from that software company again. The crooked company will go out of business without having influenced the election.

Also, once the maker of bad software has been caught, the company's executives, engineers, and all who conspired with them, risk having to pay huge fines, being sentenced to prison, and losing their livelihood. After they do their time, no software company would hire them, because customers would become suspicious of the company's product. They would not even be able to open their own computer repair business. Who would trust them to repair their computers? These convicted felons would be lucky to find jobs as taxi drivers, or doormen. How many people who are intelligent enough to run a software manufacturing business are going to be stupid enough to risk these consequences in the forlorn hope of changing some votes to favor their own political party or candidate?

Some people, especially in Ohio after the 2004 presidential election, suspected that the manufacturers of DREs (direct recording electronic voting machines with touch screens), had programmed their machines to change Democratic votes to Republican. Newspapers, broadcast media, and bloggers made hay of such suspicions. (There is even a video on You Tube of Homer Simpson watching his vote for Kerry being flipped for Bush! So, the rigging of DREs must be true!) Given the flimsy evidence, the dissenters engage in some smear tactics, using guilt by association, when they irresponsibly state in their report that "SERVE can be said to act as one giant DRE machine."40 They knew better. This statement contradicts their earlier acknowledgement that the SERVE server was secure against such security breaches as manufacturer installed malware and insider wrong-doing.

The fear of vote-flipping machines has never been shown to have any bases in fact. While lawsuits were filed against the DRE makers, no vote changing programs have ever been proven in court. The executives running those companies are not foolish enough to take the risk of being caught selling local election officials loaded equipment. To sell such software more broadly, such as to the general public online or in retail stores, would be to increase that risk greatly.

Realistically, vote changing software is not going to be routinely installed in computer assembly lines. Intelligent entrepreneurs are going to have quality control operations that will not let such loaded product go out for sale under their company's name. Pranksters, who do not value their freedom, might disseminate malicious software by disguising it as games or screen savers for free downloading to gullible consumers. Not only can the secure servers detect and block such programs, but the FBI, and agents from the Interstate Commerce

Commission, or state law enforcement agencies will nab the naughty fellows long before they can impact any election. The myth of bad software manufacturers changing an election outcome is nothing more than a scary story. While fuel for fearful fantasies, there is no basis in social science reasoning to give that tall tale any credit.

Spammers and Spoofing

The dissenters suggest that spammers can send out millions of deceptive emails, which install malware when opened. But those who have calculated that they can get away with this crime are, for that reason, probably not as clever as they think they are. The law is likely to catch them quickly, and stop them. They would have to start sending out the infected emails prior to voting day, so that people who do not read their email every day can be caught in the trap before the election. Thus, there would be time to discover the malware before it can do widespread damage.

In the early days of mass Internet usage, people were naïve about the threats out there. The "Love Bug" infected many PCs in 2000. Unsuspecting users opened an email from an unknown source with "love" in the title, and what they got was a virus that shut down their machine.

Now, however, all worthwhile security software companies have virus detection systems for email. Untrustworthy email is flagged, so people with that protection can just delete the email without opening it, and no harm will be done. Also, the public has been educated about the risks of opening email from unknown sources.

Only people who are ignorant of the need for computer protection, or those who gullibly purchase sub-standard security software, will be affected. But, once the better security companies detect a bug, they will alert law enforcement and post their findings on the Net. The word will get to low grade security companies, who can then install up-dated security scans. Few votes will be affected by this tactic.

"Spoofing" is another trick that can be sent out by spammers. Here, an email is disguised to look like it is from a trust-worthy source, such as a state's Secretary of State, Registrar of Voters, or political party. Presenting itself as a "reminder to vote," it offers a link "for your convenience." But the link leads to a fake look-alike website. Then the voter gives away his or her PIN and personal information. With this information, the bad guys can then log on to the real website and cast some extra votes.

But one aspect of public education is to inform voters of this trick, and to assure voters that no government agency will ever send out such a link. If a voter received an email with such a link from a political party, or other private source, he or she would have to decide whether to trust it or trash it. Spoofing can also be prohibited by federal law.

These protections of US elections will work equally well against spammers from within the reach of US law, and against those who operate outside that reach. The bad guys who can be nabbed by American law enforcement will do time for their crime. Our government can agree by treaty to make and enforce laws against tampering with foreign elections from within our jurisdiction, if foreign governments will do the same. In countries with extremely strict law enforcement, off shore tampering in US elections could result in harsher penalties than tampering with our elections from within our borders.

Of course, hostile elements will still exist in the World Wide Web. The same folks who send out a gazillion emails saying you are in the will of a Nigerian prince, or selling you pills to enlarge your breasts or penis, will probably attempt to engage in election fraud. But, as I have shown, voters can protect themselves from this vermin.

Thanks to competition for profits, security software companies have a high learning curve. Whenever a new virus or damaging bug appears, they find a way to stop it. For example, Newsweek reported in November 2008,41 that Obama's campaign computer system was invaded by spyware, possibly coming from a foreign country. His computer administrators discovered the intrusion, and began trying to figure-out if it was a danger to the system, and how to remove it. Clearly, these administrators were not as sophisticated in their understanding of unlawful techniques as the FBI; because the FBI came to them the next day and told them that the bug was downloading policy files and travel plan information. While no financial information was lost, and no money stolen, Obama's team wanted to get rid of the pest right away. So, they immediately hired a private computer security firm, which took care of the problem.

One lesson to be learned from this experience is that folks who are sophisticated at building attractive and complex websites, such as Obama's otherwise skillful website administrators, might still be lacking in knowledge about the most advanced security technology. For that reason, specialists in security will have a favorable employment market for far into the future. Yet another lesson is that the intruders, possibly the best that foreign governments have to offer, were no match for our security experts.

Another instance of foreign governments engaged in hacking came to light early in 2010. That is when Google announced that it suspected the Chinese government of breaking into the Google Gmail email system. But Google is not likely to gain much sympathy by playing the innocent victim in this case. Lured into China by greed, they conspired with the Chinese government to limit the freedom of speech online. Google hired several hundred Chinese computer scientists to help run their operations. Some of these programmers were government agents whose job was to block access to websites that either favored democracy or freedom of religion. These agents made regular reports to their other mischievous minded colleagues in a couple of top Chinese universities about what they had learned of, among other things, Google's email security codes. With that information the Chinese experts reverse engineered those codes and broke into the email system so they could search for human rights dissidents using Gmail.[42]

Duh! What was Google expecting? When you play with fire, you get burned.

The Old Booby-Trap Trick

The dissenters postulate another fantastic scenario about an attacker, possibly some maladjusted teen, a Commie, or an Al Qaeda saboteur, who dislikes a particular candidate. This delinquent boy or girl "might booby-trap the website of that candidate, so that those who visit the candidate's website are unable to vote using SERVE."43 Sounds scary – until its assumptions are examined. No candidate wants his or her website to infect their supporters so that the supporters cannot vote for them. So standard intruder detection systems and protections against such tricks are routinely built into candidate websites, as the Obama example shows. And, if a voter did find his or her computer blocked from a voting website, virus removal programs, and other machines, such as in libraries or other public places, are readily available.

In 2008, the website for candidate Obama had tens of millions of visits, and *not one* report of a visitor's system being contaminated. The websites of the other candidates, too, were as free of contaminations for visitors as are those for the Bank of America, Amazon, or eBay. Here, then, is an example of how the security technology for e-commerce websites can be successfully transferred to protect the information gathering of Internet voters. These protections were in use and well-known at the time the dissenters wrote their report, but they conveniently ignored them.

Besides the security companies, competent search engines have their own malware detection systems. When someone runs a search on the candidate's name, and his or her website address comes up, it will be flagged as a threat before it is even opened. Only foolhardy voters will proceed and be infected by a bad website. In practice, as opposed to fantasy, few, if any, votes will be lost due to "booby trapped" websites.

Novel Viruses

Real experience belies the dangers purported to exist by our dissenters. They say, "Since virus checking software programs defend against only previously known viruses, virus checkers often are unable to keep up with the spread of new viruses and worms."44 But the novel spyware in Obama's system was rooted out within hours of their calling the professional security experts. The dissenters underestimate the learning curve of the good guys.

As a result of this capacity to catch on quickly, one aspect of any large scale Internet-based voting fraud scheme is that it is unlikely to be carried on for long without someone soon detecting it. Novel viruses will appear, as they do in nature, but the defenders of democracy will promptly detect and stop them. As Lincoln said, "you can't fool all of the people all of the time." There is always a good guy who is just as smart, if not smarter, than the bad guys. So, any vote changing virus is not likely to last for long, especially in an environment full of smart and experienced security experts in both private business and law enforcement, who are on high alert, and looking for just such a bug. The more widespread the threat to elections, the more likely it is to be detected. Only those who are not well protected will be infected.

Employer Coercion

The dissenters spin out another fantasy, which at first might seem theoretically plausible. That is, "An employer is also in a position to coerce employees who vote at work into voting a certain way."45

OK. Suppose Mr. Meany, owner of an apparel factory, orders his sewing machine operators to line up and pass through his office and vote Republican on his computer. Would the minuscule benefit he derived from this federal offense be worth the risk of going to prison? Suppose he had 100 employees. Would these votes have any significant impact on an election? Even if all employees submitted to his coercion, surely some of them would soon thereafter alert law enforcement, and later testify against him in the trial for his crimes. They would all have a right to sue his company in civil court, and possibly win a million dollars each for the violation of their civil rights, and for their emotional distress. His coercion would only get him behind bars, and his company in bankruptcy. How many people are there with sufficient business acumen to run a company, but who are foolish enough to risk everything, freedom included, for a few votes in a national election? Not many, if any.

Multiply this scenario as many times as you please, and the results will be the same. Only the world's dumbest employers would take such an enormous risk of paying fines and doing time for so little gain. In addition,

73

employer coercion is already possible in states like Oregon, Washington, California and in all the jurisdictions where voting by mail is widely practiced. Theoretically, an employer can order all of his employees to fill out their mail-in ballots and give them to him to check and mail in.

Fantasy aside, the fact is that no such crime has been reported in any vote by mail system in the US. Clearly, such an inconvenient truth goes a long way towards debunking this frightening fantasy of our four dissenters. A thorough study of voting fraud throughout the US was recently conducted by New York University's Brennan Center for Justice. The authors found that although the irresponsible press publicizes all sorts of voting fraud allegations, when examined for the facts, such claims "often prove greatly exaggerated." In fact, between 2002 and 2005, while hundreds of millions of votes were cast, "the federal government indicted only 40 voters for election crimes related to illegal voting … obtaining 26 convictions or guilty pleas, for a nationwide average of eight to nine illegal voters a year."[46] The 2004 presidential election had over one hundred million voters, with only "eight to nine illegal voters." That is surely a tolerable margin. In addition, none of these convictions involved employer or social coercion.

Clearly, when fantasy is compared to fact, the fear of voter coercion is unjustified; and such fear was definitely not a reason to shut down SERVE.

Remote Viewing

As I have mentioned, the dissenters warn that spyware could be installed in the voter's computer by rigged products coming from the factory or being downloaded from the Net, tricky email, or visiting a bad website. Once installed, such spyware could record how the voter voted. "What is surprising," they write, "is not that such software exists, but that it is readily affordable to all; one can find such software for under $50, as well as dozens of free versions."47 Here they go again: scary scenario, silly assumptions.

No one can have meaningful sales, or even free distribution, of such spyware in secret. They must advertise. Those who make, sell, and buy any kind of software for the purpose of violating election laws can be caught and prosecuted, including the "host" websites that carry the ads or facilitate the sales, such as Amazon, eBay, or PayPal. The administrators of those websites could be charged as accessories to the crime, and co-conspirators, who could be punished as severely as the perpetrators of the crimes. Officials who enforce election laws will routinely search the Web for advertisers of election malware and spyware. They might pose as mischievous buyers of the contraband in sting operations, or they might put up their own ads, pose as sellers, and catch buyers. No wrongdoer will be safe from their clutches.

Anything seems possible to these four computer security "specialists" when they assume a sleeping police force, PC users without common sense, and personal computers with little or no protection from malware or spyware. Given these assumptions, they can *imagine* that party competition would exacerbate the wrong-doing. "It is possible to imagine widespread attacks that targeted all voters in a particular party for disenfranchisement, leaving the other party unaffected. Such an attack would have serious consequences."48

Yes it "would" – "would," that is, if all American law enforcement were vacationing in Cancun on Election Day, and everyone was using unprotected PCs. On the other hand, having the two major parties disenfranchise *each other* might not be so bad for our country. Then Independent candidates would win, and perhaps stop the partisan bickering in Washington.49

Seriously, the suggestion by our Super Sleuths that Internet based elections will be swamped with cheap or free spyware enabling every voter to spy on every other is, in the technical language of the law, prima facie nuts. That is not going to happen. They undermine their credibility as "scientists" when they so patently exaggerate the threats to the integrity of elections based on Internet voting.

Remote Control

Suppose, given their assumptions, an Evil Demon takes control of a million computers because their naive owners opened his stealth email. Then he could watch how each voter voted. If he liked the vote, he could allow it. If he did not like the vote, he could change it to his liking. Theoretically, he could swing an election.50 Of course, he would have to be a fast reader and typist to get all that work done on Election Day! (And the voters would have to be watching TV when the vote confirmation window comes up with the bad guy's vote on it, and not theirs. Then they would have to confirm the vote without looking at it – not a difficult assumption to make for our four dissenters!)

Another trick that this Evil One could use, while the law sleeps and all security software is turned off, is to become "a man in the middle." He could send out spoofing emails which would lure a million voters to his own website, disguised to look like the SERVE website. Then the duped voter would waste his or her vote, and never know what happened. The Evil One could target specific groups of voters that he wants to disenfranchise. If he did not like women, he could do it to women voters. If he did not like Afro-Americans, he could do it to them. Our Super Sleuths feel certain that "there are many ways that an attacker could become a man in the middle."[51]

These truth-loving experts actually engage in a little trickery of their own. They claim that deceptions like the spoofing of voters with a phony look-alike website are "another vulnerability of SERVE," and "threats that are not overcome in the system."[52] But one need not be a computer scientist to figure out that if this spoofing is done on the Internet without entering into the SERVE secure website, then SERVE is not responsible for what happens outside of its system. Such false and self-contradicting accusations further erode the credibility of these dissenters. Perhaps their dissembling is one reason why the other six peers, and no other experts on the SERVE project, allied themselves with these four.

The Voting Dead

No phantom votes, or votes unconnected with a registered voter, as I have said, could have gotten into the SERVE system, whether on a large scale or a small scale. SERVE would only allow one vote per registered voter. But in performing this function, SERVE must rely on the professionalism of the local election officials who provide SERVE with the list of registered voters. Those officials are responsible for the integrity of the registration process, not SERVE. While no votes are allowed on SERVE without passing the registration check, if voter rolls are not kept up to date, some people might still be able to vote in the name of a deceased person. This has happened with paper based voting. However, once all vital records have been digitalized this will not be a problem. Then, the list of registered voters will automatically keep pace with changes in the vital records, and the dead will never vote again. The use of biometric identification will help to keep the connection of one person to one set of records tight.

Denial of Service Attacks on SERVE

Every website has a limit on how many visitors it can accommodate, and on how much information it can process, before it becomes overloaded and simply freezes, thereby denying service to all who attempt to access it. Given the right assumptions, then, every website, including SERVE, is, in theory, a sitting duck for a denial of service attack.

How can such attacks be launched? One way is a Million Man conspiracy. In this fantasy, a huge number of conspirators meet on some social networking website, like Facebook or MeetUp, and "secretly" plot to ruin the next election. Then on Election Day they all log on to the SERVE website at the same time, and start clicking on various buttons in the hope that the system will become overwhelmed with trying to respond to all the requests for ballots and information.

Something like this actually happened in Estonia in 2007. A few years after tiny Estonia broke away from the control of Russia, some Russians became upset that their language was no longer being used as the official language in the government, and for other reasons, such as the removal of a Russian general's statute from a park. Disaffected Russian's actually conspired online to overwhelm a couple of Estonian government agencies on an upcoming Russian holiday. Sure enough, at midnight on the appointed day thousands of computers started logging on to the finance and education department computers in Estonia. The congestion blocked access for several days, until the vengeful Russians tired of the prank.53

However, as I mentioned before, any public invitation to engage in a criminal conspiracy made in the US, unlike Russia at that time, will be promptly discovered by the FBI, and all participants possibly sent to prison. Incidentally, since the attack on Estonia, Russia has decided to begin using Internet voting for voters in its remote areas.54 Surely their law will become far less tolerant of online Denial of Service, or "DoS," conspiracies once they appreciate their own vulnerability to such attacks.

Another DoS scenario involves, once again, that alienated "lone teenager not on US soil."[55] This time he invades a million PCs with his loaded email, without being detected. "The attacker could then take remote control of the ... machines and wreak havoc with a future election."[56] He could control computers all over the country. "We can envision scenarios in which the computers of SERVE voters have been compromised on a large scale..."[57]

Imagine, with everything all set, on Election Day the Botnet Master could send a signal to his "slaves" to go on the SERVE website and automatically start clicking on buttons. With all this traffic, or so he hopes, "eligible voters will not be able to vote using SERVE."[58] The four fanciful dissenters opine: "It seems unlikely to us that SERVE could withstand such a high volume DDoS attack."[59] (By "DDoS," these experts mean a super *double sized* denial of service attack).

Once again, our impassioned dissenters are a tiny bit disingenuous in presenting this scary scenario. They "forget" to mention all the state-of-the-art counter-DoS techniques the SERVE team built into the system. These include using a large enough quantity of bandwidth to handle the expected traffic, employing multiple servers and redundant systems to dodge attacks and to take over service if a server fails, and using several ISP entry points.

Only by ignoring these protections do their predictions of a denial of service disaster become plausible.

The dissenters predict that after the "traumatic event" of a busy SERVE website, the American people will become so disgusted with Internet voting that they will riot in the streets until Congress makes a new law going back to the old tried and true paper ballot, marked with a number two pencil in a voting booth at a polling station. Of course, all the usual assumptions, such as sleeping police and voters who automatically open every email, must be accepted for either of these fearsome nightmares to come true in practice.

But, if the law is alert, no widespread conspiracy will escape their notice. The owners and administrators of the social networking website that hosted the conspirators could be charged as co-conspirators, and would risk doing time with murderers, armed robbers, and the rapists of women and men! So, there seems to be some incentive for administrators to not allow such a criminal conspiracy to form on any popular social networking websites.

A bit of gullibility is required for anyone to believe that some Terrible Teen, acting alone, could succeed. Relying on the deference due them as experts, our four dissenters declare with certainty that "no good defenses against network flooding attacks are known on today's Internet," and "adequate protection against denial-of-service attacks is unattainable with the technology available today."[60] But this is plainly not true.

An online vote was clogged up during an election in Toronto, Canada, due to a DoS attack, in 2003, well before our dissenter's report was written. The security technology of that time *was* sharp enough to detect the source of the attack and stop it within 45 minutes. After that, voting continued as before.61 Of course, the dissenters do not mention this incident. Security technology has improved greatly since then, making even the little success of the pranksters in Toronto unlikely to be repeated.

As a normal part of their daily routine, banks fend off denial of service attacks from a variety of sources, including middle class teenagers with nothing else to do, would-be blackmailers, and possibly commercial competitors. Other e-commerce websites do the same. Iran, North Korea, and Al Qaeda could save billions of dollars by chucking their projects to make or attain nuclear weapons, if it was possible for them to shut down all the major commercial websites in the land of "The Great Satan" by launching the Mother of All DDoSs against us. They have the brains, the know-how, and the mega-sized computers, to do it. But they do not do it, because it cannot be done. Our security infrastructure is more powerful than their capacity to attack.

Finally, while a DoS attack can be launched by a clever botnet master, as I have noted, the FBI is just as clever. In 2009, John Schiefer, once known as the "Botnet King," began serving a four year term in federal prison for his escapades. Besides legal fees, he was ordered to pay nearly $20,000 in restitution. He took control of around a quarter million personal computers, using them to send spam, and stealing identities from some.

Upon Schiefer's arrest, the feds announced, "While computer criminals have many technological resources at their disposal, we have our own technology experts, as well as a host of legal remedies to punish those who exploit the Internet for nefarious purposes," said United States Attorney Thomas P. O'Brien. "As Internet-based criminals develop new techniques, we quickly respond to their threats and prosecute those who compromise our ability to safely use the Internet."[62] So much for the unreal assumption of a sleeping police force!

Their Success, Our Loss

Anyone who reads the "scientific" report of our Super Sleuths will see that they are not doing computer science there, but are spinning out goofy plots for bad crime shows. They assumed a public which is universally ignorant, gullible, and irresponsible, and which would fall for every silly scam put to them. They assumed a Keystone Cops law enforcement which would fall over each other as the crooks escaped. Opps. They "forgot" all about the software security industry. But, as I have shown, by examining actual events through the methods of social science, a person can develop a truer sense of social reality than that resulting from the unreasoning speculations of imaginations all fired up by frightening visions. This more realistic look at the voter's environment reveals numerous safeguards against PC intrusions, and a lot of folks who are rapidly learning to safely use their new technology in hostile conditions.

Crime is a natural aspect of civilization, just as sickness is a natural aspect of life. Perhaps there will always be some election related crime. Thus, Internet voting will probably result in a small number of people losing their chance to vote because of someone's malicious mischief, or criminal wrong-doing. The victims will be the unprotected, or inadequately protected, and sometimes gullible members of the electorate. As Lincoln also said, "you *can* fool some of the people some of the time."

But, in my view, as I have explained, the arguments presented by the four dissenters did not at all merit the Draconian consequences the Wolfowitz decision has caused. The members of our country's armed services overseas, and all UOCAVA citizens, were thrust back into the Dark Ages of postal voting; additionally, a crucial step in the development of American democracy had been blocked for years to come. (As I will show in the following chapters, Internet voting has much more to offer the US than mere convenience.)

The Cause of SERVE's Demise

Ultimately, the responsibility for shelving the SERVE project lies with then Undersecretary of State Paul Wolfowitz. Only he knows exactly why he took that decision. The public record is incomplete. Some questions about his reasoning that cannot be answered by the public record alone include: did he put his own career interests ahead of the nation's interest, as circumstances seem to suggest? In other words, did he choose to avoid public controversy so as to make himself seem well suited to the job he hoped to get? Or, did he really believe the scary stories told by the four dissenters, and heroically stop SERVE to prevent the election catastrophe they predicted?

Nor does the public record show whether Wolfowitz considered any counter-claims made in defense of SERVE by its supporters or members of the SERVE team. Did they privately fight back? Did they try to save SERVE? If so, unlike the four dissenters, they did not go public with their arguments. The newspapers, magazines, and online sources of opinion which gave extended coverage to the sensational claims made about the supposed risks of using the SERVE system, did not give *any time*, much less equal time, to the defense of the project. As too often happens, in the midst of their feeding frenzy, bloggers, the media, and the press failed to even mention the other side's point of view.

Of course, the SERVE team was capable of making a strong case in favor of proceeding with the project. Surely they made some effort, at least in private consultation with Wolfowitz, to defend SERVE. If so, whatever was said has yet to be made public. Not only are the arguments put to Wolfowitz in defense of SERVE not in the public record, but his reasons for finding them unpersuasive, if they were made, are also a mystery.

Also for reasons unknown, the SERVE leadership did not publish its defense of the project until nearly three years after its demise. That defense was made in a report to Congress by then FVAP head, David Chu. Chu's report shows, among other things, just how security conscious the SERVE team was when they built the system. I will conclude this Chapter with a summary of Chu's report.

William J. Kelleher, Ph.D.

Chu's Belated Reply to the Four Dissenters

In rebuttal to the four dissenters, Chu noted that "Security has always been a primary concern in the development of information technology systems that facilitate the election process for UOCAVA citizens." Just as did VOI, SERVE "addressed these concerns rigorously through the use of digital certificates and encryption to provide privacy and security for all citizen and local election official transactions." As I mentioned above, the VOI technicians were well aware of the threats posed by hackers and voter fraud schemes. Thus, adds Chu, "Intrusion detection systems and independent test and certification processes were also applied."63

Wise to the ways of would-be attackers, Chu states that to "provide a high degree of protection, the SERVE security design relied on multiple layers of redundant checks and balances throughout the hardware, software, and human elements of the system."64 Drawing from their successful experiments with the VOI project in 2000, the SERVE technology was enhanced to include "roaming digital certificates for voter identification and authentication so the voter did not need a smart card enabled computer. Encryption mitigated the threats to network security and voter privacy. Digital signatures were incorporated to combat voter fraud, and controls were used to guard against vote buying and coercion."65 Finally, the "FVAP developed extensive testing, implementation and post-election evaluation strategies that would serve to determine whether the SERVE project had satisfied its original objectives."[66]

Since the security of SERVE itself was less questioned by the dissenters than the security in the voter's environment, Chu did not need to defend SERVE's security. However, to reassure Congress that his department was sensitive to security issues, he included a table (page 12 of his report) listing the security threats anticipated by his team, and the strategies they built into the system to mitigate those threats. Here is that table:

THREAT and MITIGATION

Network Security

- Encryption

- Intrusion Detection Systems

- Redundant Firewalls

- Penetration Tests

Privacy

- Digital Signatures

- Secure Socket Layers

- Encryption

- Voter ID/Ballot Data Separation

- Voted Ballot Data Verification

Virus, Worm, Trojan Horse

- Anti Virus Scanning

- Digital Signatures

- Voted Ballot Data Verification

Spoofing

- Secure Socket Layer

- Digital Signatures

- Voted Ballot Data Verification

Denial of Service

- Large Quantity of Bandwidth

- Multiple Carriers

- Multiple Internet Service

- Provider Entry Points

- Utilization Monitoring

Voter Fraud

- Digital Signatures

Other Countries

Chu also reviewed some of the major Internet voting projects carried out in eight other countries. He observed that Estonia had become the first country to hold its national election via Internet voting. Their system was thoroughly tested before being implemented in the 2005 election. 40 international observers were invited to monitor the process. They all agreed that the event was a complete success. Participation increased. No technical or security problems were reported.67 Fortunately, Russian dissidents have not interfered in Estonian elections.

Since 2000, Canada, England, France, The Netherlands, New Zealand, Spain, and Switzerland have all experimented with various forms of Internet voting in domestic elections and as a means for their overseas citizens to vote from off shore. All of these experiments were successful. *None* of the nightmare scenarios conjured up by the four dissenters came true in any of these cases. Of course, the dissenters neglected to discuss these counterexamples to their catalogue of scary stories.

Chu's Hope

Chu notes that Congress has recently provided funds, not to the DoD, but to the Election Assistance Commission (EAC) to work in conjunction with the National Institute of Standards and Technology (NIST) to establish new electronic absentee voting guidelines for UOCAVA citizens. Once these are complete, he assures Congress,

FVAP will follow them in the development of future electronic absentee voting projects.68 While surely disappointed that Congress has taken from his team the responsibility to originate these guidelines, Chu expressed his expectation that the new "guidelines on electronic voting from the EAC and NIST will frame the strategies for the eventual development of a large-scale internet voting project [in the US] *that will most likely mirror the functionality and the security of the VOI and SERVE projects."*69 In other words, despite the success of the four dissenters at shutting down the project, even three years later Chu still believed that the SERVE team got it right.

Chu adds that the FVAP will also continue to encourage state legislatures to enable their local election officials to participate in FVAP's use of fax, email, and other "electronic alternatives [to voting by mail] for *UOCAVA* citizens who live and serve in remote areas or distant places and are mobile (e.g., ships at sea, combat areas, missionaries and Peace Corps workers)."70 Finally, FVAP is planning to invite competitive bidding from private companies for a contract to improve its current systems. FVAP will specify that these improvements must be "built as individual modules that could be integrated into future expanded services which may include an internet voting system for UOCAVA citizens."71

Chu still has hope.

Conclusion

Clearly, in 2007 David Chu was anticipating a return to something like the SERVE Internet voting system for overseas Americans. Happily, this return is underway as I write, in the 2010-2011 period. In October of 2009 President Obama signed The MOVE Act (The Military and Overseas Voter Empowerment Act). This new law requires the states to send out absentee ballots at least 45 days before a federal election, so that overseas voters will have enough time to mail them back. In addition, the states must provide some form of electronic method of sending out voting material, if a voter requests it.

To comply with MOVE, thirty-three states provided some form of online voting for their overseas citizens during the November 2010 elections. Most of them used fax or email services, but two of them – Arizona and West Virginia – offered voting on a secure website, much like the old SERVE model. Not surprising to those who have heard both sides of the security debate, there have been no reports of security breaches by any of these states. Now, the way for *domestic trials* of Internet voting has been opened by these successes.

But before celebrating this good news, I would like to discuss some of the other benefits of Internet voting besides convenience, security, and speedy and accurate results. Surprisingly, Internet voting can help the US to fulfill the original intentions of our nation's Founding Fathers for our election processes in ways that the current two-party system has never even approached. Chapter Two will show exactly what those original intentions were, particularly for presidential elections.

Many Americans realize that our election processes are corrupted by the undemocratic advantages that Big Money now has over candidate selection and the control of public debate over candidates and issues. Chapter Three will review how that corruption comes about.

Chapter Four will show how Internet voting, properly organized, can make all US elections more democratic than they have ever been. The crippling dependency that candidates now have on elitist self-serving campaign contributors can be eliminated. Then, elected officials will take office completely free of political debts to anyone but the people who elected them. Once that happens, the locus of power in American government will shift to where it should be, in favor of the nation's interests and free of the rule of special interests.

Unfortunately, the fear and false information first spread by the four dissenters still infects public opinion. Thus, Chapter Five will endeavor to further combat their propaganda. Once the unreasoning untruth has been overcome, the potential for more democracy than Americans have ever dreamed of can be realized by putting the Internet into the service of our politics, as I will discuss in the concluding pages of this book.

Chapter Two

The Original Intentions of the Framers for US Presidential Elections

Introduction:

The Anti-Party Spirit of the Constitution

Our Constitution had its beginning in the Philadelphia Convention of 1787. The leaders of the 13 states held that meeting to discuss possible solutions to the problems of governing they were having under the Articles of Confederation. Those Articles were the first agreement between the states to have a federal government. But this first central government lacked the power it needed for such basic functions as raising taxes, or printing money and regulating interstate commerce. Sometimes called "the Second American Revolution," the men at the meeting in Philadelphia decided that a new constitution was necessary to establish a stronger federal government. They understood that if this new government was to have the legitimacy it would need to succeed, it would have to honor existing state power and independence as well as win the consent of the people of the several states.

Our Founding Fathers (a group that includes all the revolutionary leaders and activists of the time) were, in their intellectual orientation, men of the Enlightenment. The Enlightenment was the time in European history when science emerged as a way of understanding life and nature, rather than unquestioning belief in the authoritative dictates of the Church. Science, of course, encourages individuals to exercise Reason, to think for themselves, and to base their thinking on experience, observation, and experiment. This new method of thought was producing new knowledge by leaps and bounds in chemistry, physics, biology, and in medicine and technology. Thus, the Framers (the actual authors of the Constitution) strove to be as rational as they could be in composing our Constitution.

The document the Framers produced won ratification in 1788. But there were many objections to it by other members of our nation's Founding Generation; most importantly, it lacked a list of specified and guaranteed rights. Thus, before the document was ratified, the Framers had to engage in a great deal of explaining and debate, and promise to add a "bill of rights" as their first order of business under the new Constitution. The Bill of Rights was proposed in 1789, and ratified in 1791.

In this chapter I will attempt to clarify and explain the original vision of the Framers for one small, yet significant, element of the document they produced in Philadelphia. That is, the intentions they shared for the workings of the presidential election process. But first, an item of disclosure, and then a note of caution.

The reader will see that some of the intentions of the Framers seem unfavorable to democratic sentiments. If it appears that I do not gloss over but rather underscore some of those intentions, it is because I read the Constitution and the intentions the Framers had for it with such sentiments. Also, I have resisted comparing the original intentions of the Framers with the practices currently followed under the two-party system. The two-party system does conform to some of the expectations of the Framers for the presidential election process. For example, a president and vice president do get elected every four years. But, other intentions that the Framers had for the process are not so well fulfilled. Principal among these are the element of *deliberation* that was meant to be the definitive method for the selection of the top two executive officers.

Curing the Mischiefs of Faction.

Many readers will be surprised to learn that among the most important original objectives of the Framers, or authors, of the US Constitution was to fashion a government that *could not* be taken over by political parties. Generally, our nation's Founding Fathers abhorred political parties. They regularly referred to parties as "factions." A brief discussion of the theory behind our Constitution will show what a prominent place anti-party sentiment played in the political thought of our Founders.

They knew from their own experience that political parties put the party's self-interests, such as winning elections and obtaining privileged legislation, before the best interests of the people as a whole. Wary of such organizations, they sought to establish a system of government that would always strive to act in the best interests of the whole country.

The Founders were familiar with the way parties distorted the functioning of a political system, starting with political campaigns. At the time of the Philadelphia Convention, party campaigns were already being conducted in New York City, and in some state politics, and for the members of the House of Commons in England. They saw the crowds being stirred-up, the false promises being told, and the votes being bought and sold. They wanted their government to be above such intrigues and vulgarities.

They had other reasons for their antipathy to parties. For example, they understood that party loyalty discourages independent thinking. John Marshall, who some say is the greatest Chief Justice of the Supreme Court, wrote, in a letter to his brother, that party politics are "despicable in the extreme... Nothing, I believe, more debases or pollutes the human mind than faction."[72]

Another independent thinker, Thomas Jefferson, had a deep contempt for political parties. A friend once asked Jefferson if he considered himself a member of any political party. Jefferson replied, that "[I have] never submitted the whole system of my opinions to the creed of any party of men whatever, in religion, in philosophy, in politics, or in anything else, where I was capable of thinking for myself. Such an addiction is the last degradation of a free and moral agent. If I could not go to heaven but with a party, I would not go there at all."73

With amazing prescience John Adams wrote, "There is nothing which I dread so much as a division of the republic into two great parties ... This ... is to be dreaded as the greatest political evil under our Constitution."74

In their efforts to have the Constitution ratified, James Madison, Alexander Hamilton, and John Jay wrote a series of newspaper articles explaining both the need for a new form of federal government, and how each provision of the Constitution would fulfill that need. These essays were later collected, numbered, and published as a book entitled *The Federalist Papers*.75 They agreed on the importance of preventing parties from corrupting government, and they give numerous reasons for their resentment of parties. For instance, Hamilton was contemptuous of parties, in part, and like Jefferson, because they could corrode an individual's sense of civic morality. Hamilton wrote that a "spirit of faction" can drive individuals to do together that "for which they would blush in a private capacity."76

Voicing an opinion shared by the Founders, Madison wrote that the need for government is "a reflection on human nature." He said, famously, "If men were angels, no government would be necessary."77 An avid reader of history, Madison observed that factions are particularly a problem in large and diverse societies, like the society being formed by the 13 new states. Where there are numerous people, individuals naturally develop different, and sometimes conflicting, interests.

Then, sounding eerily like a 21ˢᵗ Century observer, he commented, "A zeal for different opinions concerning religion, concerning government, and many other points … have, in turn, divided mankind into parties, inflamed them with mutual animosity, and rendered them much more disposed to vex and oppress each other than to cooperate for their common good. … But the most common and durable source of factions has been the various and unequal distribution of property."[78] Due to these variations of wealth, "Different interests necessarily exist in different classes of citizens."[79] Hence, there is a compelling self-serving materialistic motive for factions to compete for political power.

Expressing views widely held among the Framers, Madison wrote that because the Constitution separates governmental powers, balances those powers, and provides the different departments with checks against encroachment by the others, as well as giving the people a part in the political process, it is "the proper antidote for the diseases of faction."[80] To this end, "Ambition must be made to counteract ambition."[81] For the Framers, then, a constitutional separation of powers held out the best hope for preventing a single faction from controlling the whole of government. Madison predicted that a federal government, with more power and authority than that in the Articles of Confederation, would be able "to break and control the violence of faction."[82]

Hamilton concurred with Madison's commentaries, and, like the other Founders, thought that a *rational* system of government is one that guides officials to serve the interests of the whole community. He asked rhetorically, "Why has government been instituted at all?" He answered, "Because the passions of men will not conform to the dictates of reason and justice without constraint."[83] The new Constitution was meant to provide the needed "constraint" on the propensity of people to form factions, which would irrationally strive for self-serving advantage at the expense of the whole community. In this sense, the Constitution was meant to be a work of social engineering, a political system designed to insure that government would regularly, almost mechanically, operate to serve the public good.

The Framers of the Constitution rejected the idea of establishing a pure democracy. The main reason, explains Madison, is that "a pure democracy … can admit of no cure for the mischiefs of faction."[84] In such a system, only if "a faction consists of less than a majority," can the majority vote check the minority faction's selfish behavior. However, when "a majority is included in a faction," then merely voting will not prevent mischief, and "neither moral nor religious motives can be relied on as an adequate control."[85] Therefore, a written constitution is necessary, among other things, to insure that the rights of minorities will be protected against abusive majorities.

The Framers felt that this plan for *a representative government*, or "republic … promises the cure for which we are seeking."[86] Idealistic as it may seem from the perspective of the 21st Century, the Framers hoped that representatives would be less susceptible to "the spirit of party" than the average citizen would be. Representatives were envisioned as being persons who would have a higher sense of responsibility for the whole, the interests of which they would be elected to represent. They would resist the temptations of factions with a sense of judgment "more consonant to the public good."[87] One of the most fervent beliefs of the Founders, writes Madison, was that "no form of government whatever has any other value than as it may be fitted for the attainment of … the public good."[88]

The Powers Separated

Our Founding Fathers were also wary of having an excessively strong executive power. They had just fought a revolution against a king, so they were highly sensitive to the potential for abuse in a strong executive. They shared Madison's understanding that in "Republican government, the legislative authority necessarily predominates."[89] Hence, the *first* Article of the Constitution defines the legislative branch.

In part, to prevent any single faction from capturing the legislative power of government, the Framers divided that power into two divisions, the Senate and the House of Representatives. They intended that if one part were to succumb to party domination, the other part would jealously guard its independent powers and thereby prevent the faction from capturing the whole legislative branch.

That is why the power to elect the members of these bodies is also separated. Originally, the state legislators, rather than the people, were to elect a state's two US senators. The people could only vote directly for one federal official; namely, their representative in the House. Here is the reasoning the Framers followed: suppose the people of several states fell under the spell of a faction, and elected the faction's leaders to the House. The state legislators would, hopefully, resist capture, and at least the US senators would be elected to represent the national interest, rather than the interests of a party. As a check within the legislative system, if the House became faction-dominated, the faction-free Senate would then resist any self-serving moves by the other chamber. The Framers anticipated that their constitutional government would function rationally, like a faction-resisting clockwork.

Another way to prevent any one faction from forming in the House, and acting against the best interest of the whole country, is to have all the representatives come up for election every two years. This would give voters who had once succumbed to the temptations of a faction an opportunity to return to Reason, and rectify their ill-considered selection of a Representative. The Constitution also provides for staggered elections in the Senate, with six year terms, so that one third of the senators would be up for election every two years. This empowers the states to remove faction-prone senators and replace them with *nonpartisan officials*; yet, having two thirds of the Senate not facing elections would provide some stability to that institution's policies.

To help the presidency resist capture by any faction, the Constitution provides for an executive that is relatively independent of the legislature. In parliamentary governments, the legislature appoints the executive, or prime minister. This makes the person in office dependent upon the will of the legislators. If a faction were to capture such a legislature, the members could appoint one of their own to the executive branch, and the faction would dominate those two branches of government. But a president who is not dependent upon the legislature for his or her term in office, can execute the laws, and carry out the other executive functions, without succumbing to the will of a faction-dominated legislature.

Hence, Article Two both establishes certain independent powers for the presidency, and, as a check on the executive, specifies the powers it is to share with the legislative branch. To further insure the independence of the executive, the president and vice president are to be elected every four years by a special body of electors who have no connection to the House or Senate. This body would be constituted anew every four years by a unique election process under the authority of the legislature in each state. I will closely examine this "Electoral College" system in a moment.

In Article Three of the Constitution the Framers sought to establish a judicial branch that could not be captured by some faction, or party. This independence would be preserved by allowing Supreme Court justices and federal judges, once appointed by the president and confirmed by the Senate, to have their jobs for life (assuming "good behavior"). Hamilton explains that the Constitution separates the judicial branch from the other branches out of a "fear that the pestilential breath of faction may poison the fountains of justice."90 Dividing the appointment power between the president and the Senate would, so the Framers thought, also help to obstruct the capture of the courts by self-serving political parties.

Besides the three branches of the US government, our political system consists of separate states, each entitled to have its own "Republican form of government," as guaranteed by Article IV, Section Four, of our Constitution. Providing for separate states within a federal system is also a way to guard against the mischiefs of faction. Before the days of mass communication, Madison anticipated that with several states, "The influence of factious leaders may kindle a flame within their particular States but will be unable to spread a general conflagration through the other states."91

Washington's Farewell

Clearly, the political philosophy of our Founding Fathers included the proposition that a government based upon Reason would strive to serve the interests of the whole community. Therefore, factions, moved by selfish passion, would work an irrational corruption on the rational operation of government. Lest the above discussion has not provided enough evidence to convince some readers of the predominant anti-party intentions of the Founders, let us consider one more expression of opinion on that subject.

George Washington is, of course, widely regarded as "the father of our nation." He led the revolutionary army in its successful war against Great Britain, sometimes paying his soldiers from his own pocket so they could send money home. He was elected to preside over the writing of the Constitution during the Philadelphia Convention. After the Constitution was ratified by the states, he was unanimously elected to be the first President of the United States. In 1796, when his second term in that office was about to expire, he delivered a "Farewell Address" in which he declined to stand for a third term, and in which he gave his parting words of advice to his country.

His speech is divided between domestic and foreign policy. I will only discuss what he said about domestic policy. *Two-thirds* of that discussion is focused on the threat he saw coming to a unified government from political parties. He implored his listeners to "[let me] warn you in the most solemn manner against the baneful effects of the spirit of party..."[92] Since he was declining another term, these admonitions "will be offered to you with the more freedom, as you can only see in them the disinterested warnings of a parting friend, who can possibly have no personal motive to bias his counsel." He said:

> To the efficacy and permanency of your Union, a government for the whole is indispensable. No alliance, however strict, between the parts can be an adequate substitute ... All obstructions to the execution of the laws, all combinations and associations, under whatever plausible character, with the real design to

direct, control, counteract, or awe the regular deliberation and action of the constituted authorities, are destructive of this fundamental principle, and of fatal tendency. They serve to organize faction, to give it an artificial and extraordinary force; to put, in the place of the delegated will of the nation the will of a party, often a small but artful and enterprising minority of the community; and, according to the alternate triumphs of different parties, to make the public administration the mirror of the ill-concerted and incongruous projects of faction, rather than the organ of consistent and wholesome plans digested by common counsels and modified by mutual interests.

However combinations or associations of the above description may now and then answer popular ends, they are likely, in the course of time and things, to become potent engines, by which cunning, ambitious, and unprincipled men will be enabled to subvert the power of the people and to usurp for themselves the reins of government, destroying afterwards the very engines [of our representative government] which have lifted them to unjust dominion.   This spirit, un-fortunately, is inseparable from our nature, having its root in the strongest passions of the human mind. It exists under different shapes in all governments, more or less stifled, controlled, or repressed; but, in those of the popular form [like ours], it is seen in its greatest rankness, and is truly their *worst enemy* (emphasis added). The name of American, which belongs to you in your national capacity, must always exalt the just pride of patriotism more than any appellation derived from local discriminations.

Finally, he expressed his hope that "These considerations [would] speak a persuasive language to every reflecting and virtuous mind, and exhibit the continuance of the Union as a primary object of patriotic desire."

Washington's heartfelt warning clearly expresses the extreme anti-party sentiment he shared with the other Founders. As the man who presided over the crafting of our founding document, he understood this anti-party/pro-national interest intention as the true "Spirit of our Constitution." From his position, he witnessed how each Framer at the Philadelphia Convention strove to impress on the document his own earnest desire to establish a rational, faction-free, government for the whole. It was to fulfill those ends that they agreed upon the separation of powers with numerous checks and balances. To their minds, Reason left no doubt that life, liberty, and the pursuit of happiness depends upon having a country which forms an unbroken Union. This pro-whole/anti-faction Spirit pervades every part of the document, from start to finish.

The Electoral College, too, is infused with this Spirit. The best way to understand what the Electoral College meant to its authors is to first read the section in the Constitution that defines the institution. So, after quoting the formal provisions for the Electoral College, I will discuss some of the most apparent tacit understandings its creators shared, and which explain the meaning those provisions had for them.

The Formal Provisions for the Electoral College

Article II, Section One contains the actual language specifying how the Framers originally intended the President and Vice President of the United States to be elected. This was meant to be accomplished through the institution we call the "Electoral College." Beginning with the second paragraph of Article II, Section One, the Constitution states:

"Each State shall appoint, in such manner as the Legislature thereof may direct, a number of Electors, equal to the whole number of Senators and Representatives to which the State may be entitled in the Congress: but no Senator or Representative, or person holding an office of trust or profit under the United States, shall be appointed an Elector."

The next paragraph of this Section states, "The Electors shall meet in their respective States, and vote by ballot for two persons, of whom one at least shall not be an inhabitant of the same State with themselves."

When the Electors meet in their states and vote, "they shall make a list of all the persons voted for, and of the number of votes for each." The lists are to be signed, certified, and sealed, and then submitted "to the President of the Senate." (The Constitution gives the vice president the position of President of the Senate. However, it is mostly a "figurehead" position since, under Article One,

107

Section Three, the VP cannot vote in the Senate except to break a tie).

After all the lists have come in, the President of the Senate is to meet with the House and Senate together, open the several envelops, and for the first time, count the votes from the various state Electoral Colleges. The person with the most votes as president will become the President of the United States. The person with the most votes as vice president will take that office. But if there is a tie, or if no one wins a majority of the votes, then the House of Representatives is to elect the president, and the Senate is to elect the vice president.

The part of Section One about making "a list" became one of the first of many problems for the Electoral College. In 1800 Thomas Jefferson almost lost his election to the presidency to Aaron Burr when both men received 73 votes. In their list of vote totals, the Electors neglected to specify that they meant Jefferson to be president and Burr to be his vice president. After the confusion was cleared up, the House voted according to the will of the Electors, and Jefferson was elected president, Burr vice president. To clarify this clerical oversight, Section One was later modified by the Twelfth Amendment, which was ratified in 1804. It states that the Electors are to make "distinct ballots" for the presidential and vice presidential vote, and to submit the results on "distinct lists" for the two offices, rather than on "a list."

First, to clear up a common misconception about the Electoral College, let us look at the phrase, "The Electors shall meet in their respective States, and vote by ballot for two persons…"93 Although the term "Electoral College" is widely used in discussions about the presidential election process, that term is actually not used in the Constitution. Some people are mislead by the term into thinking that *one group* meets in one place to elect our two executive officers. But the directive phrase "The Electors shall meet in their respective States" shows that the Electors were intended to meet to vote in their own, or "respective," states, and not as a national body. Thus, the Framers did *not* intend that a single, national vote be taken to elect the president and vice president. Instead, the "Electoral College" is as many separate groups of Electors as there are states, which meet every four years in their state, and which never meet together. In other words, and I will discuss this further, the election of the president and vice president was originally intended to be a state-based operation.

To bring into a clear light this particular original intention, let us return to the first two words I quoted from the second paragraph of Section One, "Each state." These two words have an enormous significance, which can only be appreciated when placed within the nest of meanings and intentions shared by the Framers as they created their new "federal" government. We of the 21st Century, who are steeped in the political culture of the two-party system, must make an empathic effort to understand what the words "Each state" meant to the Framers as they wrote, read, and voted to approve the words during the Philadelphia Convention over 200 years ago. The best way to come to this understanding is to consider the times within which the Framers worked.

Behind the Electoral College

Small State Concerns

The Electoral College is, in part, the result of a political compromise between the small states and large states during the time the Constitution was being written in Philadelphia in 1787. Madison mentions this in Federalist Paper number 62, and in his notes on the Convention.94 The notes show that the problem came up during the discussion of how the president and vice president were to be chosen.

Large and small state representatives agreed that they should not have Congress elect the executive branch officers, as is done in parliamentary political systems. As a faction prevention measure, they wanted to separate the executive and the legislature and make each branch independent of the other. However, the small states were concerned that in any method of voting for the president and vice president, a few large states could combine, or form their own faction, and dominate the process. Because of their numerical advantage, a faction of large states would be able to choose the executive officers in every election. They could also elect only large state leaders, and exclude the leaders of the small states from even being considered for the positions. In other words, small states worried that they could be rendered irrelevant and powerless in the presidential election process.

The Framers sought to ease these concerns with several legislative devices, or rules. One rule, or provision, is that every state would have equal representation in the Senate. Each state would have two senators, no matter how large or small the state.

While this guaranteed equality among the states in the Senate, provisions were also put into the Electoral College which would guarantee more equality of participation for the small states directly in the presidential election process. For instance, each state was guaranteed at least three Electors (one for each senator, and one more since each state would have at least one representative in the House).

Each state was given an opportunity to have at least one of its leaders considered and voted for by other states in the process. This guarantee was effected by the Article Two requirement, and repeated in the 12th Amendment, that in their votes for president and vice president, one of the persons they vote for would be from another state. Thus, small state leaders could be considered by their own Electors, and had some chance of being considered and voted for by Electors in the bigger states.

Additionally, as a way of equalizing state power in the presidential election process, each state was to conduct *its own election*. That is, rather than one national election, the Framers envisioned one complete presidential election per state. The process would have two stages. First, in each state "the Legislature thereof" would decide how its Electors would be chosen. Secondly, the Electors would meet in their state capital, deliberate, and vote *directly* for a president and vice president.

The Election of Electors

As I have shown, the Constitution specifies that "Each State shall appoint, in such manner as the Legislature thereof may direct, a number of Electors." Thus, the states are free to chose their own way of "appointing" Electors. The legislatures could do it themselves, or they could delegate the responsibility outside themselves, such as to the governor, or the people. The Constitution says nothing about having the people in each state elect Electors, or otherwise participate in presidential elections.

However, according to Hamilton, Madison, and Jay, the Framers *anticipated* that the states would have Electors elected by a popular vote.[95] Thus, the people of each state were expected to play an *indirect* part by electing presidential Electors, who would then vote directly for the executives. In practice, however, several states started out with their legislature electing Electors. The people in these states objected to being excluded from the presidential election process. But forty years passed, following the ratification of the Constitution, before the people in every state won the meager privilege, which is all we have now, of electing Electors.

The Framers had agreed that letting *the people* of the states directly elect the president and vice president was a bad idea. They wanted Electors to act *for* the people, as their representatives, in the actual vote. The central reason for this convoluted approach to presidential elections was, according to Hamilton, "to afford as little opportunity as possible to tumult and disorder."96 I will discuss this prejudice against the people more in a moment.

The Framers expected that there would be no political rallies or campaigns in this process. Indeed, as incredible as it may seem in our time, such office-seeking behavior was uniformly regarded by our Founding Fathers as beneath the dignity of any gentleman like themselves. For the first 100 years of presidential elections, prospective presidents did not openly campaign for the office. (Once the two-party system got underway in the 19th Century, the parties campaigned *for* the prospective presidents. Until the 20th Century, the candidates stayed home, so that they would "look presidential.")

As the number of states with popular voting for Electors increased, a common pattern emerged. Prior to that vote, newspapers would have announced the names of the prospective Electors. Generally, before the rise of the two-party system, the candidate-Electors were put on the ballot by the governor or legislature. Editorials, articles, and letters to the editors would discuss the policies of the prospects. Some of the prospects would already have been known to the people. This could include local lawyers, judges, mayors, other state and local officials, or prominent persons in the community. Through informal meetings, in the town hall, the town square, or popular pub, some of these prospects would make themselves available for discussion with the local citizenry.

Deliberation

After the popular vote, the elected Electors would meet together on an appointed day in the state capital. They would convene in a courtroom, church, or other meeting room set aside for the occasion. In the course of their meetings they would make a short list of persons they thought best suited for president and vice president. Since there would be no presidential candidates engaged in boisterous campaigning under some party banner, the Electors would quietly draw from their general knowledge of prominent persons in their own state, and in neighboring states. They might deliberate for a few days before taking a final vote.

Once completed, they would record their votes, and send their two lists, one for president and the other for vice president, to the President of the Senate. Then they would return to their ordinary lives.

In this process, and consistent with our "federal" system, *each state* would be an independent and equal partner with every other state. In the vision of the Framers for this process, there would be no national parties coordinating groups of states. They envisioned no cabals between states, and no domination of one state over another. Each state would take care of its own business, and pay little heed to what the other states were doing. Only after all the votes had been counted in a joint session of Congress would the final results be known. Only after the newspapers reported what had happened in the various states would any one state know what the others had done.

As men of the Enlightenment, one of the highest priorities of the Framers was that the presidential election process be, like the rest of the Constitution, as I have said, in accordance with Reason. The original intention to have *procedural equality* among the states is clearly a rational principle. It establishes order among the states during the presidential election process, and includes them all without favoring any one of them. Although some states had a numerical advantage in the final vote, each state was equal to every other *as a matter of procedure*. This procedural equality is implied in the two words "Each state," and is surely one of the reasons that the small states consented to the Great Compromise, which, among other things, gave all states two senators while allowing representation by population in the House.97

When the point of view of the small states is considered in the context of that time, it seems to me that they cannot be accused of buying "a pig in a poke" when they agreed to the Electoral College procedure for presidential elections. They received several significant benefits. As mentioned, besides each state having equal representation in the Senate, in presidential elections every state had to vote for someone from another state, which gave small state politicians a chance at being considered and elected by other states. Also, at that time, the most extreme voting ratio between the largest and smallest states was only 12:3.

Today the numerical disparity between the Electoral Colleges in the states is far greater than it was then. In the first presidential election, Virginia had the largest electoral body, with twelve members. Massachusetts had ten. New York had eight. Only Rhode Island and Delaware had the minimum of three, all the others had at least five.[98]

The Framers could not have anticipated that in 2008 seventeen states would have from three to five Electors, while California had 55, and eight states had twenty or more. This huge imbalance in Electors occurred long after all the Framers were gone. So the numerical inequality then was not as great as it is today, with the most extreme ratio of 55:3 between California and several small states. Thus, in our situation, that compromise might not seem as acceptable as it seemed then. All told, the guarantee of procedural equality, plus these other benefits, made the bargain between the large and small states seem to them "fair enough."

Faction Prevention

As we have seen, one of the means by which the Constitution would protect the offices of the United States from domination by factions would be to separate federal and state power. The idea of this "federalism" is that if a faction took over the states, the federal government could resist, and vice versa.

Incredible as it may seem today, the Electoral College was intended by the Framers to be a bulwark against factions seeking to capture the presidential election process. John Jay, who became the Supreme Court's first Chief Justice, expressed the opinion shared by the Framers that the Electoral College "mode," or "system," of electing the president would have the capacity to resist "the activity of party zeal," to which popular elections are vulnerable.99

So, just in case the US Congress came under the control of some faction, Article II, Section One, states that "no Senator or Representative, or person holding an office of trust or profit under the United States, shall be appointed an Elector." Under this provision the agents of a mischievous federal legislature would not be able to penetrate and corrupt the presidential election process by putting federal officials into a state's Electoral College.

In addition to being free from any federal influence, the states were also envisioned as acting independently of out-of-state interference by privately organized parties. Each state would act on its own. If an out-of-state, or multi-state, faction took over one or two states, the independence of the other states and the federal government would enable them to act as checks against the self-serving faction becoming a national power.

The Framers feared that to have all the Electors meet together at one time and in one place would surely invite the very mischiefs of faction that they so ardently sought to prevent. By having Electors meet in "each state," the Framers hoped to prevent the formation of a *national faction* which would corrupt the presidential election process.

The authors of the Constitution seem to have assumed that Electors would be unable to combine in a corrupting faction for two main reasons. One is that different people would probably be elected as Electors every four years.

Over that period of time, just the entry of new generations of voters would tend to discourage the continued re-election of the same folks to be Electors. This turnover would prevent the kind of continuing conspiracy necessary for faction building. Secondly, being dispersed over the several states, communication would be difficult to conduct because of the limited time they would have to complete their deliberations. Both communication and transportation were dependent on horseback in those days.

Suppose a faction within a state captures the vote for that state's Electors. They will be in a position to bargain with presidential prospects for self-serving deals, contrary to the nation's best interests. But as long as this corruption is confined to one or two states, the national interest will not be significantly undermined.

The Constitution would also put a check on a state that had fallen under the influence of an internal faction by requiring that at least one of the people for whom the Electors voted for as president or vice president "shall not be an inhabitant of the same state with themselves." As we have seen, this provision would also boost the chances of a person from a small state being considered by the Electors in a large state. A private faction in a state could compel its Electoral College to consider *one* of its agents, but not two. This would also prevent a state's internal faction from penetrating the executive branch of the federal government with two of its agents, one president and the other vice president, thus completely capturing that branch.

Other Provisions

There are other provisions in the Constitution that express the anti-faction spirit of that document. For example, the first line of Article I, Section Ten says, "No State shall enter into any treaty, alliance, or *confederation* ..." (emphasis added). We fought a Civil War over that last term. In the third paragraph, Article I, Section Ten states, in part, that "No State shall, without the consent of Congress, ... enter into any agreement or compact with another state ..." Clearly, the Framers sought to anticipate and block every form by which factions could break up the Union.

Gentlemen Preferred

The Framers wrote the Constitution with an elitist bias. Yet, while favoring elites, the Founding Fathers were not aristocrats – at least not in the sense of the European societies of their time. Those aristocrats believed that the rule by those who were born among the "better few" is nature's way, and God's will.

Our Founders rejected the notion that birth should determine class. Their anti-aristocracy feelings were so strong that in Article I, Section Nine of the Constitution, they prohibited the US government from granting "titles of nobility," and they forbad any US official from accepting titles "of any kind whatever, from any King, Prince, or foreign state." They agreed with the idea that there are people in society who rank among the "better few."

119

However, entry into this "meritocracy" is to be open to anyone who earns his status by dint of his own effort and wit. Their biographies show numerous instances of "rags to riches" climbs. Alexander Hamilton and Benjamin Franklin are two of the best known examples of what the Founders regarded as men of merit. For our Founders, elite status was an achievement.

The Framers of the Constitution envisioned a "representative government" with the representatives largely drawn from the elite classes; i.e., the classes of high achievers. Thus, the system tilts in favor of that conception. In a moment I will discuss other undemocratic biases reflected in their construction of the Electoral College.

Our Constitution was designed to protect the interests of economic elites by giving them the lion's share of power in the selection of federal officeholders. The president, every member of the federal judiciary, and the Senate were meant to be selected by what were then known as "gentlemen." At the time the Constitution was written, nearly every state had laws which restricted voting mostly to white males who either owned land or were otherwise well off. For the most part, this group of "gentlemen" also supplied the candidates for state legislatures and elected them to office.

As I noted above, the Constitution originally provided that the state legislatures would elect the state's two senators to the United States Senate. Of course, only gentlemen could afford to leave their farms and businesses to do the business of legislating. So, once again, gentlemen would be electing gentlemen to office. The Constitution provided that the people could vote directly for their member of the House of Representatives, but who could afford to take two years away from work to fill the job other than gentlemen?

The members of the judiciary would be gentlemen, because only gentlemen were raised in families where the sons were educated in the law. The president would nominate a federal judge or Supreme Court Justice, and the Senate would confirm or deny – gentlemen selecting gentlemen.

Although the Constitution allows the people in the states to elect Electors, the Framers expected the members of the Electoral College to be the gentlemen of their communities. That is why no provision is made in the Constitution for reimbursing Electors for the costs of transportation, food, or lodging associated with fulfilling their duties. Gentlemen could easily defray these expenses, and take the required time off from work. Who would the people most likely elect to represent them in the Electoral College but a state's governor, a state legislator, a mayor, or some other prominent fellow? And the president they elected also must be a gentleman. Who else would have a national reputation and could afford the time required away from his business affairs?

Jay wrote, "the select assemblies for choosing the President, as well as the State legislatures who appoint the senators, will in general be composed of the most enlightened and respectable citizens." Such citizens, of course, are likely to elect as president and senator "those men only who have become the most distinguished by their abilities and virtue."100

Thus, the Framers meant the Electoral College to be a small group of materially successful white males, like themselves. These Electors were expected to elect one of their own kind for the presidency. Indeed, George Washington was one of the wealthiest slave owning white males in the country when he was elected the first President of the United States. In the republic that our Founders envisioned, the interest of gentlemen would be well protected because gentlemen would dominate the government.

Deliberative Gentlemen

In accordance with their great belief in Reason, our Founders sought to fashion a government that was as conducive as possible to rational and deliberative decision-making. Indeed, both House and Senate were expected to be devoted to rational deliberation.

Favoring gentlemen, and keeping the common man from holding offices in the federal judiciary and US Senate, and giving the common fellow only an indirect role in electing the president and vice president, were understood as ways of avoiding the kind of raucous and boisterous behavior that party politics can stir up. Gentlemen were thought to be able to rise above the sort of "tumult and disorder" that distracts the mind from clear reasoning based on knowledge. Such unemotional thinking was regarded as necessary to make rational calculations concerning the nation's best interests.

Thus, to *promote* thoughtful deliberations over political matters was as important to the authors of our Constitution as was their effort to *discourage* the mischiefs of faction. Indeed, these two intentions, one positive, one negative, are inseparable elements in the understanding the Framers had of good government. For them, factions and irrationality were two sides of the same coin. The separation of powers was originally intended, then, to facilitate thoughtful and informed deliberation.

They applied these principles of social engineering in fashioning the Electoral College. The Framers expected the Electors to engage in a *deliberative process* when choosing executive personnel. Thus, the Framers took several steps to promote reason and deliberation in the presidential election process. These steps included: 1) having Electors rather than the people vote for the executives; 2) having Electors meet in small groups, which at the time were only from 3 to 12 members; 3) confining these groups to their separate states; 4) biasing the process in favor of "men of means," who could afford to pay their lodging costs while meeting with other Electors, as well as take time off from work; and, 5) by limiting the process to a single purpose to be accomplished in a short period of time, in which the deliberations and vote would be made and the group then disbanded.

Hamilton was a strong believer that a government of gentlemen would best insure that Reason prevails over the spirit of party. Thus, he envisioned the Electoral College as providing gentlemen with an opportunity to reason together. In Federalist Paper number 68 he wrote that it "was equally desirable, that the immediate election should be made by men most capable of analyzing the qualities adapted to the [presidency], and acting under circumstances favorable to deliberation, and to a judicious combination of all the reasons and inducements which were proper to govern their choice."[101]

Most of the Framers agreed with Hamilton that "A small number of persons, selected by their fellow-citizens from the general mass, will be most likely to possess the information and discernment requisite to such complicated investigations." Also, small groups are likely to be more conducive to honest discourse than that shown by candidates in campaigns. In presidential elections, for the Framers, "Nothing was more to be desired than that every practicable obstacle should be opposed to cabal, intrigue, and corruption."[102]

Clearly, the Electoral College was intended to engage in a thoughtful and deliberative process, conducted among a few dignified gentlemen, who would discuss personnel among themselves with as much decorum, and only a little less formality, than in a judicial proceeding. What the Framers had in mind can fairly be compared to a modern corporation holding *personnel selection meetings*. The big difference is that Electors were not envisioned as considering *applicants*, but rather men who had *not* applied or campaigned for the position. Hence, the Framers expected the electors to discuss not office-seeking applicants, but gentlemen known to them to have a "continental character."

Why the President is Not Directly Elected by the People

During the debates in the Philadelphia Convention, Governor Morris proposed to the members that the president be elected directly by the people, as were the governors of Massachusetts and New York.103 This seems to have caused considerable alarm among the gentlemen present.

Fresh in their minds was the wild irrationality displayed, in their opinion, by the rioting mob in the recent Shay's Rebellion. Daniel Shays was a patriot who fought in the Revolution under Washington's command. But in 1786, he led an unsuccessful revolt against the government of Massachusetts. That government was driving Shays and other veterans into bankruptcy. Massachusetts imposed heavy taxes on small land owners, like Shays, but little or no taxes on rich merchants and shippers, while the state officials were paying themselves fat salaries. The officials tried to justify the inequalities by resorting to patriotism and arguing that the tax revenue was needed to, among other things, pay off the debts incurred by the costs of the Revolution. But to these rebels, such patriotic appeals were merely the last resort of scoundrels.

At a time when over 90% of the people lived on small farms, many of the men present at the Philadelphia Convention were landlords and creditors who rented land to the common farmer and who held the common man in debt. These gentlemen feared that if *the people* had too

125

much power they would do such horrible things as abolish debtor's prison, forgive all debts by law, and institute rent control.

In the midst of the commotion caused by Morris's proposal, Colonel George Mason of Virginia quipped that it would be as "unnatural" to refer the selection of the president to the people "as it would be to refer a choice of colors to a blind man." Inspired by the levity, one Mr. Williamson suggested that having the US legislature elect the president would promote rational choice, while allowing the people to directly elect the president would be as irrational as drawing straws!

While this comment probably provoked another round of guffaws in the room, modern democratic sensibilities would not find it funny. But the incident shows how far from the minds of these elites was any serious consideration of a popularly elected president.

One of the Framers, James Wilson, pointed out that there were several states whose governors were directly elected by the people without catastrophe. But the other Framers had heard enough. That proposal was promptly voted down. The majority of Framers did not want the masses electing the President of the United States. That position was just too important, in their view, to be left to the common sort to fill. While it is true that literacy rates among the common folk were low at the time, Framer *classism* seems to be the primary reason why the Constitution makes no provision for the popular election of the president.

The Struggle Against Oligarchy

In the republic that the Framers envisioned, the interest of gentlemen would be well protected because gentlemen would dominate the government. But the people were not entirely excluded from the selection of government officials. As we have seen, the Constitution originally provided one avenue for popular participation; that the people of each state can elect their members to the House of Representatives.

This one thin link of the people to their government distinguished our original "republic" from pure oligarchy, or the exclusive rule by the wealthy few. Indeed, a republic may be defined as a political system that guarantees a place in government to both the wealthy few, and to the less well off masses. Although the reverse order between the classes would still qualify as a "republic," in the new United States, the place for the minority of economic elites was at the top of the power hierarchy. Prior to the inclusion of the Bill of Rights, the right to elect House members was the only concession made by the Framers to the masses. That was as close as the Framers wanted to come to democracy. Favoring oligarchy, then, was among the original intentions of our Constitution.

While the Framers anticipated that the states would allow popular elections for Electors, that would be only a *privilege*, and not a guaranteed *right*. Indeed, the right to vote was severely restricted in most states at the time. As I have mentioned, many states only allowed well off white males and land owners to vote. Elements of this elitist chauvinism, with its racist and sexist undertones, have carried through in the development of our political system to this day.

One indication of the all too human fallibility of the Framers is their astonishing assumption that the farmer-soldiers who fought in the Revolution would passively accept a political system that disdainfully barred them from full participation in the self-government project for which they had fought. As we have seen, the ink on the Constitution was barely dry before the people in the states demanded that a bill of rights be attached to the Constitution as a condition of ratification. Only after the Founders agreed to this condition did the majority of the states vote to ratify.

Even before the Constitution was ratified in 1788, there were mass movements within the states demanding an expansion of voting rights. Within about twenty years after ratification, most states had abolished all property restrictions on voting for white males. The original expectation of some Framers that each of the states would allow a popular vote for Electors was not realized until the 1830s (except for South Carolina, which finally conformed its rules to the rest of the country after the Civil War).

There were, of course, other democratizing movements. After a long struggle by progressive activists, the people in the states won the right to directly elect their senators when the 17th Amendment was ratified in 1913.

Gradually, some of the states began to allow women to vote for state officials. However, the right of women to vote in federal elections was not nationally recognized until the 19th Amendment was ratified in 1920 – more than 130 years after the Constitution had come into effect.

Shamefully, all restrictions on black voting were not removed until the 1964 Civil Rights Act and the 1965 Voting Rights Act were made law. Even though slavery was abolished by the 13th Amendment in 1865, and blacks were technically granted "equal protection of the laws" by the 14th Amendment in 1868, and explicitly granted the vote by the 15th Amendment in 1870, literacy tests, poll taxes, and other deplorable devices were used to bar blacks from voting. The poll tax was not fully outlawed until the ratification of the 24th Amendment in 1964. These dehumanizing practices were consistent with the original intention of the Constitution to count slaves as but three-fifths of a person for determining how many represent-atives a state could have in the House of Representatives.

For centuries, youths have been impressed, or drafted, into military service. Yet, youths did not win the right to vote for those who are 18 years old and over until the ratification of the 26th Amendment in 1971.

Let us not Disneyfy our history by pretending that our Founding Fathers were innocent of elite chauvinism, racial prejudice, and sexism. The record of their attitudes in these matters is too well documented to be denied. They were fallible human beings, and men of their time. Their prejudices became institutionalized, and dislodging those biases has been a task that the American people have been struggling with since our political system began.

Indeed, American political history is largely the story of people who were denied the opportunity to participate in self-government, struggling to overcome their barriers so that they could have some influence in making the decisions that would determine their fate. The original American Dream – to have the right to participate in self-government – has not been fully forgotten. The people, who struggled, fought, and sometimes died to overcome the smug institutionalized oligarchic exclusions from our political system have kept that Dream alive. It has made them feel driven by a strong desire to further democratize the Constitution. Of course, this popularly shared intention runs counter to the oligarchic intentions of the Framers.

Here, then, is the central contradiction that still underlies the dynamics of American politics today. Democracy cannot be won without a fight. Its opponent is oligarchy. The struggle is an old one, which was well underway even before the Philadelphia Convention had its first meeting.

Conclusion: The Original Intentions List

As I have noted, the Framers met in Philadelphia to discuss solutions to the problems of governing that the country was experiencing under the Articles of Con-federation. In writing the Constitution, they sought to establish a federal government that would, in their shared view, serve the best interests of the country as a whole. To that end, they fashioned a complex blueprint to, among other things, facilitate commerce among the states, provide for the safety of the nation, and protect the liberty of the people.

To assure the success of these aims they designed a plan for a government which they strongly desired to be free of self-serving factions. They separated the powers of government into three branches. They provided distinct methods for placing personnel in each of the general departments of this government. Senators would be elected by state legislators. Representatives would be elected by the people of the states. Justices, and other specified officers, would be appointed by the president with the advice and consent of the Senate. The president and vice president would be elected in a well-defined process that came to be called the Electoral College.

I have stated how the authors of our Constitution originally meant the President and Vice President of the United States to be elected. To support my thesis I have quoted the Article Two, and Twelfth Amendment, provisions for the way by which the two executive offices were intended to be filled. I have given an empathic interpretation of this language, in combination with other writings, speeches, and the facts known about the men and their time, so as to sketch out their underlying original intentions for the presidential election process. In sum, then, the intentions which were the most salient for the designers of the Electoral College include the following:

A) They intended that the presidential election process be *nonpartisan*; that is, free of the corrosive influence of passion-stirring political parties.

B) They also intended that this process be conducive to Reason by being orderly, deliberative, and dignified. The Framers anticipated small meetings of from three to twelve Electors. The Electors would meet only for the single purpose of electing a president and vice president, not for policy making, or other purposes. There would be no self-promoting, office seeking "candidates," nor party generated campaigns to pressure Electors into some form of "group think." The Electors were supposed to be especially responsible persons, who would represent the people of their states, be independent thinking individuals, and who would discuss personnel selection in a judicious and dignified manner, free of "tumult and disorder," and striving to put Reason above emotion and prejudice.

C) Out of solicitude for the states, and consistent with the commitment of the Framers to federalism, the process was designed so that *each state* would have an equal part in the procedure. Each state would conduct its own presidential election, and report the results to the President of the Senate. Each state was expected to act independently of the others, and each was required to vote for at least one person from another state. These provisions were intended to avoid jealous competition among the states for advantage over one another by colluding either among themselves, or with privately organized parties.

D) As a further bulwark against factions, federal officials were barred from participating in any state's Electoral College.

E) The process was assumed to cost so little that each Elector could easily defray his own expenses. Of course, the Framers originally expected that the president and vice president would have *spent nothing* in the process because no one would have campaigned for those offices.

F) The process would have two phases. First, each state legislature would determine how Electors were to be chosen. The Framers anticipated, but did not require, that this first phase would allow the participation of "the people" of each state. These voters would elect Electors to represent them in their state's Electoral College. The Framers figured that the risk of irrationality incurred by letting the people vote for Electors would be minimal, as eligibility to vote was limited mostly to free white males (to the exclusion of such irrational creatures, in their view, as slaves and women). But the second phase, the actual vote, would be free from any irrational degradation by ordinary folks. This phase was intended to preserve decorum and encourage Electors to deliberate freely and rationally over which of the prospective presidents under consideration would most likely act for the common good.

G) Because the Framers regarded the people as being less capable of orderly and rational deliberation than gentlemen like themselves, their Constitution largely empowered elites to guide the formation and continuation of the "republic;" which they understood to be a form of government that favored leadership by an oligarchy of *merit*, as measured by a fellow's material success, as well as permitting the masses a little participation.

Now that the original intentions of the Framers for the presidential election process have been set forth, the actual practices followed by US political elites in the 21st Century can be evaluated for the degree to which those intentions are honored and fulfilled. That will be the task of the next chapter.

Should some of the present practices be found to significantly vary from the original intentions of the Framers, perhaps the Supreme Court may be prevailed upon to enjoin the anomalous practices. After all, as *Bush v. Gore* and *Citizens United* suggest, the current Court has both a penchant for actively participating in the presidential election process, and a much vaunted commitment to abiding by the original intentions of our Constitution. If the members of the High Court are to be true to their professed beliefs in "original intent," the country may soon see some interesting activity in the Hallowed Halls of Justice.

Chapter Three

Plan and Practice – How Current Practices Deviate from the Original Intentions of the Framers

Introduction

In the previous Chapter I discussed the anti-party spirit of the Constitution. I showed that the Constitution is a complex set of intricate separations and balances of governmental powers. These divisions are designed to insure that the framework of government keeps the governing process focused on the best interests of the nation, and not let government be captured by self-serving factions. The Framers meant the Constitution to be a mighty bulwark against "the Spirit of Party," and "the violence of factions." One of their great fears was that factions would render the Constitution, to use Hamilton's phrase, a "mere parchment delineation of the boundaries [of government]."104 Little did these leaders in a land of farmers know that soon their "parchment delineations" would, indeed, prove to be about as effective as a scarecrow in a freshly seeded corn field.

Their plan didn't work. The Constitution's separation of powers has been smeared over by the two-party system. Its operatives occupy every office of government, in all three branches, and at each level, federal, state, and local. Congress is split in two. An "aisle" divides Democrats and Republicans. That aisle is not in the Constitution. The presidency regularly changes hands between a "Democratic administration" and a "Republican administration." In 2000, a Republican dominated Supreme Court disregarded judicial restraint and ruled in *Bush v. Gore* so as to insure the election of a Republican president. As of 2011, the High Court is still dominated by a Republican Party ideology, which the Democrats hope to swing their way with more appointees by President Obama's "Democratic administration." The two-party system has created its own self-sustaining political culture, which so fills the minds of Americans that this socially constructed, party-dominated system appears to them to be as natural as trees and rain.

I centered my discussion in the prior chapter on how the antiparty spirit of the Framers is manifested in the provisions for the Electoral College. The Framers hoped that these carefully crafted provisions would protect the presidential election process from party corruption. In this chapter, I will compare the original intentions of the Framers for presidential elections to the actual practices followed in our country today. Because those elections are dominated by the two-party system, the inquiry will be as to how well the current system fulfills, or fails to fulfill, those original intentions. If the plan of the Framers is considered as a measuring stick for how well politics and government are operating in the US, then this chapter will read as a kind of report card. In Part 2 of this chapter, I will review Barrack Obama's 2008 campaign as the most recent example of how the deviant process currently works.

Part 1: Our Deviant Times

The Framers Originally Intended Nonpartisan Presidential Elections

Times have changed since the first Electoral College performed like clockwork, and twice unanimously elected George Washington the President of the United States. Some of these changes have not been of the sort that the Framers thought desirable. Indeed, some parts of today's presidential election process are quite the contrary of what the Framers had hoped to bring about.

George Washington specifically advised us that the "name of American … belongs to you in your national capacity," and that this name "must always exalt the just pride of patriotism more than any appellation derived from local discriminations." He warned that factions are "the worst enemy" of popular government. Nevertheless, in the political culture of the two-party system, strong party identifiers, which number in the tens of millions, now equate short-term election victories for *their party* with the best interest of the *whole nation*. Contrary to Reason, they attempt to subsume the universal into the particular. And this sort of irrationality is precisely what our Founding Fathers feared most. Such ill-logic can only be sustained by frenzied emotions. Heedless of Washington's warnings, by exalting the spirit of party we have become our own "worst enemy."

A comprehensive account of the follies into which the two-party system has led the US would require volumes of words, and take me far from my immediate purpose. My concern here is not to dwell on all the damage the two-party system has done, but to show how we can stop repeating the errors of the past. Working within the two-party system will never produce results other than partisan follies. But modern electronic technology now gives us, the American people, an opportunity to correct the design flaw in the Constitution that permitted the rise of the two-party system.

That flaw, as we have seen, is the smug, classist, racist, sexist, oligarchic intention of the Framers to limit the people to exercising only puny power in our system of self-government. At first, just white males with land or money were permitted to vote in federal elections, and then *only* to elect representatives to the House. Although not required by the Constitution (as explained in the preceding chapter), under pressure by the people, the states permitted the people to elect Electors, who would in turn meet, deliberate, and vote for the president and vice president. But the election of Electors was not free of elite control, and the power of the people in this process was quite small and secondary. Their power is no greater now, as I will show in this chapter.

The Framers originally intended *nonpartisan* presidential elections *by Electors*. Those two expectations, like a ship on a stormy sea, have been dashed on the rocks of politics. In the two-party system, Electors have *de facto* lost the power to elect, and partisanship reigns supreme.

The American people continue to have a deep desire for *full power* in the presidential election process. Unfortunately, from the democratic point of view, their lack of power is what the Framers also originally intended; and, that oligarchic intention to marginalize the power of the people in the presidential election process is sustained in the two-party system.

Indeed, the yearning of the American people to live in a more democratic political system is exactly what the two-party system has deviously exploited to sustain itself. Its genius is to create the illusion of full democracy where very little actually exists. But, to their great credit, the Framers have made reform possible by bequeathing to us a constitution that can be amended. Many of the current amendments, from the Bill of Rights to the abolition of slavery, to the eighteen year old vote, have incrementally enhanced the power of the people. The process based on internet voting, presented in the next chapter, can be a great leap forward in that democratizing tradition.

The Framers Originally Envisioned Prospective Presidents as Men of Continental Character and Above Office-Seeking

I wonder how our Founding Fathers would feel about the shameless money-chasing and office-seeking of presidential hopefuls in the two-party system. This is not what they originally envisioned a man of continental character doing. They expected the job to seek the man, not the man to seek the job. They never imagined that money would be an issue. They wanted elites in control of the process, to be sure. But they uniformly disdained "office seekers." That custom was so strong in this country that no one publicly campaigned for the presidency for nearly 100 years after the Constitution was ratified. Not Washington, not Jefferson, not even Jackson. Lincoln engaged in public debates with Douglas, but not for the presidency. That contest was for a seat in the Illinois state Senate (which Lincoln lost). In the late 1800s, William Jennings Bryan publicly campaigned for the office several times, but he never won it. His opponents stayed home, and sat on the front porch "looking presidential."

Some people may say that dignity, like beauty, is in the eye of the beholder. But no culture has a story praising a handsome young man for falling in love with a toothless old witch covered by warts. That image is too awful. In other words, some values come naturally. And, outside the political culture of the two-party system, no culture holds up leaders who beg for money as models for their youth to imitate. For people who have not been conditioned to accept it, such behavior offends the natural sense of dignity in leadership.

So, another, and tacit, original intention was that only people with too much dignity to publicly beg for money would be considered for the nation's highest office. That intention bites the dust in the two-party system.

The Framers Originally Intended that Electors would be Independent Thinkers with Unfettered Freedom to Deliberate and Vote on Prospective Executives

As the quotes of the Constitution and Federalist Papers in the previous chapter show, Electors were meant to be responsible representatives of the people, and who, like senators or members of the House or Justices of the Supreme Court, would exercise their best judgment independently of any faction. The Framers anticipated that once Electors had been chosen, they would freely consider a wide range of potential executives. The only con-stitutional limits on who the Electors could elect were that the person be at least 35 years old, a natural born citizen, 14 years a resident of the US, and that at least one of the people for whom they vote, not be an inhabitant of the same state with themselves. Within those parameters, anyone could be seriously considered as presidential timber.

There were no other limitations on the decision-making process. Electors were free, if they had so desired, to make a list of all persons on the census rolls who fit those four simple criteria, and discuss them all one-by-one. Hypothetically, there might be over 1000 people on such a list. Of course, being practical people, Electors would not waste their time on so tedious a procedure. Instead, as the Framers imagined it, they would immediately make a short list of persons known to them to be of "continental character." In other words, in Virginia a group of twelve, in New York a group of 8, in Rhode Island three, etc. would brain-storm and come up with a list. This short list would be folks of their own choosing, with no outside pressure. They would discuss the merits of each person on the list, perhaps take several elimination votes, and in short order, eliminate all but two. Then they would vote for president, and the one with the fewer votes would be the vice president. (The original method of one vote was changed by the 12th Amendment to have separate votes for president and vice president.) Each state would then report its results to the President of the Senate, and wait to find out what the other states had done.

The Framers anticipated honorable, intelligent, independent thinking, politically sagacious men, like themselves, to be chosen by the people as Electors. That is why the Framers did not try to over control the process. They trusted the Electors to do the right thing.

Except for reporting to the President of the Senate, the originally intended process does not happen under the two-party system. Instead of independent minded gentlemen, Electors have become party cronies, who get on the list of Electors as a reward for their party loyalty, service, or financial contributions. But even these qualities are not fully sufficient. They must also *pledge* to vote for whichever candidate wins the popular vote. The current practice is so topsy turvy that now Electors are *prohibited* from exercising the independence of judgment that the Framers originally meant them to exercise. Their function has been reduced to a ritualistic rubber stamping of the popular vote.

The political culture of the two-party system has so contorted the minds of elected officials and political activists, that they have become blind to the values of free thought and free speech, which were central in our Founding Generation. Under today's warped way of seeing things, Electors who act as the Framers had intended – that is, think independently and vote their own judgment – are vilified as "faithless." Even though the vote is a sacred act in America, protected vigorously under the First Amendment as political speech, several states have laws making it a *misdemeanor* for an Elector to do as the Framers intended.105

The parties screen their crony-Electors carefully. While there have been several thousand Electors in US history, less than a dozen in any century have gone against their pledge. In this century there has only been one; in the 2000 election. No independent minded Electors have yet been punished by law for their "deviant behavior;" instead, they are ostracized by their fellow party members. Ironically, the Communist Party rule that *the party* should dictate correct thought and action for individuals, was ended with the demise of the old Soviet Union. But in the political culture of the two-party system deluded minds see this discarded Soviet practice as in the best interest of our nation!

Ray v. Blair

One eminent critic of this practice of pre-pledging Electors has commented that under the control of the parties, Electors "officially became voluntary party lackeys and intellectual nonentities to whose memory we might justly paraphrase a tuneful satire:

They always voted
at their Party's call
And never thought
of thinking for themselves
at all."

These biting words were written by Supreme Court Justice Robert H. Jackson, with whom Justice William O. Douglas dissented, in the case of *Ray v. Blair* (1952), 343 US 215, 232. In that case, the majority of Supreme Court Justices voted to *uphold* the constitutionality of such "pledging." Even though the Court acknowledged that this practice is not what the Framers originally intended, they held that it was "a time-honored custom," and therefore should be given the High Court's imprimatur. Of course, all the honorable Justices were the products of an appointment process dominated by members of the two-party system.

Oblivious to the contradiction they are creating, this "Vinson Court" is widely praised by party-loving jurists and legal scholars for handing down opinions following "original intentions" and "judicial restraint." Despite all the words, in this deed the Court not only legislated from the bench, but actively turned a practice, which our

Founding Generation would surely have regarded as an abominable corruption, into a de facto Constitutional Amendment. The opinion did not consider what the Constitution means by the words "The Electors shall meet … and vote …" If a "vote" is the expression of the intent *of the voter*, then a ritual parroting of party dictates is no vote at all. *Ray v. Blair* has amended the Constitution to read, in effect, "The Electors shall meet … and rubber stamp the winner of the two-party system vote."

In the two-party system, Electors must leave their personal judgment, and their other mental faculties, at home. They do not deliberate thoughtfully any more than they think independently. The intelligent agency that the Framers meant for them to use is suspended, and in the Electoral College they function with no more humanity than a telephone line delivering another's voice. Hence the original vision of Electors deliberating with human dignity goes out the window in the two-party system.

The *Ray v. Blair* opinion was the death blow in the final conquest of the presidential election process originally intended by the Framers of the Constitution. From then on, a rubber-stamping Electoral College became the new constitutional intention. Political parties, the corrupting force that the Framers had designed the Constitution to keep out of presidential elections, has been installed by the High Court as the administrative power for those elections. The fox has been put in charge of the chicken coup.

The Original Intention to Severely Constrain Popular Participation in the Presidential Election Process Contributed to the Rise of the Two-Party System

As I explained in the previous chapter, the Framers informally envisioned that in each state the legislature or governor would present the voters with a list of several possible Electors, and that the people would vote for the number to which their state was entitled, somewhere between 3 and 12. They did not specify this procedure in the Constitution. They left out any mention of a role for the people in the presidential election process as a show of respect for the ideal of "Federalism." That is, that the federal government would limit its demands on the states as much as it could. Thus, they *anticipated* a role for the people, but did not formalize their expectation.

Under the Constitution, the state governments are free, even today, to leave both the people and the parties out of the process of choosing Electors. But they are unlikely to do this, because the two parties control the state governments. Also, state officials know how deeply the American people want to feel that their presidential election process is democratic. This desire among the populace is as old as the nation.

We have just seen that as the people in the original states demanded an expansion of the right to vote, they also sought more power in presidential elections. Most states immediately gave them the vote for Electors. But at the same time, the state retained control over who would be on the Electoral ballot. The people could only vote for the names given to them. Prior to their vote, the people would not have the power to nominate personnel to be on the slate of Electors. Nor would the people, after voting for their Electors, have any say at all about who the Electors deliberated over and voted upon for the two executive offices. This constraining arrangement did not satisfy the hunger of the people for more power in self-government.

The Revolution had sparked a momentum among the people which was aimed at fighting for Liberty through self-government. Their desire for the power to participate in choosing personnel for public office could not be satisfied by such a stingy concession as the states made to them in permitting them to vote only for preselected Electors. The people desired more than that. Thus, while the Framers meant the Electoral College design to keep factions out of the presidential election process, it would soon have the opposite result. The extremely narrow opportunity afforded the people for popular participation would prove to be self-defeating.

The mounting frustration caused by the constraints of the Electoral College system found a channel of release when, beginning in the 1820s, General Andrew Jackson used his fame as a war hero and Indian fighter, plus his flair for military organization and group manipulation, to establish the Democratic Party. With his presidential election victory in 1828, the Democratic Party swept into power. His re-election enabled him to place more party members in office, and the Era of Party Government was underway.

Soon enough, staggered opposition forces learned to form the Republican Party. Thereafter, the worst nightmare of the founding Fathers came true. American politics and government had been captured by privately organized, a-constitutional, self-serving factions. Contrary to the most fervent intentions of the Framers of our Constitution, and with a deaf ear to George Washington's heartfelt admonitions to the nation, American politics and government have been running off their constitutional track since Jackson's time. Instead of preventing factions from capturing the presidential election process, the Electoral College scheme proved to be the Constitution's Achilles' heel.

By 1840 the parties nominated candidates in conventions, paraded their candidate's image and policies around in campaigns, and competed over the popular vote for the president. By the end of the Civil War, the two-party system had captured most of the state legislatures in the United States. Then those legislatures surrendered their original constitutional authority to compose a slate of Electors, and gave that power to the parties. Consequently, in a majority of states today the Electors are nominated by state party conventions, while the party central committees do the nominating in several other states. In those few states which follow the old tradition of allowing the governor to place Electors names on the ballot, he or she must chose from a list drawn up by the parties.

While the people once voted for Electors from a list given them by their state government, in the two-party system the voters usually do not even see the list of prospective Electors, much less learn their names. Instead, ballots in the November election list the names of presidential *candidates*; thus, fooling many voters into thinking that they are voting for candidates, while their vote is actually for Electors who are pledged to vote for the candidates. Whichever candidate receives the most votes determines which slate of Electors, Republican or Democrat, will go to the state capital in December for the ritual Electoral College "vote."

In sum, looking back on the early days of our republic, it seems to me that, rather than preventing the rise of the parties, the Electoral College provision in the Constitution actually forced the people into the two-party system. People who had just fought and won a revolution for the right to self-govern were not going to suddenly cease the momentum they had begun and passively accept elitist exclusions from that which they had fought to have.

One of the greatest mistakes of the Framers, then, was to institute an elite dominated presidential election process. Had they originally provided channels for the kind of direct popular participation that would have satisfied the people's democratic desires, the US might never have had the two-party system.

The Original Intentions of the Framers for Order and Procedural Equality among the States are Lost in the Two-Party System

The success of the two-party system is due to its ability to provide politically attentive people with channels through which they can act upon their need to participate in self-government. By providing these people with numerous ways of expending energy, the two-party system gives them the feeling of meaningful participation. But a close examination of their actual power in the process shows that all their campaign "sound and fury" is, unhappily, "much ado about nothing." The power of the people in presidential elections today is no more than it was when they voted for Electors who were pre-selected by their governors or state legislatures. As I will show, their role remains secondary and their power really quite small.

In all the states, the two-party system provides the people with presidential election events, such as primaries or caucuses, in which they can participate. During these events, the people vote for candidates who have been *pre-selected* for them. Most voters and party activists are ignorant of how these initial selections were made. (I will explain this *pre-primary process* in my discussion of campaign financing below.) Activists in the primaries choose a candidate to rally around, as if they were making the original choice. No one questions how that particular hopeful has appeared before them. They just learn from the media, and through party communications, that "Joe Dokes" has announced his candidacy, and that "Mary Smith" has announced hers. Then, for some, Joe becomes "their" man, while for others, Mary becomes "their" candidate. The officials of the two parties give these activists plenty to do to boost their favorite person. Volunteers are needed to knock on doors and pass out campaign literature. Someone has to offer voter registration forms in shopping centers. People are needed to man the phone banks in the rented offices of their candidate. Websites are set up to feed information, and space is provided for online discussions, and online fund raising.

The primary and caucus votes are cast for the state's delegates to the respective party national conventions. These delegates like Electors, pledge to vote for a particular nominee in the summer convention. (Electors do not vote until the Electoral College meets in December.) While the candidate selection process is scheduled to drag on for several months, usually only a few early primary and caucus votes are needed for the two parties to make an informal decision as to which candidate will be their nominee. The count of pledged delegates predicts the nomination. By the time the two parties have their conventions in July or August, who the conventions will nominate as their presidential candidate is no surprise.

Conventions have several functions. The formal naming of their party's candidates for president and vice president is the most apparent function of conventions. However, if feathers were ruffled among party activists competing against one another in the primaries, convention hoopla can also provide the upset egos with a cathartic experience so that they can all feel like one team again. The conflict between Clinton and Obama supporters in 2008 is an example. Some frustrated Clinton supporters threatened to vote for McCain if Obama won the nomination. But during the convention everyone had a grand old time, and formerly disappointed Clinton activists returned home ready to go out and boost their party's pick.

Certainly this two-party primary/convention process is a far cry from what the Framers had in mind for presidential elections. As I showed in the previous chapter, the Framers envisioned each state holding its own distinctive presidential election at roughly the same time, and thereby enjoying *procedural equality* in the process. The two-party system obliterates all procedural equality between the states. From the beginning of the primary season, New Hampshire and Iowa grab all the early media attention because they are the first two contests. This has made some state officials extremely envious. So in recent years the jealous states have attempted to steal some of the limelight, and the profits from campaign spending, by moving their primaries as close as possible to the primary in New Hampshire and the caucuses in Iowa.

In 2000, Iowa held its caucuses on January 24th, and New Hampshire held its primary on February first. The bulk of the other states did not hold their events until March. But, suspecting that some states were plotting to butt-in on their place at center stage, by 2008 Iowa and New Hampshire had both scampered up to early January. Craving more attention, over a dozen states, including the most populous like California and New York, crept up to Tuesday, February 5th. As a result, the primary season has become so "front loaded" that after one "Super Tuesday," the rest of the season can be rendered irrelevant, leaving a lot of sore losers, which is what happened during the Democratic Party primaries in 2000 and 2004. The Obama/Clinton contest in 2008 was a rare exception in which uncertainty about who would be the nominee was extended until June, when, among other things, Obama won a majority of delegates, and Clinton quit.

An embarrassing event took place in 2008. In their lust for the limelight, Florida and Michigan conspired to beat the February Super Tuesday pack by moving their primaries to January. But, fearing that New Hampshire and Iowa would start competing with Christmas for media attention, and incur the ire of the retail lobby, the elites of the two-party system attempted to restore order to the process. In an unusual display of unity, the Republican National Committee and the Democratic National Committee extracted commitments from Florida and Michigan to refrain from holding their primaries in January, and stay behind the Super Tuesday crowd. However, unable to control their jealous urges, the two states *broke their promises*, and held January primaries. As punishment, only half of their delegates were allowed a place in the party conventions. What ever happened to the original intent for dignified behavior in presidential elections?

The two-party system's use of primaries and caucuses explodes several of the original intentions of the Framers. The Great Compromise between the large and small states is one victim of the new system. During the Philadelphia Convention, small states feared the large states would dominate them in the presidential election process. So, the Constitution treated all states equally, giving each two senators and procedural equality in electing presidents. Unhappy with mere equality, we now have two Mighty Mouses, Iowa and New Hampshire, taking the lion's share of attention in a process that is effectively over before the vast majority of states, big and small, even take part. So much for procedural equality. Other victims are orderliness and rationality. The Founders had set up a rational, orderly process; each state would have its own procedure for electing Electors, and they would meet in their respective states, rationally deliberate, and vote.

Now we have the states literally climbing over one another's backs in a greedy stampede for power, profits, and media attention. Throwing composure to the wind, two large states have dishonored their promise to stay in the pack behind the two Mighty Mouse states. Stirred by petty jealousy, the states are creating chaos. The original Enlightenment intentions to subdue emotion and follow Reason, and to act with dignity, have been jettisoned in the political culture of the two-party system.

The two-party's "general election campaign" is, of course, the most humongous deviation from the original intentions of the Framers for presidential elections. Deserving a place in Ripley's "Tales of Believe it or Not," is the true story that the Founders abhorred campaigns, and thought that the Electoral College system would prevent campaigns from happening. They envisioned each state calmly and quietly carrying out its own election process, and no national factions campaigning whatsoever. How wrong they were! Two factions have combined into one system to control and to denigrate nearly every aspect of the originally intended presidential election process.

In the political culture of the two-party system, fawning intellectuals vie with one another to find new ways to make the people think that the two parties are as American as apple pie and the Constitution. At least since the 1950s, party-loving revisionist scholars have reported that terms like "federalist" and "Jeffersonian" were bandied about in the days of our Founders. From this fact they disingenuously leap to the unwarranted conclusion that our Founding Founders actually *began* the two-party system! They simply disregard all that the Founders said reviling factions. The truth is that political parties as formal organizations with elite leaders and mass followers, agendas forged in national conventions, and which conducted nation-wide presidential election campaigns, did not emerge in American politics until General Jackson made his unique and toxic contribution to our history. Tragically, within this political culture, such mendacious myths are the main fare in every school's civics curriculum. Small wonder why Americans have "forgotten" their nation's original intentions for presidential elections.

The Framers Originally Intended that Each State would Initiate and Independently Conduct its own Presidential Election

As we have seen, the Constitution says that "Each state shall appoint, in such manner as the legislature thereof may direct, [its] Electors …" It goes on to say that "The Electors shall meet in their respective states, and vote …" Clearly, the Framers envisioned a nearly simultaneous process happening independently in each state, and under the control of each state's legislature. I have shown that the two-party system has co-opted the entire process, and reduced the role of the states from being initiators under their own power, to mere pawns in a process of primaries, conventions, and general election. Another means by which the power and importance of the states is reduced in the two-party system's process is the way campaigns are conducted.

While there are 50 states, they are not of equal importance to a presidential hopeful's election team. For an enterprise with that ambition, media markets, not states, are the first focus of attention. Election experts define the parameters of these markets, and quietly poll the people in them to sound out how well their client would do in a presidential election campaign. These experts have behavioral science techniques for testing the reactions of ordinary voters to a variety of policy formulations. Roughly speaking, the problem is to find out such things as whether their client would trigger more votes by using the words "I'm a compassionate conservative," or "I believe that everyone is responsible for his own conditions." Or, how many more votes would the words "workfare, not welfare" trigger as compared to "single mothers get enough government assistance as it is"?

The aim of such public relations techniques is not to present the electorate with arguments as to the nation's best interests based on logic, facts, and sound practical judgment, but to manipulate the minds of voters with emotion triggering words. Fawning intellectuals disguise the dishonesty of this practice by calling it "framing." Numerous formulations, or frames, must be tested in each of several media markets. A candidate's public image must also be framed. So, behavioral tests are done on this as well. These PR trials are conducted in order to shape the image and appeal of a person with presidential aspirations.106

Of course, the Framers could not have dreamed that one day media markets would be more important than states in presidential elections. But, technology changes history, and US politics have adapted with our current practices. One consequence of these practices is that the ideal of the Framers for separate presidential elections in each state has been trashed. Media markets are based on concentrations of huge urban/suburban populations, which cross state lines. A state's electoral votes are still necessary to win presidential elections, but the electoral votes of several states can be won by the shrewd management of cross-state media markets. All that is required is millions of dollars to hire the right experts, and to pay the costs of advertising.

As I have mentioned, in the 18th Century the Framers originally intended that when Electors met, each small group would make its own unique pick of prospective presidents and deliberate over their choices. The two-party system usurped that function in the 19th Century, when urban party bosses and other elites bargained over candidate selection during conventions. 20th Century primaries were supposed to reform that process and make it more democratic. But in the 21st Century, the all important *initial* selection of prospective presidents is made by a different group of elites, and long before both the primaries and conventions.

These elites operate in private, unknown to most of those party activists who so energize primaries and the general election campaigns. Their business is conducted in the new "pre-primary process," two to three years before the Electoral College meets in December of the presidential election year. Their "hush-hush" propaganda machine, in the press and the academy, keep them unheard of by nearly all of our nation's voters. The only way to understand the power of this shadowy group is to re-examine the presidential election process from the point of view of campaign finance. This I will do next.

The Framers Originally Intended a Cost-Free Presidential Election Process

As I suggested in Chapter Two, the Framers informally envisioned Electors as being "gentlemen," like themselves. Gentlemen, they assumed, would have no need of reimbursement by the states for the meager costs of lodging, food, and travel in order to elect their country's president and vice president. Indeed, the honor of the office, and their own dignity, would move them to gladly bear the expenses. Times have changed.

During the 20th Century, organized campaigning ascended to normalcy in the US. Then the money spent on presidential elections rose rapidly. Supporters of Lincoln reportedly spent about $100,000 of their own money to campaign for him, although he did not campaign. The first campaign manager to tap corporations for contributions was Mark Hanna. He raised over $7,000,000 in Republican William McKinley's successful 1896 bid. Progressive reformers then pushed for the first curb on corporate contributions, and Congress passed the 1907 Tillman Act. But the costs of campaigns continued to rise, and so did the amounts contributed.

Gradually, the two-party system's process for presidential elections evolved to the point at which superrich persons and special interest groups could secretly deliver suitcases full of cash to candidates, and no laws were broken. Since the public did not know about this money, or who gave it, they could never discover any quid-pro-quos between special interests and elected officials. The last campaign where this is known to have happened was in Richard Nixon's successful re-election bid in 1972. The practice became well publicized during the Nixon impeachment hearings. To a public that desires to live in a democracy, this practice smacked of unfair superrich and special interest privilege.

In response to public outrage, Congress enacted the Federal Election Campaign Act (FECA), with amendments, in the early 1970s. Among other things, this law established contribution limits for individuals, political parties, and PACs. A "PAC" is a political action committee formed by some corporation, union, or other special interest organization, which must register with the FEC. The FECA also set up strict requirements for candidates to report campaign contributions, and instituted the Federal Elections Commission (FEC) to enforce compliance. Federal law now requires, in addition to contribution limits, detailed record keeping by candidates, and full disclosure to the FEC of contributions over $200.00. This law was presented to the public as a way of democratizing

William J. Kelleher, Ph.D.

presidential elections by limiting the control that wealthy interests can have over the process. However, as I will show, the actual consequence of the law is to *enhance*, not limit, the power of what I call "the Contributing Class." That is the class that makes the lion's share of contributions, and which in our time holds the ultimate power in presidential elections – the new "gentlemen."

In 2002 the McCain-Feingold law came into effect. That law was presented to the public as fine-tuning the FECA. For example, it restricted some political advertising, including that done by independent groups, such as the infamous 527s, which are tax exempt organizations that engage in political activities Independently of candidates and political parties. (One example is the Swift Boat Veterans that ran an ad in the 2004 presidential election campaign casting doubt on John Kerry's courage in the Viet Nam War.) 107

However, like most campaign finance reform measures, the actual consequence of McCain-Feingold was to further empower the superrich, rather than curb their power, in the presidential election process. First, PACs and parties could give *more* under this law. Also, it more than doubled the amount of money an individual could contribute. Under the prior law, an individual could only give $1000 to a particular candidate in the primary season, and another $1000 in the general election. McCain-Feingold raised each $1000 limit to $2300. But in 2008 the total annual limit an individual could give to multiple candidates, PACs, and parties was over $115,000. Most folks do not have to worry about exceeding such a "limit." In fact, the superrich do not have to worry about exceeding it either. Not only is the size of the so-called "limit" insignificant to them, but *limits* in themselves are merely for show. Money, like water rushing downhill, will always find a way around obstacles.

McCain-Feingold also put new regulations on "soft money." "Soft money" was another way for superrich people to get around their contribution limits. After maxing-out on their individual contributions to candidates, they wrote their checks to a political party, seemingly for its general use; but they earmarked the check by attaching a note or a letter directing that the money be spent on a particular candidate's campaign. This way, the really rich guys could contribute to a candidate without contributing to a candidate! That was banned. However, the money found a new way to flow around this obstacle.

Now, instead of "soft money," candidates can open a "joint bank account" with their party. When the rich guys max-out on their individual contributions to candidates, they write another fat check to the joint bank account. This generous loophole more than doubles the amount that an individual can channel specifically to the candidate. According to FEC records, Obama raked in an extra $87,000,000 from party transfers to his campaign.[108]

Besides contributing to a candidate as an individual, a person can contribute to a special interest group PAC. Contributions to PACs are "limited" to $5000 per person. Not to worry! This restriction is just for fooling the public into thinking that the wealthy special interests have been reined in. There are no limits on how many PACs a wealthy person can contribute $5000 to, up to the $115,000 max. Theoretically, if there are 23 PACs that support a rich guy's favorite candidate, he can contribute $5000 to each one of them before reaching his "limit." Then his wife can write her checks, and all the children theirs.

PAC contributions to candidates are also limited to $5000 per candidate. That "limit" is supposed to contain the amount of influence one PAC can buy. But this limit, too, is easily skirted. Here is one way PACs can skirt the law: first, PAC members contribute $5000 apiece directly to their PAC, which writes its own checks to the appropriate candidates, and other PACs. Then the PAC members write additional checks to a particular candidate's campaign for the maximum amount. But they do not send the check to the campaign office individually. Instead, the PAC's Washington lawyer, or lobbyist, collects the checks from the members. Then he or she delivers all the individually written checks, not as a PAC contribution, but as "individual contributions."

They call it "bundling." A "bundle" of just over 200 checks can total a one million dollar contribution from the PAC via its members. At first, bundles were delivered in a briefcase, rather than a suitcase. The candidate understood that the bundle was an enhancement of a PAC's contribution, but his accountant only had to report the *individual checks* to the FEC. Thus, the PAC got extra credit with the candidate, and no laws were broken – at least technically.

When the press exposed this tricky practice as giving the wealthy an upper hand in the presidential election process, a new federal law required candidates to report bundles that are *personally delivered* by lobbyists. In 2000, the Bush campaign, under Carl Rove's leadership, pioneered a way around that requirement. He would give each of those Washington lawyers and lobbyists a special number. They would tell their clients to write the number on their checks, and send in the checks individually.

The accountant would keep *three* sets of books. Two sets of books would be for the public to see. One set of those public books would have a list of seemingly unconnected individual contributions, and the other would have the list of PAC contributions. The third set of books would be by the numbers that identified the special interests. Rove had the best of both worlds. To all appearances there would be no suitcases or briefcases delivering dough, the campaign would appear to comply with the law, and the PACs could purchase extra credit with the president.

According to Public Citizen, a government watchdog group founded by Ralph Nader, bundlers for the Bush campaign who raised at least $100,000 were given the honorary title of "Pioneer." On its website, Public Citizen quotes a solicitation letter by Bush Pioneer Thomas Kuhn. He was the head of the Edison Electric Institute, the lobbyist group for much of the energy industry. Here is a quote from the letter: "As you know, a very important part of the campaign's outreach to the business community is the use of tracking numbers for contributions. [For] our industry [please] incorporate the #1178 tracking number in your fundraising efforts."

After his election, President Bush wasted no time promoting the "Clear Skies Act," a deceptively named regulation buster, advocated by Kuhn and the energy industry.[109]

Public Citizen provides several facts that explain the benefits of bundling. For example, more than 40 percent of Bush's bundlers in the 2000 campaign eventually received government jobs, such as ambassadorships or cabinet positions. One of those bundlers was Jack Abramoff, now in prison for other devious matters. Before Enron CEO, and Bush Pioneer, Ken Lay was convicted for several felonies, he had sent the White House a list of eight candidates for positions on the five-person Federal Energy Regulatory Commission. Two were named. More than 60 of Bush's bundlers in 2004 were federal lobbyists. Top Bush bundlers received more than $1.2 billion in federal contracts for their companies and their clients between 2001 and 2005.[110]

No one fully appreciated it at the time, but Rove's strategy of bundling-by-numbers gives another special advantage to the wealthy interests. In effect, it nullifies the FECA requirement that PACs register, and comply with the law's limitations. When a PAC registers with the FEC, everyone can know of its existence, and can know what it wants from the government. Then pesky watchdog groups, like Public Citizen, or Center for Responsive Politics, can use campaign contribution reports to uncover any quid-

pro-quos, such as special legislation, government contracts, jobs, etc.

But suppose those Washington lawyers and lobbyists
give a private "tracking number" to some superrich
individuals who share a special interest, without them
registering as a PAC. The candidate's campaign
accountant would report a long list of "individual
contributors" to the FEC, and no one outside the campaign
would know which, if any, of those donors were united by
their special interest. Only the accountant, and the
candidate, would know by the common tracking numbers
who really belongs to some self-serving organization. As I
will show in a moment, this *liberation of the special
interests* would reach its full potential in the 2008
campaign.

The "smart money" engages in this bundling-by-
numbers to give to several candidates, and contributes like
this to candidates of both parties. That way, the superrich
in the contributing class always win, whoever the person
or party in the executive branch may be. When the time
comes, an undisclosed special interest group, which has
contributed hundreds of thousands of dollars in bundled
checks, asks to write just one self-serving line in a 1000
page bill that the president is preparing to send to
Congress, and their wish is granted.

Long lists of "individual" contributors on FEC reports
create the appearance of an open process. The stacks of
paper work make it look like there is plenty of
"disclosure." Undisclosed, however, are the dominate
small groups of folks who are informally organized within

the Contributing Class. With all the named individual contributors on publicly available records, apparently complying with the law, the public accepts the entire process as "legal," and therefore "legitimate." Meanwhile, the bundlers who specifically want to insert lines in bills, get jobs heading regulatory agencies, etc. and yet remain undisclosed so no dots can be connected to them, are free to carry on.

The Center for Responsive Politics has attempted to uncover united bundlers by grouping together the names of individual big money contributors according to their common employer.111 Guess who the leaders of these unregistered, and hence invisible, PACs are. Hint: remember how Congress fell all-over itself to pass Bush's 750 billion dollar bailout package with no requirements to make the recipients accountable? That's right! It's the firms that line Wall Street. These include Goldman Sachs, Citigroup Bank, J.P. Morgan Chase, UBS, and Morgan Stanley. In September 2008, these folks went way beyond simply inserting a self-serving line in a Bush administration bill. Using their man Henry Paulson, Bush's Treasury Secretary and former Goldman Sachs CEO, they got to write the whole bill! Individuals who named these financial corporations as their employer have contributed millions, and, just by coincidence, their employers have received *billions* in return. Not a bad investment! Some of the senators who voted to be so generous to the superrich were McCain, Biden, Clinton, and Obama.

FEC rules are designed to frustrate the discovery efforts of public interest groups. For example, the FEC allows many special interest group members to hide their interests behind the rubric "retired." This is one of the most generous groups of contributors. However, their corporate associations are unknown, because they don't have to say "retired" from *what company*. Consequently, they appear to be simply somebody's little old civic minded grandparents – reminiscent of the wolf in Little Red Riding Hood.

Also, FEC rules, as of 2008, did not require candidates to disclose which of their donors are involved in bundle-by-numbers schemes. However, OpenSecrets.org states that both the McCain and Obama campaigns have admitted to using over 500 bundlers each. These bundlers have given over $270,000,000 to the two campaigns.112 But no one outside the campaigns knows what the bundled donors want from the government in return, nor whether this is a complete accounting, or just scratches the surface. Public Citizen estimates that there may be as many as 2400 informal bundle groups.113

Campaign finance reform laws have also helped to correct a dangerous trend towards the fragmentation of political elites that once existed. For example, stresses started to emerge between conservative and liberal elites in the two-party system after WWII. Newly rich con-servatives, largely from southern, western, and Mid-western states began challenging New Deal liberal Democrats as well as liberals within the Republican Party. Barry Goldwater's nomination in 1964 highlighted an emerging conservative faction that threatened to rupture into a powerful third party if not integrated into the existing US power structure.

To smooth over this fissure the FECA was passed in the early 1970s. Its provisions, which limit the amount that individuals and organizations can give, require more cooperation among the rich, such as forming PACs and bundling. This cooperation assures power sharing among the oligarchs, encourages working within the two-party system, and thereby reduces potentially destructive one-sided domination within the Contributing Class. The law worked so well at facilitating the integration of new entries into the power structure that the "Reagan Revolution" of the 1980s took place without political violence.

Not coincidentally, incumbents benefit greatly from such "reforms" as the FECA and McCain-Feingold. When groups within the Contributing Class must work together, they are more likely to agree to back known politicians than to risk backing untested outsiders that would like to run for the White House. In this situation, who has a better chance of successfully soliciting money than an incumbent senator, congressperson, or governor? Not only have they demonstrated that they know how to win an election, but they have probably already provided the superrich with all the services it was in their power to give. Why would wealthy contributors take a risk by granting money to unknown hopefuls? The more difficult it is for unknowns to garner start up money, the less competition there will be for familiar faces in the money chase.

This system also tempers radicalism among the rich. When big donors are pressured by law to work together, the odds are lowered that one renegade rich guy will put all his contributions behind an extremist candidate. Dennis Kucinich and Hunter Thompson are examples of left and right extremists who were filtered out of the 2008 campaign when the more centrist rich withheld contributions.

The Contributing Class understands the prejudices of the American voter, and turns those to its advantage. Out of their desire to live in a democracy, Americans resent superrich individuals running for the presidency. John Connelly, Ross Perot, Steve Forbes, and Mitt Romney are some of the superrich presidential hopefuls who have felt public rejection over the years due, in part, to their personal fortunes.

The public will accept moderately well-off people, but such people do not have the kind of initial funds needed early on. Ironically, then, the only candidates acceptable to the people are those who must depend upon the early money of the superrich. Every con man knows that he cannot succeed without his mark's cooperation. Because the public in the US so desperately want to live in a democracy, many will accept the current charade as the real thing. As we have seen, in our "republican" form of government, the many are manipulated into voting for politicians who really represent the interests of the few; that is, the oligarchs of the Contributing Class. A brief look at Obama's spectacular rocket ride to the top will show how this works.

Part 2: Deviancy Continues

Obama's Oligarchy

Barack Obama seems to have been born with political charisma and ambition. Obama was elected by his law school classmates to be the first black president of the Harvard Law Review in 1990, when he was 29 years old. Immediately, people in the press began speculating that he could be "America's first black president," although he was not old enough to hold the position.114

After graduating law school in 1991, Obama took up practice in Chicago. In the same year his first book, *Dreams of My Father*, came out, in 1995, he began his successful run for a seat in the Illinois state Senate. His campaign finance money came from just a few distinct groups. These included white builders of low cost housing on the south side of Chicago, local professionals and liberal professors who opposed Mayor Daley, and from some black business people in the area. Once in office he made the right friends in the state Senate, and he was able to influence policy and public contract-making in ways that profited his early backers.

He played the game of state politics with such success that when an opening for one of the two Illinois seats in the US Senate came up, he decided to try for it. By this time he had help from a wide variety of the richest Chicagoans, white and black. These included TV personalities, magazine publishers, musicians, lawyers, bankers, and other business people. Penny Pritzker, a Chicago billionaire financier, later headed Obama's national fundraising machine. Some of his new friends introduced him to the wealthy in New York and Hollywood. Through these folks he forged his connections with the liberal wing of the Contributing Class.115

Long before Election Day in 2004, he had enough money to pay his own US Senate campaign expenses, and then, according to the New York Times, contribute "hundreds of thousands of dollars from his campaign to [other] Democratic candidates and party committees."116 In this way he made so many friends in the national Democratic Party that they invited him to speak during the July 2004 Democratic Party National Convention in Boston. He made the most of that opportunity with a display of breath-taking oratorical skills. He had folks weeping and cheering at the same time. Immediately, all over the country people with an interest in politics recognized that this man had the potential to become the first black president. Needless to say, that November he won his US Senate race.

Hardly more than a year into his career as a US Senator, and Obama was already sounding out his wealthy connections with an eye on the biggest prize. At every intersection he came to, his light turned green. Three years before the first 2008 primary and caucus votes, Obama was already raking in more dough than anyone except Hillary Clinton. He needed big money early, so he could hire very costly consultants like David Axelrod, of the pricey PR firm, Axelrod, Kupper, Plouffe & Del Cecato

(AKP&D). Politico.com reports that Obama's own senatorial election PAC, The Leadership Political Action Committee, "paid AKP&D $133,000 from 2005 until Obama entered the presidential race last February [2007]."117 After that, he paid them from his presidential campaign fund.

Well before Obama announced his intention to run for the presidency, he began his appeal to an Internet audience. He presented himself on "social networking" sites such as MySpace and FaceBook, as well as YouTube and Linkedin. He also reached out by using the huge email lists that he purchased from MoveOn.org, and the Dean and Kerry campaigns, which they had assembled in 2004. He gathered more e-mail addresses at his rallies. His "audacious hope" was that he could create an Internet base of contributors and activist supporters, many, if not most, of whom had never heard of him before encountering him online. Like magic, his interpersonal magnetism manifested through cyberspace, and audacity was soon transformed into reality.

Of course, Obama did not do all of this online campaigning alone. He hired a team of web wizards to help him. The Internet geniuses who had made Howard Dean the Wonder Boy of political fundraising in 2004, were a part of a budding company known as "Blue State Digital (BSD)." Thanks to them, Dean's campaign achieved fundraising history by attracting small donations, often from first time donors, over the Internet. In the 2004 campaign season, Dean raised nearly $60,000,000 over the Internet. While, during the same period, Kerry and Bush

raised more in the old fashion way, Dean's total was far
beyond what any other candidate had raised using the new
technology. Then came Obama. In just one month,
September 2008, his wizards raised $150,000,000 – almost
three times what Dean had done in a year!

On the day Obama formally announced his campaign,
in February of 2007, BSD opened his personal website,
MyBarack.com. The site asked for money based on the
"subscription model." That is, contributors were modestly
requested to give small amounts, like $10, $15, $25, or
whatever they could afford in the moment. Then,
periodically, they would be asked to give the same
amount, or perhaps a little more.

The site also encouraged people to hold fundraising
"meet ups" with like-minded supporters, much like the
sellers of cosmetics, and plastic food storage containers. It
invited independent fundraising entrepreneurs to raise
funds in their own way, and send the money to Barack's
campaign. Hundreds acted on their own initiative. Tens of
millions of dollars in small checks came pouring into
Obama's campaign coffers – and none of them with
"tracking numbers."

The fellows at BSD are more than gifted fundraisers.
They are master electronic illusionists that created a
mirage for folks who thirsted to feel politically significant.
They sparked enthusiasm by using the website to promise
participants direct access into the Obama policy-making
process.

Supporters were given space to write their own blogs. They could form subject matter groups and debate the fine points of specific policies, like ending the war in Iraq, saving the environment, legalizing undocumented immigrants, prison reform, allowing the medicinal use of marijuana, single payer health care, and other matters of domestic social, economic, and foreign policy. They were promised that Barack would listen to them – as if he would adopt the policy positions that his supporters presented to him.

He did listen. He posted videos in response to some website discussions, and sent out emails, which showed that he was listening. This positive feedback generated both new supporters, and greater intensity of participation in prior supporters. The acceleration of energy and activity online created a phenomenon the likes of which had never been seen in presidential campaign history. The "netroots" felt empowered, and the money came pouring in.

Keeping track of the money is not always an easy matter for watchdogs, because FEC rules allow plenty of room for campaign accountants to game the system. However, FEC.gov reports that by the end of December 2008, the Obama campaign had received around $745,000,000 in total contributions. Of that, reports the FEC, over $657,000,000 came in as individual con-tributions. It also reports that of those individual contributions his campaign received around $335,000,000 in amounts of $200 or less.[118] At first, then, it seems that over half of Obama's campaign contributions had come in from small donors, thus giving his campaign a very democratic appearance.

Knowing that the public longs to live in a democracy, the Obama campaign carefully crafted their public image. To that end, the Obama campaign claimed to have had over three million donors, and that 2.5 million had donated in amounts of $200.00 dollars or less. Indeed, rumors widely spread over the Internet stated that *half* of Obama's money came from these small donors. It was just what many people had wanted to hear.

However, upon studying the FEC records, after the campaign was over and all reports were in, the campaign finance watchdogs at the Campaign Finance Institute (CFI) found that actually about 26% of Obama's *individual donors* contributed $200 or less, some making many small contributions. CFI reported that other candidates have done as well or better. For instance, 25% of Bush's contributors gave $200 or less in 2004, and 38% for Howard Dean in that year. They were 21% for John McCain in 2008.[119] Thus, despite appearances created by campaign hype, the Obama campaign did not create a revolutionary democratic "change" in campaign financing, but was just more of the same; that is, a heavy reliance on those donors who gave more than $200.

Well before his online operations were underway, Obama was hard at work raising large sums of money from wealthy donors. The friends he made in the fundraising days for his US Senate campaign now became his base for the presidential campaign funds he would need. These efforts began with his inner core of superrich supporters, and moved out in concentric circles.

No one can hope to succeed in a presidential campaign without huge amounts of early money. One reason for this is that campaigning in January and February primary contests is extremely expensive. Lots of advertising must be purchased several weeks in advance for Iowa and New Hampshire. Then there are over a dozen different state contests on Super Tuesday.

Another reason why early money is so vital is that *momentum* is the key to success in political fundraising. Indeed, it is a Law of Political Science that, when fundraising among the superrich in the US, monkey see monkey do.

Thus, when the superrich in Silicon Valley got wind that megastar entertainers in Hollywood were starting to hold private fundraising parties for Obama, the Hi-Tech guys got jealous. They sent emissaries to Obama, and he sent feelers out to them. In no time, Northern California superrich were in competition with Southern California superrich to be a better friend of Obama. When Wall Street bankers and financiers heard about this, they wanted in on the deal. They offered their friendship to Obama, if he would reciprocate. He would. And so it went, *two years* of collecting elites in the Obama-For-President Booster Club *before* his official announcement in 2007, and the opening to the public of MyBarack.com.

As I have suggested, Obama's initial appeal was to the liberal sector of the Contributing Class. He charmed them with the "authenticity" of his personality, and with his own seeming commitment to their policy preferences. Ideologically he seemed to be a natural fit with them. While at first he felt uncomfortable asking for money, once he saw the results, as he confesses in *The Audacity of Hope,* "it eliminated any sense of shame I once had in asking strangers for money." Indeed, with surprising candor he described how his political ideals shifted so as to better comport with a broader spectrum of the Contributing Class. He writes, "I found myself spending time with people of means [and] avoiding certain topics during conversations with them ... I had no problem telling [them] that the tax cuts they'd received from George Bush should be reversed. ... Still, I know that as a consequence of my fund-raising I became more like the wealthy donors I met ... you learn to rationalize the changes as a matter of realism ..."[120]

Also, when contributing their money, they did not require him to make explicit promises to do X, Y, and Z. As he writes, few Money Men "proffer an explicit quid pro quo." Generally, insiders understand that according to the rules in this game, money buys "more access" than that allowed "the average voter."[121] All the details can be discussed later.

These rules distinguish campaign contributions from "bribery." A "bribe" occurs when money is given in exchange for an *explicit* promise to do something. However when no explicit promise is made, but only a "gentleman's understanding" that the candidate knows the giver's needs, or that the giver will have access after the election, there is, technically, no violation of law or political ethics. Whether *morality* differs from "law and political ethics" is a matter of varied opinion. Thus, when US Senator Obama voted to pardon telecommunication companies for having facilitated government spying on American citizens, his vote, of course, had no direct connections with the money they had already contributed to his presidential campaign.122

Then there is the matter of $18,000,000 in earmarks, which Obama has admitted to authoring during his first two years in the US Senate. Their connections to his campaign contributors have yet to be fully traced. Nevertheless, however it may appear to cynics, there surely is insufficient evidence for an accuser to reasonably challenge any provable quid-pro-quos by his earmarks. Technically, Obama's record is clean – as one would expect from a Harvard trained lawyer.

Another technical distinction can be seen in Obama's publicly announced refusal to accept any "PAC" money during his campaign. According to FEC records of PAC contribution disclosures, it's true, technically he didn't. (Well, almost. FEC.org does show a measly $1830. But that would not even cover the costs of paperclips and staples for his campaign.)

But did Obama's promise mean that PACs played no part in building up his campaign war chest? Does the lack of disclosure in the FEC records mean the absence of PAC involvement? Probably not. Would special interests sit idly by while the opportunity to befriend a possible President of the United States slips passed them? Hardly.

The Obama campaign simply borrowed a practice invented in 2000 by "Bush's Brain," Karl Rove – a special form of "bundling-by-numbers." Suppose, as the Obama campaign has suggested, that something like half a million donors contributed in amounts above $200. Each person would then be listed in the campaign's report to the FEC. That would be a list of at least 500,000 names, along with the required name of their employer, unless "retired," and the amount contributed. It is hard, if not impossible, to discern any special interest activity from such a long list of individuals. Thus, by not accepting "PAC" money, Obama's campaign could file reports with the FEC which did not reveal any special interest involvement.

So, when Obama told everybody that he would "change" the way campaigns are financed by refusing all PAC money, he got extra credit with public-spirited voters for seeming to wash his hands of corrupt contributions. At the same time, his campaign used the technically legal art of keeping separate sets of books – one with a long list of individual contributions, the other with contributions classified by the group numbers written on the checks. Technically, the Obama campaign did not take any money from *organizations* that were registered as PACs, it just took money from the *individuals* who belong to those organizations. While this practice may seem like deja vu all over again to anti-political corruption purists, Obama's campaign was the first to grasp its full potential. Like Rove in Bush's winning campaigns, the Obama campaign had the best of both worlds; big money from PAC members, without having to disclose PAC identities. For lawyers, this is a genuine distinction, although members of the general public might be left scratching their heads.

Oblivious of Obama's efforts to raise big money from Big Donors, his online supporters felt like they were a part of something new. Unfortunately, political reality is often not what it seems. Because so many of the participants in Obama's web-politics felt empowered, heard, and meaningful, they will surely not want to hear any suggestions that they were acting out an illusion; or, what's worse, that they were conned into thinking that they would have any impact on Obama's policies. But politics is not pinochle, and all the players in politics are not equal.

The locus of real power in the American presidential election process, as I have said, resides in early big money. The game begins long before the candidate announces his or her campaign to the public. By that time, the candidate's core policies have been set, and his or her political promises have been made to those generous early donors. Late-coming big money may buy access, but it cannot change those early promises. Small money, whether early or late, buys no access and has no significant influence on the candidate's policies, campaign rhetoric to the contrary notwithstanding. However, as I will show in a moment, small money *in the aggregate* can make a significant difference in a close contest.

As an empirical measure of how much influence Obama website participants actually have had over policy, his vote on the "telecoms" and his position on health care are instructive. People writing on his website were both overwhelmingly against sparing the telecoms from justice, and in favor of a single payer health care system. But in both instances, Obama has opted for the corporate powers over the will of his online supporters.123

Obama's clever website managers opened a "Citizen's Briefing Book" on Change.gov, for his supporters to propose and vote on policies. The most popular suggestion had over 92,000 votes. It proposed "Ending marijuana prohibition." The third most popular was "Stop using federal resources to undermine state medicinal marijuana laws." When that news came out, an Obama spokesperson, Jen Psaki, quickly assured the general public that "President Obama does not support the legalization of marijuana." There goes the hope that Obama's policies would be guided by the "netroots."124

Clinton v. Obama

One of the major dramas within the Obama saga is that by March 31, the end of the first 2008 FEC reporting quarter, he and Hillary Clinton were *tied* in fundraising. Both candidates had already raised millions in the two years before the 2008 FEC reporting requirements came into effect on January 1. I have mentioned some of Obama's very early sources. These are his dearest friends; his oligarchy. These friends, and newer ones, continued contributing during the first quarter of 2008. Obama's first quarter money continued coming from both traditional and nontraditional contributors. These included the newly rich liberals in such industries as entertainment, Hi-Tech, law, finance, real estate, construction, telecommunication, health care, insurance, black wealth, and from Internet savvy ordinary, or middle class, folks.

Clinton's 2008 first quarter money continued to come from the old Clinton-coalition, established in the 1990s, before the PC Revolution had fully flowered. This included the old line Democratic Party establishment in government agencies, unions, Eastern seaboard wealth, high finance, and Bill Clinton loyalists from among the same groups that were also giving to Obama.

Both candidates reported a total intake of about $26,000,000 at the end of that March. However, FEC.gov records show that 91% of Clinton's money came from checks written for more than $200, while that was the case for 78% of Obama's money. In other words, 32% of Obama's *first quarter* donations were in amounts of $200 or less, while a mere 9% of Clinton's money came in such small contributions. Compared to Clinton's paltry intake from small donations, Obama's Internet appeal for small contributions was very lucrative.

Therefore, if Obama had, like Clinton, relied on the old fashion way of raising early money – simply tapping the superrich – he probably would not have been able to compete with Clinton. This is suggested by the FEC.gov records, which show that 39% of Obama's early money came from checks for the maximum amount allowed, $2300 per person during the primary season. Generally, only the superrich give away that kind of money at such an early stage in the presidential election process. However, Clinton received a whopping 67% of her first quarter money from such checks.

Because the Contributing Class uses contributions to control the initial candidate selection process, if Obama had simply relied on traditional methods of appealing to the superrich, he would have lost the "money primary" to Clinton. Thus, while having no significant influence on Obama's policies, early contributors of small amounts via the Internet did help him to tie with Clinton in the first quarter, to the surprise of all the pundits and talking heads on TV.

Few will deny that Barack Obama is an American hero for breaking the color barrier to our nation's highest office. He will always be remembered for that very important achievement. But he, like Jackie Robinson in professional baseball, or Jack Johnson in heavyweight boxing, only wanted to get into the game, not to change the rules by which it is played. Obama won the presidency because he played by the established rules – one of which is to raise lots of money early – better than any of his opponents, except Clinton, with whom he tied. In the next quarter, he would go on to out raise her, causing her to go so far into debt that she had to quit the race.

According to campaign finance expert Michael Malbin, "the bulk of Obama's $213 million in large-donor contributions during the primaries came from about 85,000 people who started out giving big and stayed there. Much of this large-donor money – *perhaps close to a majority* – came to the campaign through bundling methods initially perfected by Bush."[125] In other words, by raising early money the Rove Way (including the use of "invisible PACs" each with a group identity number), Obama was able to impress his social networking audience with his abhorrence for registered PACs and his love of democracy. Seeing what they wanted to see in him, they rushed, in the millions, to give him their lunch money.

Obama's victory in *the money primary* was conclusive by the end of the second FEC reporting quarter, in June 2008. The August convention helped to heal wounds, and the sailing was smooth to victory in the November general election. After his inauguration in January 2009, Obama began announcing his appointments to agency positions and ambassadorships. Of course, his top bundlers were well represented in his selections.[126]

One might ask at this point how the realities of American presidential elections compare with the original intentions of the Framers of our Constitution. The ascent of money, the rise of the two-party system, and the decline of Reason, are, in my view, the most significant deviations from those original intentions. As we have seen, a main original intention was that Electors would meet and calmly reason together in making their choice of a person of Continental Character. Cost played no role in the process. Yet another original intention, tacit in the minds of the Framers, was that the Rule of Law would prevail in the presidential election process. Campaign finance shenanigans clearly make a mockery of that naïve assumption.

Bargaining, strategizing, and the art of the con have displaced both deliberation and respect for law. In the art of the con, the desires that will move the public are cunningly discerned and manipulated. They are given the illusion of getting what they think they want, and in exchange, they give the con what he knows he wants – their money and their votes. Presidential campaigns have become a mass confidence game financed by and for the wealthy few. And, how large a part of the American population are these "few"? According to Barack Obama, they, the Contributing Class, are "the top 1 percent or so of the income scale."127 Who would know better?

Conclusion

As the reader has surely noticed, the writer cannot hide his judgment that the two-party system deserves a failing grade when assessed for how well it fulfills the original intentions of the Framers for presidential elections. The two intentions that have been most damaged by the modern era are that Reason prevail, and that money be immaterial in the selection and election of presidential candidates. Rather than facilitating informed deliberation, campaigns, which could be an education to the electorate, consist almost exclusively of competing behavioral science techniques for the deception and manipulation of voters. Campaign finance laws are nothing more than an extension of this underlying intent to deceive the public, and to manufacture legitimacy.

Unfortunately, the distain for the intelligence and political sagacity of the people that these practices display, seem consistent with the oligarchic contempt and distrust of common folks, which is shared with the original Framers. That is one original intent, which, from the democratic point of view, we can do without. Fortunately, the next chapter will show precisely how the deviant behavior in our presidential election process can be corrected.

Chapter Four

How Internet Voting Can Restore All the Original Intentions of the Framers for Presidential Elections, Save Elitism and the Electoral College

Of Boxers and Beauty Queens

The past two chapters have shown that the presidential election process in the US was originally conceived as a set of rules, which were soon disregarded. Then another set of rules emerged that served the combined interests of the wealthy elites and the two major political parties. Our current process is guided by those rules. But with the advent of modern electronic technology, presidential elections can be conducted in accordance with a new set of rules, which I will lay out in this chapter. Together, these rules comprise what I call "the new election game." Of course, this is not a "game" in any frivolous sense of the word. Indeed, it is a game that can result in world peace or world war. But because rules make games, that word, when taken seriously, seems appropriate.

Upon a first reading, a new set of rules can appear overwhelmingly complex. However, after some reflection, the reader will understand that these rules are no more complex or difficult to comprehend than the rules for the Golden Gloves Boxing Tournament, or the Miss America Beauty Pageant. In these two popular contests, the competition begins locally. That is, the guys duke it out in high school gyms, or at the YMCA. The winners of these matches go on to a town or city wide competition, where many hopefuls are eliminated. From there, state wide matches are held. These could produce a State Champion in each weight division for each state. In the National Golden Gloves Tournament, one victor for each weight division emerges. He will bask in glory until some other ambitious boxer beats him in the next elimination series.

The gals follow a similar process of elimination. The high school Home Coming Queen tries out for the beauty queen of her state. Then in a grand pageant, the State Champions compete for the top position as Miss America. These "games," or contests, are uniquely American insti-tutions. They are as home grown as baseball, basketball, and football. By the way, those sports all have their own sets of rules, and the "pros" all get their start at the local level.

So, while reading this new set of rules for electing the President and Vice President of the United States of

America, keep in mind that if they seem complex at first, Boxers and Beauty Queens fully understand the rules of their respective games. Give it a little time to digest, and the rules of the new election game will become as familiar as the rules of your favorite professional, or amateur, sport.

Political Happiness

The 1998 six volume, 10,000 page, multimillion dollar report of the Senate Committee to Investigate Corruption in Presidential Election Fundraising, led by Senator Fred Thompson (R-TN),[128] reached a conclusion which everybody already knew. The two-party process of candidate selection, campaign, and election of the president and vice president is so money dependent that the superrich few can buy the candidates which they then allow the electorate to choose from. As a result, ordinary people feel left out, alienated, and resentful. Less than half of those who are eligible to vote bother to do so. Why should they dignify the deception that we have a democratic election process?

This political unhappiness is not what the American people want. Furthermore, it is not what the Founding Fathers intended. As *The Federalist Papers*, *Madison's Notes*, and other writings of the time show, our Founding Fathers believed that a people who live by the rules of a republican form of government would find political happiness. They understood that the great virtue of a republican form of government is that it provides an opportunity for all segments of society to participate in the self-governing process. They were also convinced, in their wisdom, that the "spirit of party" could only result in strife and a misguided understanding of the nation's best interests. Our own times are evidence that they were right.

As I showed in the previous chapter, a great disparity exists between the original intentions of our Constitution's Framers for the mode of electing the president and the vice president, and the actual process currently followed. The Framers, as both makers and products of the Enlightenment, intended presidential elections to be an exercise in Reasoned Judgment. They abhorred the partisan spirit precisely because it can corrupt Reason. They rejected the direct popular election of the president because they felt that the people were not fully capable of rational deliberation. Instead, they envisioned the direct election of the president by elites after orderly deliberation in the Electoral College.

The plans of the Framers of our Constitution for electing the president were abandoned by the ambitious within 25 years after Washington's retirement. Since then the two-party system has come to dominate the process. This condition is just what the Framers had hoped their Constitution would prevent.

Of course, the original intentions of the Founding Fathers are not absolute laws, but they set a constitutionally guided direction for the nation which could prove foolish to casually disregard. The Framers established a written Constitution so that future generations could stay the course of *Liberty through self-government*. But their idea of "self-government" was limited to elites. They felt the common man was too uneducated, and too easily misinformed and misled by demagogues, to be entrusted with direct and popular presidential elections. They were concerned about preserving public order and keeping policy focused on the best interests of the nation. They feared that if the common man were allowed to vote directly for the president, "combinations" and conspiracies would form among the people, factionalism would prevail, and the voters would lose sight of the national interest. It is a little known fact among the American people that the Founders condemned political parties precisely as a primary cause of political unhappiness.

Despite their wariness of the political competence of the people, the Framers were republicans and they recognized the importance of including the populace in the process of governing. Thus, they settled on the compromise idea of allowing the people to elect representatives to the House, but not to the Senate. In the presidential realm, the Framers left it to the states to decide how to select the Electors that would elect the president and vice president. Thus, if the people in the states wanted to participate in the selection of Electors, they could demand the right to do so.

The Framers envisioned Electors as people who were better informed than the general populace about public affairs. Since the Electors of each state would consist of small groups meeting in their own state capitals, and assuming a communication system limited to horse back, the Framers thought that nation wide combinations and intrigue among the Electors would be highly unlikely.

Also, because the Electors would be informed and politically experienced, there would be less possibility of demagoguery. The Framers hoped these Electoral College meetings would be as orderly and conducive to deliberation as was their own Philadelphia Convention.

At least since the time of Andrew Jackson, the country has moved far away from any form of rational deliberation preceding a presidential election. The Electoral College has failed to prevent combinations, demagoguery, and the disorder fostered by the unforeseen two-party system. Indeed, the Electoral College has become a rubber stamp of the two-party system. The only intention of the Founders that the Electoral College continues to fulfill is that the meetings are orderly – not deliberative, not meaningful, but at least orderly.

Public Sophistication

The conditions which made the Framers chary of popular elections have changed significantly, thus justifying a departure from this aspect of their original intentions. The American people are now far more politically sophisticated than they have ever been.

Americans have proven their political maturity by the success of their demands for a greater share in the process of self-government, despite an often vicious opposition. This history is well-known. First the struggles of white males without wealth or property expanded the suffrage. Afro-Americans, from the Civil War era through the struggle for Civil Rights, made huge strides in their political education. Women, too, learned about politics through struggle when they won the right to vote. Later, youths broke down more barriers to the vote. The people demanded, and had enacted, the direct election of their US Senators. The successes of the labor union movement further demonstrate the political sophistication of the American public. Experience in numerous wars has also contributed to the political education of the public.

There was little public education in the 18th Century, when the Framers wrote the Constitution. Many Americans were illiterate. But now the US has the benefit of over 100 years of public education. Eighty-five percent of Americans have a high school education or more, and 28% have at least a BA.[129] At first, the social and political experience of the vast majority of Americans was limited to that of farm families without electricity. Now, most Americans live an urban/suburban life, with all sorts of information media, near universal literacy, and 200 years of experience with self-government. Back then, folks rarely moved from the farm. But over the past 150 years, our population has been highly mobile. Over 15% of the US population relocates every year. These experiences have broadened and deepened our economic, cultural, and political self-knowledge.

We are a much more capable public now than the one the Founders knew. We the people are now ready to directly elect our president and vice president. The emergence of the Internet brings with it an election technology that can make a new chapter in American history possible. In the following pages I will show how this new presidential election process can be organized to fulfill the desires of the Framers for rational deliberation in a nonpartisan choice of presidents, and the desire of the American people for more power in our political system.

Self-selection

First, if our presidential election process is to be made more democratic, then it should be open to all qualified citizens, and not just a few well-connected elites. A basic principle of the new election game, therefore, is that every person who is constitutionally eligible for the presidency has a corresponding constitutional right to be a candidate without being restrained by his or her lack of wealth or connections. Article Two, Section One of the Constitution states that any person who is a natural born citizen, at least 35 years of age, and a resident for at least fourteen years is eligible to be president. In my view, the enumeration of these requirements implies a right, to everyone who meets them, of an equal opportunity to at least be considered by the electorate for the office.

The Framers put no formal limit on the number of people who could be considered as prospective presidents. The Electoral College was expected to consider every eligible person known to the Electors. However, when the Framers wrote Article Two, they probably envisioned a small eligibility pool of elites like themselves – well educated, well off, white males. This snobbish, oligarchic intention influenced the shape of the eligibility pool for over 200 years. Not until 2008 was this "glass ceiling" shattered. Then, as we all know, both a woman and a black man became serious contenders.

As yet another sign of the American public's increased political maturity, we have elected our first black president. Today, for most people it seems utterly unjustifiable to exclude any person from the presidential election process simply because of race or gender. In the two-party system, the eligibility pool has traditionally been restricted to people, mostly white males, who have had the free time and the financial resources needed to run for the presidency. The two-party system keeps the pool limited to a dozen hopefuls or less during any given primary season, and after the two conventions there are only two presidential contenders from which to choose.

Thus, under the two-party system the right of everyone who is constitutionally eligible to be considered by the electorate is systematically denied to all but a few. All of those without big money connections and approval, no matter what their ability, are, in reality, excluded from public consideration for the presidency.

Could there be a more patent violation of the "Equal Protection" principle? That principle, embodied in the Fourteenth Amendment, requires that every person be entitled to equality before the law. But what kind of equality does the two-party system give to over 99.9% of those who are constitutionally entitled to be considered for the nation's highest office? The two-party system unconstitutionally discriminates against these people in favor of a tiny number of servants to the special interest bundlers. I say an election system like this is not worth having.

The new election game provides the perfect remedy for this wrong. This reorganized process will be completely open to all self-selected candidates. There will be no dependence on the wealthy. As I will show, it will be publicly funded, and yet cost far less to the taxpayers than presidential elections now cost. It will satisfy the original intentions of the Founders for nonpartisanship precisely because it will be open to candidate self-selection without any party intermeddling. The parties may exist as "public education" organizations, but they will not be necessary to a candidate's success at any point in the process. And, while all groups will be free to buy as much media time as they wish, this new publicly funded process will give equal exposure to all candidates, thereby eliminating the need for individuals to worry about advertising budgets. Because Internet voting, properly organized, will equalize the opportunity for candidates to be heard by the electorate, the lack of wealth need not inhibit candidate self-selection, and the possession of wealth will provide no significant advantage.

But without the two-party system to do it all for us, how can serious and qualified candidates be conveniently screened out of the huge eligibility pool opened up by this new election process?

Of course, some method of screening the candidates is essential. Under the Article Two requirements there are perhaps 50, 60, or even 100 million people eligible to run for the office. No election system can accommodate so many people. Imagine the chaos if one third of the population were to actively petition the others to elect them to the presidency! But that is not likely to happen. Not everyone who is eligible would run. Many would not want the job. It is too much responsibility and too little privacy for most people. Nevertheless, this new process can accommodate all comers, as is required by the Equal Protection principle in our Constitution.

The New Election Game

Because every constitutionally eligible person has a right to be considered for the presidency, a means by which that right can be realized should be provided. The new election game provides that means. It is essentially a screening process. It consists of six separate steps. These are:

The Six Steps of the New Election Game

1. The Presidential Literacy Test
2. The State Selection Debates
3. The Regional Run Offs
4. The National Primary Debates
5. The National Nominating Debates
6. The Presidential Election Debates

Nobody knows how many people there are in this country that both want to be president and are qualified for the position. But in the history of presidential elections there have never been more than a small handful of contenders. After the convention system began in mid-18th Century, there has not been one contest in which more than a dozen men, and only one woman, were considered serious contenders before the conventions. Indeed, it is big news when after the convention there are three presidential candidates left in the race. Since 1948, there have been only a few contests with more than two men who were serious candidates. Storm Thurmond, George Wallace, John Anderson, Ross Perot, and Ralph Nader were news makers because they stayed in the race and challenged the two leading candidates. Still, few third-party candidates have ever received a significant percentage of the vote.

But the number of candidates who have actually run in an election does not necessarily indicate how many people would like to run, or are qualified. FEC records show that for the 2008 election 533 persons filed a Statement of Candidacy, which is required on the way to become eligible for federal matching funds in presidential elections.130 Perhaps this figure is more suggestive of the number of hopefuls that might take part in an open process like the one Internet voting makes possible.

However, for the sake of explaining how this system would work, let us suppose that *1000 people* feel that they are qualified for the presidency, want to be considered by the electorate, and are constitutionally eligible. In past election years, when there were about a dozen candidates before the conventions, that was considered an unusually large field. Compared to that number, 1000 seems impossible! Yet with electronic technology we in the U.S. can easily screen twice that number. Here is how it would work:

Step I. The Presidential Literacy Test (PLT)

The first step in the screening process is a written examination. There are some things a president or a vice president should know before he or she assumes office. These are things that should not be left to on-the-job training. The written exam would test this knowledge. The exam would be offered at no charge on the first Saturday of May in the year of the presidential election.[131] It will cover five of the basic areas in which the presidential candidate should be literate. Following political scientist Clinton Rossiter, these are:[132]

The Five Areas of Required Presidential Knowledge

1. The Constitution, the Bill of Rights, and the theory of federalism.

2. Basic economic theory and current economic conditions.

3. The military and diplomatic history of the United States, and current international conflicts.

4. Current social problems, and US history.

5. The bureaucracy and principles of public administration.

The exam will look for a breadth and balance of learning rather than for expertise in any of these areas.

Professionally operated testing services have con-siderable experience in administering the type of exam that would be used. For example, the Graduate Record Exam (GRE) has subject area tests that it gives to college students who want to apply for graduate schools. The questions that are used for history, economics, political science, etc. can also be used for the presidential literacy test. The Law School Admissions Test (LSAT) is another exam from which questions can be taken. The PLT can easily be administered to any number of people on one Saturday session in locations across the nation. However, since the states have election administration responsibility, some may decide that online testing can be done with integrity equal to that of professionally supervised in person testing. In those states an online procedure can be used.

Professional testing services, under contract to state election officials, will grade the tests and rank the scores by computer. Only those who score in the 80th percentile or above will qualify for the next step.[133] Such a score would mean that the test taker probably knows as much or more than a better than average upper division college student knows about these several subject areas. This may be more than many presidents in the past have known upon taking office.

Thus the knowledge level of college students who are interested in graduate or professional school would set the standard for what a presidential candidate should know. The standard would be high enough to eliminate those whose ignorance makes them unworthy of consideration by the electorate, yet low enough to pass well informed people who may not be super intellectuals.

The 80th percentile would be a realistic reflection of a better than average score for the educated segment of the whole American population. While this score will not be a guarantee of competence in office, at least if there is incompetence it will not be due to ignorance.

Why not, one may wonder, make the minimum score higher than the eightieth percentile? Experience shows that excellent scholars sometimes make poor executives, while middling scholars can be quite adept in practical affairs. Those who follow the careers of professional school graduates know that the students who score little better then a "gentlemen's C" in school often become the high achievers in the practical world. The purpose of the Presidential Literacy Test is to weed out the ignorant, not to enthrone the intellectual.

The grading computers should be programmed to stop scoring a test after it is clear that the test ranks in the 80th percentile. That will be the "pass/not pass" line for this test. The public record would not show any more than "P" or "NP." If numerical scores were computed and recorded, they would become debating points in the later stages of the selection process. But it is trivial and irrelevant to measure a presidential candidate's potential for leadership by whether or not he or she scored an 85 or a 95 on the test. Therefore, scores above the 80th percentile should not even be computed.

The Framers originally anticipated that the electorate would consider only well to do Caucasian men of "continental character" for the presidency. That original "continental character" standard would be honored in the new election game, but there would be a difference. The new process would differ from the original intentions in that the term "continental character" would be defined to include *all* persons of sufficient learning for the executive office. Passing the PLT would be a new requirement of eligibility for office, made mandatory by a Constitutional Amendment. (A suggested Amendment is offered at the end of this chapter.)

Only those who will be 35 years old or older on Inauguration Day, and otherwise eligible, can take the test. At 35, most people will have been away from school for more than a decade. Thus to pass the PLT will require that the test takers have been active readers of history, current affairs and other social science writings.

A military person who is well versed in the history of his field, but has neglected the study of economic and social problems and the Bill of Rights, will probably not achieve a score in the top 20%. A lawyer who knows constitutional law and economics but who lacks a basic familiarity with international relations, current social problems, and the principles of public administration will also probably not pass.

To repeat, a person need not be a super knowledgeable expert in each tested field to pass. Indeed, to score well enough on the test, one need only know roughly the equivalent of what is expected of a university student after completing two or three upper division college courses for each field. That's not much. Adequate preparation for the PLT would require less study than an upper division college student does in his last two years of school. Thus, the demands of the PLT, while challenging, are not too difficult for any intelligent, self-disciplined person to meet.

Still, people who have kept themselves so well educated are rare. This rarity adds to their worth as presidential candidates. Imagine a business person, teacher, professional, or military careerist who kept himself or herself so well read. This in itself would make him or her a fine example of a person who lives by the values of self-discipline, hard work, concern for learning and self-improvement. Aren't these qualities that every president should have? Don't such people merit the accolade "continental character"?

There are additional benefits to testing presidential aspirants for their knowledge. One of these is that the PLT would allow the people to watch the candidates debate without having to worry about the intellectual credentials of the debaters. If someone gaffes, gets a fact wrong, or otherwise slips, the mistake will be kept in its proper context as just a mistake. No one will have to wonder if the debater is intellectually incompetent as they did in 1976 when Gerry Ford, in a debate with Jimmy Carter, announced that "there is no Soviet domination of Eastern Europe."[134] Ronald Reagan raised concern in 1981 when he confidently asserted that trees cause more pollution than automobiles.[135]

In the October first, 2008, vice presidential so-called "debate," a questioner asked Governor Palin what Supreme Court decision she disagreed with besides *Roe v. Wade*. Palin searched her mind for a full minute, but could not think of any (not even *Dred Scott v. Sandford*, which helped spark the Civil War).[136] In the same year, a travel weary candidate, Barack Obama, misstated during a press interview that he had campaigned "in 57 states" in the US, but had not gone to Alaska and Hawaii!137

Everyone makes mistakes in speaking. Sometimes people under pressure say the wrong thing. If their intellectual qualifications have already been certified, then candidate, public, and press can let little errors pass. Two years after Governor Palin's vice presidential campaign, approximately 70% of American voters still had a dim impression of her qualifications to be president.138 But if she had taken the PLT, along with scores of other hopefuls, and done well, doubts based on her lack of knowledge would have been dissipated.

The PLT will make it unnecessary for the candidates to feel that they must prove their intellectual competence, because they will know that the public accepts their intellectual qualifications. In one of the Nixon v. Kennedy TV debates time was lost (as well as the attention of the audience!) when the debaters got mired in a trivia contest about two tiny islands in the South Pacific – Quemoy and Matsu. Such irrelevant displays of detailed knowledge may be amusing as a parlor game, but they are a waste of time in presidential debates. In a crisis the president does not compete in the recall of trivia, he or she engages in decision making under pressure concerning the nation's best interest. There are teams of experts on every subject which the president can use to recall necessary details.

Another basic function of the PLT is to show that the candidate is as "job ready" as any candidate can be for the presidency. That is, he or she is already in possession of the elementary knowledge needed by the president. Once in office, there is no grace period for on-the-job training. Events can happen fast. The new president must be ready to act on the day of his or her inauguration. Every new president must be prepared to converse fluently with highly specialized technical advisors. A president who cannot communicate with the experts in their jargon risks becoming dependent on their judgment.

The idea of a written test for office is not new. Benjamin Barber notes that during the Golden Age of Greece, when Athens was the shining star of democracy, written tests were a common practice in the selection process of the great city-state's highest magistrates.139

This practice was also common for centuries in Confucian China. Thus the practice of testing magistrates is almost as old as government itself, and was basic to the world's first democracy. In the US, we have hundreds of exams for civil service administrators. Why not do the same for the chief administrator?

As I noted earlier, of all the people in the United States who meet the constitutional requirements for eligibility to be president, in 2008, only 533 actually made the effort to sign-up with the FEC. Clearly, the vast majority of Americans do not want to be president. Most of our country's well educated and professional people are quite satisfied with their current positions. Few people would want to give up a life that they are satisfied with in exchange for carrying the world's heaviest responsibility in history's toughest job.

However, all sorts of people will hear the call to glory and accept the challenge to take the test. I have supposed that one thousand people might take the test. Let us suppose further that *five hundred* qualify. There could be more, or less. However, the people who qualified would be some of the finest examples of humanity our nation has to offer. Any one of them would be an excellent model for parents around the world to point to and say to their children "I want you to grow-up to be like this man or woman."

Surely this nation has 500 exceptional people who are ready, willing, and able to take on the job and to do their best at it. The next problem is, how do we choose just one of these persons of continental character to be our president? But what a blessing this burden is! No longer are we choosing between two mediocre men that a band of the superrich has presented to us. The American electorate will have some of the most superior self-educated, self-made, socially conscious, concerned citizens of the nation to choose from – truly the right stuff!

If more than 500 people pass the test, the next step will take relatively longer. But the American people should not be deprived of quality presidential candidates by setting some arbitrary limit on how many can qualify. Whoever passes the test deserves consideration from the electorate.

Step II. The State Election Debates

The second step in the process is the State Selection Debates. Within each state, the residents who passed the PLT will engage in a series of debates to determine a state champion. Suppose these debates begin on the first Tuesday in July, following Independence Day.

When a person takes the PLT, he or she will declare on the answer sheet what state he or she prefers to debate in. That will be his or her state of "residence" for the purpose of the presidential election process. Most people will select the state they normally live in, but they are free to choose any state they want to. However, each person can only declare one state. After the tests are scored, each state will use its computers to arrange the debating schedule by randomly pairing off those who qualified. The persons who pass the test will be notified of their appointed debate time when all the test results are sent out on June first.

Remember that the Framers originally intended Procedural Equality for the states. Each state was meant to have its own unique process, with no special advantages. In the original vision, every state would be an equal player right up to the time they reported their votes to the President of the Senate. Thus, each state was *guaranteed* an opportunity to have at least one of its citizens considered for our nation's top job every presidential election year.

That guarantee has never been honored by the two-party system. In that system's history, at least 30 states have never had any favorite sons or daughters in the contest. But in this new election process, the original intention of the Framers will be more fully honored than ever before, and every state can have one of its own under consideration.

The five hundred people who take the second step will probably not be evenly distributed among the fifty states. Some states might have 20 candidates, while others only one or two. If we suppose that 500 pass the PLT, then this would be an average of 10 candidates in each state. So, to illustrate how this elimination process would work, I will use the example of 10 candidates debating per state.

Let this series of debates be real debates, managed by the debaters, not softball questioning by TV celebrities. Each state will have a moderator to introduce the debaters, instruct the audience as to the procedures, oversee compliance with the rules, and keep the time. The debates will be broadcast online, and on state-wide radio and TV within the state where the debates are being held. The voters in each state will watch the debates during the early evening hours. (The debates will be available for replay online, and can be rebroadcast on radio and TV during the next morning for the convenience of those who cannot listen to or watch them in the evenings.)

Two one-hour debates will be held per evening. Each debate will have one winner, as determined by the voters. Assuming 10 contestants, the first week's elimination round will be completed in three evenings, as the following Table shows:

State Selection Debate Schedule

1st Week
Tuesday	Wednesday	Thursday
1v2	3v4, 5v6	7v8, 9v10

2nd Week
2v4, 6v8	4v10, 8v10

The winners of the first round will face each other the next week. Assuming five winners, four of them will face off in two one-hour debates on Tuesday. They can draw lots to decide on the pairing, and who will be the "odd" person. As there are two debates, there will be two winners. The "odd" person will debate one of the Tuesday night winners on Wednesday. The winner of Wednesday's debate will face the other Tuesday night winner for the final contest on Thursday.

At the end of the first debate each night, the state moderator will ask the viewing audience to write down their votes. When the second debate concludes each evening, the state's secure website will begin accepting votes. Votes will be accepted until the next round of debates begins so that there will be no voting for a previous debate while a new contest is in play. Following the final debate in the series, voting for that debate will be open for 24 hours. Thus, voters who like to mull over their decisions will have time to sleep on it, and perhaps talk it over with friends and fellow workers, or read newspapers or blogs, before voting. Each state can contract with a fact-checking service, which can report factual errors made by debaters. The models for these services already exist, such as Factcheck.org and Politifact.com.140

Preferential Voting

Throughout this new election system a preferential vote will be used. That is, people will be able to record the intensity of their pro and con feelings *for each candidate*. Voting scores will range from 0 to 9. A voter who thinks little of one debater can enter a 0 for him, and then enter a 9 for the debater of whom he thinks very highly. In this process, each voter has a right to rate each candidate. The debater with the most points is the winner.

In the current two-party system the voter is confined to one vote for one candidate. He or she is not allowed to express his or her true feelings about each of the candidates, but only a single mark for a single person. Expressing one mark for one candidate entails the absolute minimum of intellectual involvement by the voter. However, in the new election game the voter is given the opportunity to use his or her rational faculties to form a thoughtful assessment of *each* candidate, decide on a numerical rank on a scale of from 0 to 9 for each, and record those assessments as a "vote."

Voting Online

When the time comes to vote, voters will go to their state's secure website. Each will then enter his or her PIN to log on. The PIN will have been issued at the time of voter registration. While every state has authority over its own election administration procedures, one secure method of registration would be to have each voter appear once for biometric registration, either at a DMV, Voter Registrar's office, or other social services office. Thereafter, all changes of address or other communication with state elections officials can be conducted online.

After logging on, the voter can request a ballot, which will list the name of each debater for the current round of debates. The voter can rate each candidate from 0 to 9. When the ballot has been completed, the voter clicks on the "vote" icon, a window will appear with the voted ballot asking the voter if this is how he or she wants to vote. If the ballot is correct, the voter again clicks on the "vote" icon. After that, a vote receipt will appear with a unique vote number, which is different than the PIN. The receipt number can be copied, or emailed back to the voter. It will thank the voter for participating, but will not show how the voter voted. The entire process of voting can easily be completed in less than two minutes.

Voter Verification

After voting, the voter can use the vote receipt number to verify that his or her vote has been counted. To make this verification, the voter can return to the state's website, log on, and request to see the list of counted votes. If the voter's vote number is on the list, he or she can rest assured that there are no problems. If the number is not there, the voter can request an investigation. Even in the worst case scenario, when, due to some technical difficulty, the vote number is not there, the voter will not be disenfranchised from the presidential election. There will be several more opportunities to vote in this series of elimination debates, and plenty of time for website managers to catch and correct technical snags.

As I mentioned, voting will be conducted for 24 hours following the final debate. The winner will be announced 24 hours after the close of voting. He or she will be "the State Champion." Ties are almost a mathematical impossibility with millions of preferential votes being cast. However, in case of a tie, the tied competitors can hold a tie-breaking debate the night after the results have been announced.

In this scenario the American people have just screened 500 of the best presidential potential that the nation has to offer. This batch has been sheared down to the 50 finest people in the land. *Each and every state* has selected its own champion. This feat has been performed by well over one hundred million voters spending only two minutes online each night after watching one or two hours of debates on TV. Not bad for just a few evenings of citizenship work.

Now every state, large or small, in the middle of the mainland, or far off shore, has an *equal opportunity* to see its favorite son or daughter competing for the presidency.

But 50 are still too many for a *national* debate competition, so again the responsibility for candidate screening must be divided up among the electorate. Such division of labor is a natural element of the republican form of self-government.

Step III. The Regional Run-Offs

The third step of this new election process will continue screening by dividing the states into four sections of roughly equal size.141 These will be the Northeast, the Midwest, the South, and the West. (See the following Table.) In the Regional Run Offs, there could be 12 to 14 debaters per region, assuming that each state provides a champion. A series of six or seven debates will be broadcast in each region, beginning on the first Tuesday in August.

Two one-hour debates will be aired each night. Twelve State Champions can be screened in three evenings in the first week. (If there are 14 contestants in the West, three debates can be held on one of the nights, or one debate on a fourth night.) The winners of the first round will debate during the second week. Then one final debate will be held on Tuesday of the third week. (See the illustration below.) One victor will emerge from each region.

Regional Run-Offs: Four Regions

	West	South	Midwest	Northeast
1	Washington	Virginia	Ohio	Maine
2	Oregon	West Virginia	Indiana	Vermont
3	California	Kentucky	Illinois	New Hampshire
4	Montana	Tennessee	Wisconsin	Massachusetts
5	Idaho	Arkansas	Michigan	Connecticut
6	Nevada	Louisiana	Iowa	Rhode Island
7	Arizona	Mississippi	Minnesota	New York
8	Wyoming	Alabama	North Dakota	Pennsylvania
9	Utah	Georgia	South Dakota	Maryland
10	Colorado	South Carolina	Nebraska	Delaware
11	New Mexico	North Carolina	Kansas	New Jersey
12	Oklahoma	Texas	Missouri	Florida
13	Hawaii			
14	Alaska			

Regional Run-Offs Schedule

1st Week

Tuesday	Wednesday	Thursday
1v2, 3v4	5v6, 7v8	9v10, 11v12

2nd Week

2v4, 6v8	10v12, 4v8

3rd Week

8v12

The four Regional Victors will be the greatest examples of leadership that America has to offer. The voters of each region will have selected these four as the best presidential timber in their region. These four people will be well worth getting to know. Therefore, the process will pause for a September break. During this time the nation will have an opportunity to familiarize itself with its prime presidential potential. Students will have time to get settled at school and discuss the issues. The candidates will take part in media interviews. Their views will be publicized, analyzed, and discussed. They will have time to address civic minded groups and to meet people personally.

Costs to the Candidates

Media interviews are free, and civic groups can pay the travel expenses of those they invite to speak to them. Travel costs incurred by the candidates to and from the TV studio for the debate will be reimbursed by the state governments. Federal law will require employers to give the four candidates paid leave of absence for September so that they will have time to make themselves known to the public. Thus the rich candidates and those with leisure time will have little or no significant advantage over the working candidate.

At last, a presidential election will cost the prospective presidents exactly what the Founders originally intended it to cost –nothing!

First Amendment Freedoms

Constitutional law currently forbids legal restrictions on how much money a person, a party, or an independent group can spend to promote a candidate. Also, candidates who do not accept federal matching funds can spend as much of their own money in self-promotion as they please. These laws are appropriate because they are consistent with our Constitution's First Amendment. That Amendment states, in part, "Congress shall make no law … abridging the freedom of speech." The Supreme Court has rightly concluded that restricting how much money someone can spend on political speech violates the First Amendment. These new election procedures will honor the Supreme Court's rulings.

The Moment of Reason

To repeat, allowing unrestricted campaign spending will not result in an unfair advantage for the rich or well-connected. Most campaign money is spent on advertising. This advertising has two primary objectives. One is to drill a candidate's name into the heads of voters, so that they will recognize that name on the ballot when the time comes for each to cast a single vote. The other objective of ads is to condition either a negative or a positive association with the name of a candidate. Both tactics try to by-pass the reasoning of voters, and instill automatic responses in their minds.

But these behavioral science techniques of conditioning the minds of voters are only useful to the manipulators when, after a long campaign, voting consists of making a mark for one candidate on a ballot with a selection of names on it. The idea of conditioning is that the unreasoning voter will go to the polls, see the name he or she has been trained to select, and automatically put a mark by that name.

The new electronic election method presupposes an intelligent and reasoning voter. Here, the public will vote shortly after it sees the candidates debate. The voter will vote upon his or her thoughtful impression of each candidate's character, speaking ability, intelligence, issue position, and political sagacity. This impression will be fresh in the minds of the voters when they use their personal judgment to rate the debaters via the preferential vote. The voters will not vote upon mere name or attitude conditioning, like a pigeon conditioned to peck a red button rather than blue; instead, the voter will be exercising his or her civic wisdom.

All the spending done on advertising prior to a set of elimination debates will have little or no effect on a voter's judgment in comparison to the experience of actually witnessing the candidates debate. This experience will be the primary basis for the voter's decision. Thus, the voter will be engaged in *a moment of reasoning* that is free from the corruption of advertising, and based only upon his or her personal experience as a thoughtful citizen assessing candidates.

Big spending by some corporate special interest or superrich candidate could backfire by arousing resentment, as has happened in the past. So, let those with lots of money spend, it will give them no advantage, and it could work against them. This electronic election system is structured to guarantee a deliberative process, just as the framers originally intended.

Step IV. The National Primary Debates.

A new procedure will be introduced in the fourth step of the process. In the National Primary Debates there will be *two* evenings of debate, one on domestic issues, and the other on foreign affairs. The four regional winners will be such prominent people that their opinions on these separate subjects will be well worth knowing. The debates will be held on the first Tuesday and Wednesday of October. There will be two one-hour debates each evening. Contestants will be randomly matched by computer. The Wednesday night pairs will not be the same as the Tuesday night pairs. This setup enables the electorate to see each candidate in action against the others. Also, the second night will be a test of stamina and will let the people see how well the debaters hold up under stress.

The National Primary Debate Schedule

1 Week

Tuesday	Wednesday	Thursday
1v2, 3v4	4v1, 3v2	two-day vote totals announced

Preferential voting will be used, as with the previous steps. Also, the FEC, which was created by Congress to monitor compliance with federal election law, will supervise these debates. On Thursday evening the *two-day vote totals* will be announced. The *two persons* with the highest scores will go on to the next step in the contest.

Why will there be two winners of the National Primary Debates rather than one? Because the people of the United States might want to replace both the incumbent president and vice president in the final election. If only one person won the primary debates, then at least one of the other two incumbents would be assured of retaining office. However, if the voters feel the two challengers are more worthy of the nation's two highest offices than the present occupants, they should have the opportunity to "throw the rascals out."

Taking Stock

Let us pause for a moment and consider what has transpired in these first four steps of the new election game. We supposed that, after passing the PLT, 500 American citizens qualified for the presidency and wanted to be considered by the electorate for the job. The number 500 would include all types of Americans, rich and poor, black, red, yellow, brown, tan, and pink, men and women, all starting from the same line with no advantages.

Here is a group of 500 mature, intelligent, and knowledgeable people representing all walks of life who have proven their presidential literacy. Imagine the wealth of talent in this bunch! Did the two-party system ever give the voters such a variety to choose from?

None of these prospects will be party hacks picked in a back room by a few wheeler-dealers. Nor will any of them be at all dependent upon the charity of the contributing class, the leaders of which are unknown to the public. From this mountain of talent the American people can select their very best. Their final choice will not be two "old boys," one representing the Republican elite, the other representing the Democratic elite. The winners in the new election game will have no political debts. They will owe their positions only to the people. In steps two, three, and four a field of 500 superb prospects was screened and pruned until only two people remained to be pitted against the incumbent president and vice president in one more contest before the final election.

Step V. The National Nominating Debates

The National Nominating Debates will present two candidates to square off with the incumbent president and vice president. The format will be the same as the National Primary Debates. (In the following table the Primary winners are 1 and 2, with the president "P," the vice president "VP.")

The National Nominating Debate Schedule

One Week

Tuesday	Wednesday	Thursday
1vP, 2vVP	VPv1, Pv2	two-day vote totals
announced		

The contest will be held in mid-November, in the week before Thanksgiving. There will be two one-hour debates per evening. The Tuesday debate will be on domestic issues. The Wednesday debate will be on foreign affairs. On Thursday, the FEC will announce the preferential vote totals. Again, the *two* debaters with the highest scores will go on to the last debate and the final election of the president and vice president.[142]

The vote in these nominating debates cannot be used to elect the president and vice president because four contestants are still too many candidates to choose from. With four of the most prominent people of the nation in the field, the odds are that all four would receive very high scores. One candidate could win with only a slightly higher score than the others. But that kind of victory could end up frustrating the hopes of nearly three fourths of the electorate. In a democratic election process, elected officials should have the support of the majority. To govern effectively the president should have as much popular support as possible. President Lincoln once said that without popular support a president can do nothing, but with it he can do anything. Thus, to avoid having a president with less than a clear majority of support one more step is necessary.

Step VI. The Presidential Election Debates

The final step in this procedure is designed to assure that the man or woman who assumes the presidency does so with the approval of a majority of the electorate. Thus, in the Presidential Election Debates there will be two candidates. On the first Tuesday in December they will have two one-hour debates. The first debate will be on domestic issues, the second on foreign affairs. Preference voting will take place for 24 hours after the second debate. This will give the voter sufficient time to ponder his or her decision. The person who is awarded the highest number of points will be the president. The second place person will be the vice president. Incidentally, this "first place/second place" way of deciding who would be president and vice president is precisely what the Framers originally intended.

In the current two-party system, the presidential candidate *and his party* pick the vice presidential candidate. But that method is *unconstitutional.* The Framers of the Constitution originally intended that the Electors themselves, not parties or presidential candidates, pick the vice presidential prospects.[143]

Now, for the first time since the Eighteenth Century, both the president and vice president will be chosen by the electorate because each is qualified for their office. This is what the Framers intended. The vice president will be one of the two most highly regarded political figures in the nation. Selected by the folks back in his or her home state, promoted above all the competition by the people in his or her region, honored by the nation as among the two most worthy challengers to the incumbent president and vice president, the occupant of the vice presidency will have been proven worthy of the highest office because he or she will have been selected by the nation as top presidential timber.

A tie in a presidential election is most unlikely. Well over one hundred million people will be voting their preference for the two candidates on a scale of 0-9. The odds against these totals being equal are extremely high. But if this unlikely event occurs, a one hour tie breaker debate can be held with the voting lines open for 24 hours afterwards. If a second tie occurs, the election will go to the House of Representatives, as the Constitution now prescribes.

If there is no tie or other irregularity, the President of the Senate will officially declare the election results before a joint session of Congress on the second Friday following the Tuesday debates. (This period will provide time to hear and investigate the grounds for a challenge to the process, if any.) The inauguration of the new president will take place on January 20 in accord with the 20th Amendment.

An Education of the Electorate

The pace of the new election game is designed for the convenience of everyone involved. The PLT is given in May on a Saturday so that the work week won't be disrupted.

Then the states have about three weeks to grade the tests, arrange the debating schedules and inform the candidates. After the June announcement, the hopefuls will have about one month to prepare for the State Selection Debates, and to make themselves known within their state.

The electorate does not begin to vote until the series of debates in July. The people in some states might not have any debates, while in other states there could be several hours, depending on how many residents pass the PLT. After the State Champions have been selected, there will be a pause of about thirty days. During this time the media will be bringing people information about the fifty Champions. The candidates will be interviewed in print, online, on the air. Pundits will be speculating about who has the best chances of victory in the regional contest. Political advertising will occur, for sure; but the performance of the debaters will weigh more heavily in the minds of voters than any ads they saw online or on TV.

After Independence Day, every four years, the presidential election will be "in the air." Newspapers, websites, blogs, and other media will keep the issues alive. Because there will be so many viewpoints to discuss and such a variety of new ideas coming from the candidates, this new election process will truly be an education to the electorate.

There will not be time to learn about all fifty candidates before the Regional Run Offs begin. Just to learn about the background and views of the dozen or so candidates in one's own region will be an education. Still, many

Americans will hunger to know what's being talked about in the other regions.

After the regional debates, the electorate will be able to focus in on the details of each candidate's views. The press will have time to pick apart each of the four contenders. The September break will give people time to think over and integrate what they have learned.

A wiser and well-informed electorate will view the National Primary Debates in October. Central issues and questions will have emerged during the long break. While each region will know its candidate, three quarters of the country will be seeing three of the candidates in action for the first time. In this process, people will rarely complain about seeing the same old faces on TV every night. In each series of debates there will be new faces with new opinions for the viewers to consider. Candidates will always be facing new opponents and new challenges, so they will have to stay on their toes. There will not be any droning on of the same old superficial slogans that the candidates in the two-party system were so obsessed with. People will be encouraged to engage in rational deliberation about the candidates and the issues.

When the National Nominating Debates come around in November, the public will be on the edge of their seats, waiting to see how the challengers do against the incumbent president and vice president. When this round of voting is over, the people will surely give thanks for the leadership they have, and for the election process that empowered them to select such candidates.

December will almost be anticlimactic. The two best people will already have been selected. But the vote will be necessary to decide who will be president and who will be vice president. After the decision is made, America will be full of people glowing with a sense of accomplishment. Not only were the offices filled, but the people filled them, and an education was acquired in doing so. The pride that the voters will feel will make their investment of time well worth it. The sense of efficacy they feel will be the measure of their "political happiness."

A Question of Time

And what about the time? At first, that would vary depending on how many hopefuls qualified in each state. For example, in states where only four hopefuls qualified, the State Champion could be selected in only three hours of debate for the entire month. The amount of time required to watch the debates and vote in states where the unlikely number of ten hopefuls qualified, would be but nine hours.

Of course, if someone tries to watch political debates online or on TV for nine hours straight, their eyes would pop out of their heads! But that is not how the game is played. The debates are spread out. A series of debates with ten contestants would only require three evenings for the first round; two hours for the first two nights, and one hour on the third. Then there is a four day respite before the second round of only four hours of debate spread out over three evenings. Is that too demanding on the time of the voter?

The typical American watches four to six hours, sometimes eight hours of TV per day. Increasing numbers are online that long. At six hours per day, that's 180 hours per month. In July when all, or most, of the states will be at work screening state candidates, the process could be finished at the utmost in only nine hours of debates, and probably less. That is a mere 1/20th of the typical person's TV time for a month.

Then in August, during the Regional Run Offs, total TV time for the month would be, at most, eleven hours – a mere one-sixteenth of regular TV time! This is the greatest sacrifice anyone will be asked to make, and then only once every four years.

True, somebody's favorite program may be preempted so that the voters of our nation can screen the candidates and elect their president. But the networks can reschedule these shows so that everyone can watch the debates and their favorite programs too. In return for this small sacrifice, each citizen will get the good feelings of being a real power in the presidential election process. Plus, the country will get a president who truly represents the people. Isn't that a bargain?

The challenge of this new system is not that people will be asked to watch a lot of extra TV, but that people will be asked to watch a few hours of different programming. Is that too much to give up for democracy? Hopefully, the reader will agree that the new election game will not crucify the electorate on an electronic audiovisual cross.

While involving the people more, the new method will actually *shorten* the time in which the presidential election process is conducted. Under the current two-party contributor-centered system, the candidate must start fundraising two years before the election. Press speculation and candidate "trial balloons" also start appearing during that time. Election year primaries begin in January, and run through June or July. While everyone is subjected to TV political advertising, often less than a third of the eligible voters bother to participate in primaries.

The two conventions are usually held in August or September. Of course, the public has no involvement in these, except as passive spectators watching TV highlights. In September the general election campaign begins in full force. The public is bombarded with mass manipulation tricks, but have no power. There are some debate-like events between the candidates, but they are not real contests.

This circus drags on until the November vote. Here is the one time where all the people have their first chance to record their single mark for a president – nearly two years after the process had begun! To complete the mockery of "democracy," even this one vote is *not official*. The official vote comes in December when the various Electors meet and vote as the Electoral College.

In the new election process the electorate in every state is totally involved from the very first debate – just as they should be in a republic, and as the Framers originally intended Electors to be. The debates can be real, allowing spontaneous confrontations between the candidates. The public votes after each debate. Their votes are not symbolic, as they are now in November, but determinative. And instead of one symbolic vote, the electorate will have several meaningful preferential votes eliminating candidates until the final choice is made. Since all of these votes will be by modem or phone, the total time spent casting these several votes will be far less than the time consumed by driving to the polls, parking, waiting in line, and casting one symbolic gesture in November.

This new system will completely eliminate the wasteful, exhausting, degrading, and often boring primary and general election campaign activities. It sets up five rounds of debates, which start in July, break in September, and finish in the first week of December. Thus, not only is the time for public attention reduced from nearly 24 months down to five, but because the people will be exercising real power, it will all be quality time.

The candidates will not have to crawl around begging for money, because participation in the debates will not cost them a penny. No more hopefuls with sore knees, brown noses, and enchained by political debts! They can spend more time with their families and at their careers. And the "lame duck" period of the incumbent will be reduced from the last three months of his or her presidency down to a few weeks.

The new election game will save taxpayers money. Currently, hundreds of millions of federal dollars are simply "granted" to the two candidates, and to the two-party organizations. The new process will be publicly funded, and yet, cost far less than the two-party system's circus of deception. No new agencies will be required, just some changes in rules and the personnel (who are now party hacks) at the Federal Election Commission. The only major costs will be the initial outlay in the counties for their secure voting website servers.

The air time needed for the debates on TV can be donated by the networks as a condition of licensing. There would be no loss of First Amendment rights on the part of the networks, because the public owns the airwaves already. Most of the free and democratic nations in the world require TV stations to contribute substantial amounts of time for political purposes. Among these are England, France, Germany, Canada, Mexico and Japan.

In the forty years between 1968 and 2008, the Republican Party has presented the American people with but seven presidential candidates: Nixon (CA, 1968, 1972), Ford (MI, 1976), Reagan (CA, 1980, 1984), Bush 41 (TX, 1988 & 1992), Dole (KS, 1996), Bush 43 (TX, 2000, 2004), and McCain (NV, 2008). Seven white males in 11 presidential elections is not much of a selection. In the same period, the Democrats have given us eight white men: Humphrey (MN, 1968), McGovern (SD, 1972), Carter (GA, 1976, 1980), Mondale (MN, 1984), Dukakis (MA, 1988), Clinton (AR, 1992, 1996), Gore (TN, 2000), and Kerry (MA, 2004). Obama(IL) shattered the old racist pattern in 2008, but still, the record is not very impressive.

The Republicans only drew candidates from five states in these forty years. The Democrats only drew from seven. Thus, during this time, only 12 states have seen one of their own be selected as a presidential candidate. Thirty-eight states have been, in effect, orphaned by the two-party system.

The State Selection Debates will produce 50 highly qualified candidates, one from each state, for every presidential election. Not only is that all inclusive of the states, as they agreed to in The Great Compromise, but it gives the people much more of a choice!

As I have noted, this process will fulfill the original intentions of the Founding Fathers for nonpartisanship in presidential elections precisely because it will be open to candidate self-selection, and candidate screening directly by the electors, without any party intermeddling. The parties may exist as "propaganda organizations" for their special interest groups, but they will have NO CONTROL over *any step* of the process. Nor will any political party receive any government money. Political parties are simply private organizations, and should be self-supporting as such.

As I have shown, the intentions of the Founders for an orderly process conducive to the use of Reason will also be fulfilled. Individuals will be making their own in-formed decisions in their own homes, undisturbed by techniques of mass manipulation.

Of course, a Constitutional Amendment will be needed to remove the Electoral College, and to establish the PLT and electronic technology as a part of our election law. Article V of the Constitution provides alternative methods for enacting an Amendment. The more efficient way is for

Congress to write the Amendment, and let the state legislatures vote on its ratification. Here is an example of what such an Amendment could say:

SUGGESTED AMENDMENT

Section 1.

The President and Vice President of the United States shall be elected by the people. In addition to the qualifications stated in Article Two of this Constitution, candidates for these offices must pass a written examination. Those who pass the exam will participate in a series of electronically broadcast elimination debates. Following each set of debates there will be a period during which votes will be cast and recorded electronically. All candidates will be eliminated in this manner until two remain. A final post-debate vote will be taken to determine by the greatest number who will be President, the Vice President to be determined by the lesser number.

If a tie occurs, a one hour electronically broadcast debate will be held, followed by a second period of voting electronically. If a second tie occurs, the election will be taken by the House of Representatives wherein votes will be cast for one or the other of these two candidates. This vote shall be taken by states, the representation from each state having one vote; a quorum for this purpose shall consist of a member or members from two thirds of the states, and a majority of all the states shall be necessary to a choice. If no such majority is achieved prior to the 20th day of January, the provisions of Section 3 of the

Twentieth Amendment shall take effect until such a majority is reached.

The President of the Senate shall, in the presence of the Senate and House of Representatives, announce the results of the determinative vote.

The incumbent President and Vice President at the time this Amendment is implemented will not be required to take the written examination, but they will be required to participate in the debates at the appropriate time to seek reelection. The Congress shall have power to enforce this Amendment by appropriate legislation.

Section 2.

Paragraph two, Section 1, of Article Two to this Constitution, and the Twelfth Amendment to this Constitution are hereby repealed.144

Chapter Five

The Reasonable Person Standard and the Critics of Internet Voting

Liberty and Reason as Original Intentions

Chapter Two explained the original intentions of our Founding Fathers for the conduct of presidential elections. As originally intended, a calm and orderly process, conducive to reason, would result in the selection of someone with a continent-wide reputation for political sagacity and a personal commitment to the best interests of the whole nation. Trusting in human reason, the Constitution envisioned groups of Electors judiciously deliberating, each in their own state, and thinking of their state's best interest, as well as that of the nation. In this process their votes would be the result, to borrow Washington's words, of "common counsels and modified by mutual interests," rather than the product of "the ill-concerted and incongruous projects of faction."

The Framers of the Constitution anticipated that by specifying their intentions in a written document, future self-governing generations would have clear guidance. This guidance was meant, among other things, to preserve the founding principles of *Liberty through self-government*, and of *self-government through Reason*. It was to these ends that the Framers employed the constitutional devises still admired around the world. These include the separation of powers, the checks and balances, the federal system, regular elections, popular participation, etc. The Framers had hoped to establish a political system that would remain free of party domination.

Our nation's founding moment endures, then, as a model for mankind because its participants strove to be reasonable persons. What more could be asked of any group of human beings? As Madison observed, one reason that the Philadelphia Convention succeeded is that it was free of "the pestilential influence of party animosities."[145] A second reason was the willingness of its individual participants to compromise for the sake of "the public good."[146]

Like the Philadelphia Convention, the success of "Republican self-government," as that conception was understood in our Founding Generation, requires that all people put reason above *passion* (in the sense of unreasoning emotion). As Hamilton wrote, "Why has government been instituted at all? Because the passions of men will not conform to the dictates of reason and justice without constraint."[147] Madison echoed the same sentiments, "it is the reason, alone, of the public, that ought to control and regulate the government. The passions ought to be controlled and regulated by the government."148

In this chapter, I will examine the current debate over the merits of Internet voting in the light of the original intention of our Founding Generation that Americans, as a self-governing people, use reason to forge policies that will preserve and enhance their Liberty.

Reason v. Emotion in the Internet Voting Debate

In Chapter One I recounted the story of the SERVE project,149 which was abruptly terminated on January 30, 2004. At the behest of Congress, the Department of Defense (DoD) had invested over twenty million dollars, and two years of work, on setting up an experimental system of Internet voting. The system would enable nearly 100,000 UOCAVA citizens (overseas Americans, both military and civilian) from seven different states, to conveniently vote in the 2004 presidential election. Upon its completion, the DoD team contracted with ten computer scientists to inspect the SERVE system, and to make recommendations for its improvement, if need be.150

After only two days of inspection, four of them became determined to *stop* the project, rather than try to improve it, because they feared it was headed straight for "catastrophe." Despite the understanding that the team of ten would file a joint report at the end of the inspection period, the four dissenters immediately "went public" with their accounting of all the disasters they feared the project was sure to bring about.151

Their sensational claims created a media blitz. Undersecretary of State Paul Wolfowitz, who headed the department with the SERVE project, ordered the halt. Whether that decision was self-serving, or an emotional over-reaction spurred by the four alarmists, or a matter of prudent caution prevailing over the SERVE team's reckless adventurism is still a subject of dispute. In any case, that 2004 event stopped the federal government, to this day, from participating in any further trials of Internet voting based on the use of a secure website for overseas citizens. Progress in the states was also halted, until 2010 when a few daring election officials undertook some small trials.

Chapter One examined the specific reasons offered by the dissenters for going public, and criticized each of their notions for falling short of the degree of rationality rightly to be expected of "scientists." However, that pivotal moment in the history of Internet voting in the United States is well worth a second look so that any doubts about whether these dissenters acted with reason, or with unreasoning emotion, can be dispelled.

The Reasonable Person Standard

But how can anyone say what is "reason" and what is "unreason" in an action? Aren't these mere subjective judgments, with one person's reason being another's unreason? If so, then isn't the informed judgment of a high government officer to be preferred over the Monday morning quarterbacking of some author?

While these questions might provide fuel for endless debates among philosophers, the issue of the supposed equality of subjective opinions has long been settled in the practice of law, where practical decisions must be made. Throughout the history of the common law, courts have recognized that the best source for determining the degree of reason in a person's actions is the common person. That is one reason why juries are impaneled in trials. Everyday, judges instruct juries to assess for themselves, and for the court, the degree of reason in someone's actions. A prosecutor, for example, must prove his case "beyond a reasonable doubt" in order to have an accused person convicted of a crime. In breach of contract cases, a jury may have to assess the degree of reason in the expectations of the parties to the contract. A court may enforce the reasonable expectations of one party, and deny enforcement to the party with expectations deemed unreasonable by a jury.

In a civil suit for harms allegedly caused by a defendant's negligence, a jury may be instructed to apply the "reasonable person standard" to appraise the degree of reason in the defendant's actions. If the defendant has been determined by the jury to have acted with an unreasonable disregard for the rights and safety of others when he caused the plaintiff's harms, then the court will likely award compensatory damages to the plaintiff. But if the defendant shows that he exercised "reasonable care," and that plaintiff's harms were unforeseeable by a reasonable person, then the court may not hold the defendant responsible for plaintiff's harms.

The reasonable person standard used in these cases consists in each juror forming a *personal judgment* as to whether or not a reasonable person would have acted as the defendant did under the same or similar circumstances. In both civil and criminal cases, the jurors are instructed by the judge to use their own judgment, based on their own life experiences, in deciding what is reasonable under the circumstances. Courts recognize that all normal human beings have the natural capacity to use empathy to form such judgments about the degree of reason in another person's conduct. Without that natural capacity, the common law, followed in England for almost 1000 years and in the US for over 200 years, would collapse in disarray.[152]

The *intersubjective agreement* of jurors provides the court with a sufficiently objective standard by which to decide a legal dispute. In this way, the practice of the common law daily replicates the chief principle followed in the making of our Constitution – that is, for a self-governing people to resolve civic conflicts by striving to be reasonable.

This same method can be used by you, the reader, as juror, to appraise the degree of reason in the actions of those who brought the SERVE project to its sudden end. Assuming that Wolfowitz would have allowed SERVE to proceed but for the public demands of the four dissenters, we can focus on the reasonableness of their acts, as the primary cause of SERVE's demise, and leave the question of *his* reasonableness under the circumstances for another day.

Publicly demanding the end of a government program is certainly not, of itself, an unreasonable thing to do. Indeed, it may be heroic. So the question to be considered is, were the *reasons* of the four dissenters for demanding the termination of SERVE reasonable? Since they were trained computer scientists, the question can be asked more specifically. That is, would reasonable persons, trained in computer science, have acted as the four dissenters did under the same or similar circumstances?

Several matters must be considered in the making of this determination. Among these is the consensus of the experts, at the time, about what security risks actually existed for Internet voting in general. Were the four dissenting computer scientists acting consistently with expert consensus, or against it?

Another factor to be considered in this chapter is the consensus of the experts as to whether the measures the SERVE team had taken to mitigate the security risks were adequate for providing a reasonably secure system of Internet voting. If the dissenters acted against the consensus of the experts in both instances, that may be sufficient grounds for adjudging their reasons and their actions as having been unreasonable.

In Chapter One, I presented the arguments of the four dissenters as to why the SERVE system was unacceptably insecure. I also discussed the measures taken by the SERVE team to mitigate those security risks. Here I will show that when the consensus of expert opinion in the few years leading up to Wolfowitz's order is added to the mix, the weights on the Scale of Justice tip the balance steeply against the four dissenters.

The evidence of this expert opinion is readily available. It was gathered at the time for a book on the very subject of the pros and cons of Internet voting. The authors are two political scientists with extensive experience in the Internet voting community. Thad Hall and R. Michael Alvarez researched and wrote their book, *Point, Click, and Vote: The Future of Internet Voting*153 during the years of 2001 through mid-2003.

Ironically, the book was completed and submitted for printing prior to SERVE's termination, and then published, unchanged, after SERVE was stopped. Thus, the authors collected their data and wrote their findings with a distinct optimism about the prospects for Internet voting; and, of course, in ignorant bliss of what was about to happen. In their self-understandings, they were recording "the state of the Internet voting debate"154 in the period leading up to what they thought would become Internet voting's greatest triumph – the success of SERVE.

Because they had no idea of what was about to happen, they gathered their information and drew their conclusions without rancor or resentment for the critics of Internet voting. Their lack of bias makes them excellent witnesses as to the consensus of expert opinion prior to the cancellation of SERVE. Without intending to do so, Hall and Alvarez provide some of the best expert testimony now available as to the degree of reason in the arguments used by the four dissenters against SERVE. The testimony of other witnesses will be presented after we hear from Hall and Alvarez.

The State of the Debate Prior to the Demise of SERVE

First Period 2000-2002

Hall and Alvarez show that the same arguments that were used against SERVE in early 2004 had already been in circulation for at least three years. Thus, these arguments were well known to the community of experts during that time. This community had considered those arguments on several occasions. The community of experts that I refer to includes computer scientists who are knowledgeable about voting technology and Internet security, political scientists, and government officials at the local, state, and federal level.

At the federal level, for example, the Department of Defense had begun planning for its first effort at voting over the Internet for overseas citizens, called "VOI," a few years prior to its implementation. This was a 6.2 million dollar trial of the new voting technology.155 Hall and Alvarez both participated in the evaluation of this project.156 Pro and con arguments were considered at the planning stage in the DoD, and again in congressional committees when the decision was being made to allocate the funds. Clearly, the consensus of opinion among the government elections experts and the independent computer experts was that the security challenges for VOI could be managed. That they did manage those challenges was proven by the success of the project in 2000, when several Americans cast their votes via the Internet from overseas. This was the first actual voting online for a presidential election, and it was free of security problems.157 Indeed, it went so well that in 2002 Congress saw fit to provide up to forty million dollars for SERVE.

The Republican Party held a straw poll in Alaska via Internet voting in the 2000 presidential primary season. The Democrats in Arizona also held their primary vote online that year. Pro and con issues were discussed by state party leaders before going ahead in both cases. A lawsuit was filed in federal court by anti-Internet voting activists in Arizona, but after considering their reasons, the judge ruled that the online voting may proceed.158

In both these states, then, the prevailing consensus, including the informed opinion of a federal judge, was that security problems could be managed by the contractors who would set up the systems. Like the VOI, both of the state trials went off without security problems. The practical experience in these *three* instances tended to confirm the expert opinion, and to inform the public, that Internet voting can be conducted in a way which will mitigate, if not completely prevent, security breaches.

In addition to these pioneering trials, the community of experts was busy in other ways with work on Internet voting issues. Hall and Alvarez report that in the 1999-2001 period, well before the 2004 termination of SERVE, three major studies on the feasibility of Internet voting for elections in the United States were conducted. Alvarez had been a participant in all three. These were the California Internet Voting Task Force, the Internet Policy

Institute study commissioned by President Clinton, and a CalTech/MIT study, in which Hall also participated.

Hall and Alvarez were among the peer review group that inspected the VOI system in 2000, and they were also included in the group of ten that DoD invited to inspect SERVE's security features.159 Their CalTech/MIT group had a several million dollar contract with the Department of Defense to evaluate the success of the SERVE project once it had been implemented and used by UOCAVA voters. Indeed, they participated in the selection of the other eight peers.160 They are deeply embedded in the community of Internet voting experts, where they are highly respected.

Hall and Alvarez write that scholars and government officials in the US first began to think seriously about the prospects for Internet voting in "the late 1990s."161 Thinking reached the level of legislation in 1996, when the California legislature passed Assembly Bill 44. Four years before the Internet voting trials in Alaska and Arizona, that bill provided funding for a task force to look into the possibility of Internet voting in California. Just the fact that this funding proposal could pass in the legislature shows that reasonable and responsible people were willing, then, to seriously consider Internet voting. These legislators would not have acted thus if their constituencies had thought they were embarking upon a reckless or unreasonable adventure.

Indeed, citing the burgeoning use of computers in California, and public opinion polls of the time, Hall and Alvarez suggest that if there had been a referendum, "internet voting could easily [have been] adopted in California."162 Apparently, both government and public attitudes during the late 1990s, and in several states, were very receptive to the idea of experimenting with Internet voting.

However, not every California official was enthusiastic about instituting Internet voting. Republican Governor Pete Wilson vetoed the bill, citing concerns over the costs of such a study and worry that the Internet was too susceptible to voting fraud.163

A fellow Republican, Bill Jones, was the Secretary of State at the time, with the responsibility for conducting elections in California. Jones was a pioneer in the e-government movement. He was among the first to put government information online, including campaign finance reports. His opinion of Internet voting shines brightly in his slogan, "California citizens should be online – not in line."164 Thus, in 2000, a couple of years after Wilson's veto, and using his office's funds, Jones commissioned California's first official study of the feasibility of Internet voting.165

The task force consisted of over 30 members, including experts in the fields of computer science, political science, and state and county election officials. In January of 2000, before the VOI and the two state trials took place, the California task force published its conclusions. Their report found, among other things, that some specific security issues for home computers, such as vulnerability to viruses and spyware, were not fully resolved by the current state of the technology. There were also the problems of reliable voter registration technology, voter authentication, and ballot security. The home computer security software industry was still in its infancy, and secure cell phone technology had not yet been invented.

The report expressed a concern about the problem of the "digital divide." That is, at the time a large number of folks, especially minorities, lacked Internet access. So the task force thought it would be unfair to offer the convenience of Internet voting to the "haves," while the "have nots" still had to stand in line. Of course, this is no longer a problem. Everyone in the US now has convenient access to online voting technology. Those very few people without their own PC or cell phone can easily use the equipment made available at schools, government offices, or public libraries.

Primarily due to these access and PC security concerns, the report recommended against an immediate and wholesale shift to Internet voting for the state of California at that time.166 However, the task force did suggest that *small trials* of Internet voting be conducted. For example, those with computers could apply to vote online, like they currently apply to vote by mail as absentee voters. (Presumably, these applicants would be security conscious, and have security software already in-stalled in their machines.)

Also, secure online voting stations could be made available in polling places on Election Day for those who wanted to try the new method of voting. The report suggested that Internet voting could be gradually increased in California, as the security problems were worked out by technological advances.167 Cautious optimism was the shared attitude of the task force members.168

During the Clinton administration, in the 1990s, Vice President Al Gore led a movement to modernize the way government managed information and interacted with citizens. Using electronic technology was a major theme in the process of "reinventing government."169 Inspired by the idea of Internet voting in federal elections, in 1999 President Clinton ordered the National Science Foundation (NSF) to fund a study of the subject.

The NSF awarded a $95,000 grant to the Internet Policy Institute (IPI) to conduct the second major feasibility study of Internet voting. This study considered the readiness of the whole United States for an immediate shift over to the new technology. Like the California report, the IPI study concluded that "significant risks" existed with Internet voting. In addition, to the security and digital divide issues, plans were needed in case of massive electric power failures during the voting time, and further study was needed on how Internet voting would affect voter participation, and studies of the quality of political information the voters would receive via the Web should also be done before making any drastic changes in voting procedures. While the time was not ripe for a full scale leap, these experts also thought that controlled experiments using secure computers in some polling places could be carried out, and gradually increased if successful.170

The third major report of that period came out of the 2001 CalTech/MIT feasibility study of Internet voting.

Noting that Alaska, Arizona, and the DoD had already conducted actual trials of Internet voting in the 2000 election, these experts announced that "Internet voting is here."171 The CalTech/MIT report recommended re-defining the challenge facing the nation as not *whether* to proceed, but how best to continue with the process of implementing Internet voting. To that end, two of the most technically sophisticated universities in America pooled their resources and expertise, and prepared to conquer all the technological obstacles to a nation-wide system of Internet voting. Confidence in the technology was much higher in this study than in the other two. "Everyone knows that an Internet voting system can be built," declared Hall and Alvarez.172 The consensus of the experts in the CalTech/MIT study was that the rise of Internet voting seems "inevitable: Internet voting is the future of voting in the United States."173

Clearly, the attitude of the experts in the 1999-2002 period was one of confidence and cautious optimism about the feasibility of one day building a secure Internet voting network in the United States.

The Critics in 2003

While Hall and Alvarez reported the optimism of expert opinion at the time, they were fully aware that not all the experts agreed. The critics of Internet voting were well-known to Hall and Alvarez. Some of the critics sat on the same committees as the two authors. In fact, three of the four SERVE dissenters sat on committees with Alvarez. Those three are Barbara Simons, David Jefferson, and Avi Rubin. These three also participated in the Internet Policy

Institute (IPI) study group along with Alvarez and two dozen other computer scientists, political scientists, and government elections officials. David Jefferson also worked on the California task force with Alvarez.174

Simons and David Wagner, the fourth SERVE dissenter, were not mentioned by Hall and Alvarez as opposed to Internet voting prior to the cancellation of SERVE. Their notoriety as critics emerged only after they endorsed the report calling for the termination of the SERVE project.

However, Hall and Alvarez did have something to say about Avi Rubin in recording their observations prior to Wolfowitz's fatal order. The authors observed that during this period there was "a small but strident group of computer scientists who have issued strong criticisms of Internet voting..."175 Of course, as they wrote they had no idea that SERVE would be stopped, or who would be responsible for stopping it. Ironically, however, the first of the "strident" critics of Internet voting they choose to mention was none other than Avi Rubin, who would turn out to be the most strident, and perhaps the instigator, of the four SERVE dissenters.

While the IPI group consensus was generally optimistic about the ability of science and technology to overcome the current obstacles to a trustworthy Internet voting system, Rubin, a university professor of computer science, disagreed. Not satisfied with having his dissenting opinions merely footnoted in the final IPI report, Rubin independently published his own report on Internet voting security.176

Besides establishing himself as a maverick, Rubin also laid out the central doctrine that he would continue to insist upon in the future. Indeed, the arguments he made in 2001 became the main reasons he and the other SERVE dissenters called for a halt to that program. I have discussed these criticisms in Chapter One. In sum, for Rubin, the user computers, i.e., laptops, desktops, etc., are the weakest point in any proposal for "remote Internet voting," that is, online voting from home or anywhere else. During the time for voting, argues Rubin, these computers can be spied on, controlled remotely, or infected with a disabling virus. Voters could be tricked, or spoofed, by look alike websites into wasting their votes, and giving away personal information. Also, the vote server can be crippled by a flood of automated messages, which could cause long delays or even stop the voting process – the infamous denial of service attack (DoS).

Of course Rubin is making his standard assumption, as I pointed out in Chapter One, that both home computers and Internet voting servers will be free of protection. Given that assumption, Rubin began insisting as early as 2001 that Internet voting should not be tested in *any* public elections; at least not until the current technology can be replaced by something that he would certify as way more secure.[177]

Hall and Alvarez note that even more shrill and extreme than Rubin, at the time, was another computer science professor, Rebecca Mercuri. She has declared that the risks of Internet voting "are far worse than ones found in manual balloting [or, paper-based] systems."[178] Her list of charges included the susceptibility of Internet voting to large scale fraud, vote buying and selling, DoS attacks, lack of anonymity for the voter due to spyware, difficulty of voter authentication, and lack of audibility for recounts because there would be no paper trail. While Rubin was willing to entertain the idea that future improvements in security technology might make Internet voting feasible, Mercuri grandly pronounced that these problems with voting online are "inherently unresolvable," and so, no matter what the circumstances, "Internet voting should not be used for public elections."[179]

While Mercuri was not involved with the evaluation of SERVE, and thus not one of the four dissenters, they included many of her well-known arguments in their criticism of SERVE. Drawing upon the consensus of expert opinion at that time, Hall and Alvarez specifically rebut each item on Rubin's and Mercuri's lists. Hall and Alvarez also emphasize the essential *unreason* in Mercuri's and Rubin's methodology.

Critique of the Critics

First, Hall and Alvarez suggest that both critics, but especially Mercuri, write with unscientifically dogmatic attitudes and language. How can anyone, Mercuri or anyone else, know whether those security problems are "inherently unresolvable," and therefore can *never* be resolved? Consider the spectacular ability of science and technology to solve "unsolvable" problems over the past two hundred years. This path of progress is littered with the arrogant declarations of experts that one thing or another "can't be done."

Given the track record of science and technology, the more reasonable view would seem to be that determining whether a problem can be solved is most reliably decided by hypotheses testing and experimentation; in other words, intelligent trial and error, not expert decrees. How much reason is shown by a computer "scientist," like Mercuri, who issues dire warnings and dogmatic declarations, but who "does not offer any hypotheses that could be tested in the field"?180 Her disregard of the scientific method marks Mercuri as an unreasonable critic of Internet voting.

Mercuri's final proclamation, that "Internet voting should not be used for public elections," is a self-fulfilling prophecy, not a scientific hypothesis. If no Internet voting trials are done to try to solve existing problems, then the problems will not be solved and they will appear to be "inherently unresolvable." Such self affirming proc-lamations are hardly good science.

Rubin may at first seem a little more flexible than Mercuri. He, too, insists upon holding off on testing Internet voting in public elections, but only *until* the technology is developed "that will make stronger network security possible."181 But he actually sets up the same dogmatic bind as Mercuri. For, how can anyone know if a voting technology is "stronger" until something is done to test it? Besides that, why would an Internet voting technology company invest its resources in research and development, if no government agency is going to try out any Internet voting system? This is why first steps must be taken. Reason suggests, at least for Hall and Alvarez, that if governments hire companies to test such systems in public elections, other companies will strive to construct a better system in competition for the government contracts.182

Both critics were also being unreasonable, according to Hall and Alvarez, by framing the choice as all or nothing. The critics insisted that because no current system of Internet voting has been proven safe for the entire country to use, none should even be tried. But, for Hall and Alvarez, a more reasonable view would seem to be that using small scale trials can gradually work up to a secure large scale system.183 Indeed, this *gradualism* was the consensus opinion in all three of the major studies reviewed by the two authors.

Rubin and Mercuri declared there were several means by which an Internet based election could be ruined. But they have offered no science in support of these assertions. As experts on the literature, Hall and Alvarez point out that up to the time, "not a single publicly available study has attempted to quantify the risks associated with different types of security threats to Internet voting systems."184 For Hall and Alvarez, reason requires that testable facts be acquired before any solid conclusions about the likelihood of an event can be drawn. "There is no way to know whether any argument regarding Internet voting is accurate unless real Internet voting systems are tested, and they should be tested in small-scale, scientific trials so that their successes and failures can be evaluated."185

In expressing this standard of reasonable thought, they echo Founder James Madison, who modeled reasonable thinking. He wrote, "Let us consult experience, the guide that ought always to be followed whenever it can be found."[186]

Not only were there no studies showing what the likelihood is for any particular type of Internet voting attack to be successfully executed on a mass scale, but three trials of Internet voting had already been conducted without any security incidents. Thus, Rubin and Mercuri not only had *no facts* in support of their shrilly presented speculations, but they had to ignore existing facts.[187] That is hardly a reasonable practice for supposed "scientists."

As professional political scientists, specializing in elections issues, Hall and Alvarez are both deeply committed to the use of the scientific method as the only way for reason to discover truth. Their intellectual integrity, experience, and expertise explain why they are repeatedly asked to participate in Internet voting studies and trials. They chide Rubin and Mercuri for not adhering to the same values.

"Instead of wasting time on heated rhetoric and uninformed debate," say Hall and Alvarez, "researchers should gather solid information about the relative importance of different threats for different types of Internet voting architecture."[188] They observed in this period that the critics of Internet voting are relying "on heated but often poorly informed arguments about its potential benefits and problems. What is needed, however, are facts."[189] Only then can reasonable estimates be made about the likelihood of any particular type of attack succeeding.

Besides the lack of science to back up the claims of these naysayers, the two political scientists remind us that very reliable Internet security is demonstrated thousands of times per day in the areas of online banking, and by buying and selling in e-commerce all across the World Wide Web. If the threats of a remote bad guy changing votes on a mass scale before they are recorded, or a hacker stealing voter identities on a mass scale so that he can cast multiple votes, are more than a nightmarish fantasy, then these tricks would be widely used to drain the money from banks and businesses. Yet, the actual data shows that such disasters are *not* prevalent in "online banking and commerce."190 Here, then, are more facts that Mercuri and Rubin ignore, or dogmatically dismiss as "irrelevant."

Voting from Home

If voting from home was truly an invitation to such abuses as coercion, and buying and selling votes, as Mercuri claims, then the incidents of these crimes would be high in places where absentee voting by mail is widely practiced. But the facts are that this does not happen. For example, California has a popular vote by mail absentee voter system. It allows voters to vote from home or anywhere else by mail. However, in the six years between 1994 and 2000, California had only one voter *fraud* conviction for "every 1.3 million votes cast!"191 Voter *coercion* convictions are non-existent. The experience is similar in Oregon, in which all voting is by mail, and in Washington state, which has a very high percentage of voting by mail. These supposedly potential crimes are, in practice, not a big problem, because voters tend to be people of high integrity, and law enforcement is skillful at catching wrongdoers. In other words, the facts show an extremely low likelihood of these events occurring in vote at home systems.

There have been cases in which thieves have stolen voting by mail materials from mail boxes, and cast votes by forging a voter's signature. This happened in Miami in 1997.[192] Such cases are *known* because the perpetrators were caught. However, well-tested Internet voting technology, such as secret personal identification numbers used on a secure server, as in e-commerce, can prevent a hacker from intercepting a voter's vote in order to tamper with it. Military quality encryption methods can keep a voter's identity and vote undecipherable to a spy.

Given their experience in the field, and their reading of the scientific literature, including studies by the FBI, Hall and Alvarez found that, according to prevailing expert opinion, "an effective Internet voting system can be created which is as secure, and likely more secure, than traditional absentee voting systems."[193] So the *facts* compel a conclusion which is the exact opposite of Mercuri's baseless declaration that the risks of Internet voting "are far worse than ones found in manual balloting [or, paper-based] systems."[194]

Does this "scientist's" persistent disregard of facts seem reasonable?

The Experience in Europe

In addition to the prevailing scientific opinion, and the three successful experiments in 2000, there are numerous other examples that show a widespread confidence in the efficacy and security of Internet voting technology prior to the ending of SERVE. For example, Hall and Alvarez discussed Internet voting trials which were then being conducted in several European countries, including England, Germany, Sweden, and Switzerland. Some trials used voting by cell phone texting. All of them worked as planned, with no security problems. In fact, Switzerland hired a team of hackers and gave them three weeks to try to break into the system. According to Hall and Alvarez, the hackers "failed."195 After successful trials in local elections in England, plans were made to extend the experiments to other localities.196 The German government was so enthusiastic about Internet voting, that it started planning a gradual build up to national elections.197 Estonia has gone entirely to cell phone voting.198

Accenture Honors Award

Back in the USA, and still prior to the cancellation of SERVE, Accenture, the lead consultants for that project, had become a finalist for Computer World's Honors Award. Computer World is a highly regarded information technology magazine with a world wide circulation of over 120,000 subscribers.

Each year, according to the Computer World website, a panel of information technology experts "identify those organizations whose use of information technology has been especially noteworthy for the originality of its conception, the breadth of its vision, and the significance of its benefit to society."199 Accenture was specifically nominated for "creating the most comprehensive system to date for secure online voting. ... In addition, SERVE provides a valuable blueprint for the future development of reliable online voting systems."200 Past honorees include Microsoft, Cisco, Verizon, EDS, Sun Micro-systems, and Unisys.201

That Accenture's role in the SERVE project brought it enough recognition to become a finalist for this prestigious award shows that the worldly expert judges of this contest thought quite highly of SERVE's achievement, and that they believed a secure Internet voting system was possible. (Needless to say, the sacking of SERVE put a stop to the consideration of Accenture as an honoree).

Michigan

Also prior to the cancellation of SERVE, the Michigan Democratic Party, in 2003, debated and then decided to offer online voting as an option in its 2004 February caucuses. The Democratic National Committee debated and then voted to approve the experiment. According to the New York Times, the vote was taken *after* objections were heard that "major security problems had not been resolved and that online voting discriminated against low-income blacks and Hispanics, less likely than whites to be computer-literate."202

Michigan Democratic Party chairman Mark Brewer, told the Times that he had promoted the Internet option as a way to make voting easier and increase turnout. "Polls [in Michigan] show that this is very popular, particularly with young people, and they have one of the worst rates of participation," Mr. Brewer said. "If this helps them, that's terrific."203

Nine candidates campaigned in the Michigan caucus, and several strongly supported the online voting project, including John Kerry, Howard Dean, Richard Gephardt, and Gen. Wesley Clark. All the candidates had websites, and several offered to bring lap tops to the homes of their supporters so that they could vote online. Voters also had the options of voting by mail, or at polling places. Although voting at polling places was to be held on February 7, online voting had already begun, and, according to the Times, by January 8, "11,000 people had applied for ballots, three-fourths of them over the Internet."204

Here is yet another instance of highly responsible, politically experienced American elections experts, along with presidential candidates, who considered the pros and cons of Internet voting, including security issues, and enthusiastically embraced the new technology. As Mr. Brewer said, and as the number of ballot applications show, the idea was popular, and Michigan voters eagerly participated. For all these folks, then, an experiment with online voting seemed to be a very reasonable idea.

Internet Voting Technology Alliance

Also, in the year 2000, before the Alaska, Arizona, and VOI trials, another group of optimistic computer scientists, business people, and public officials, including former Alaska Senator Mike Gravel, met in Washington, D.C. Calling themselves "the Internet Voting Technology Alliance" (IVTA), they anticipated the growth of Internet voting in the world, and intended to become the central source of technical information, and to set uniform standards, for such voting systems. Their current website says they started with "approximately 50 participants."205

According to their mission statement, "The primary goal of the Alliance is to ensure a high level of quality and integrity in the resources and information provided, in order to foster public confidence in Internet voting." Displaying the group's optimism, Ed Gerck, IVTA Chairman, wrote on the website, "the challenges facing Internet Voting are actually fading away as privacy and security issues in Internet communications and voting protocols are, more and more, being clearly solved."

Of course, the fall of SERVE slammed the door on such optimism about the future of Internet voting, and the IVTA has been reduced to little more than one website among billions. In the US, Congress has assigned the responsibility of setting standards for all voting technology to the Election Assistance Commission (EAC); thus depriving the IVTA of one of its main purposes.206

The Science of Secure Electronic Voting

For several years prior to SERVE's abrupt ending, universities, like MIT and CalTech, and corporations in the computer industry had been conducting research into the prospects for Internet voting. The corporations understood that profits could be made from a secure, convenient, and accurate Internet voting system. Some of them helped finance the university research.

A collection of technical papers resulting from this research was published in early 2003. These papers addressed the security and operational issues of every step, from end-to-end, of Internet voting. Entitled *Secure Electronic Voting*,207 some of the articles showed, in technical language, how to make an Internet voting system, based on typical home computers, that is as secure as any system in e-commerce. Hall and Alvarez had studied these writings, and cite them with approval in their book.

One example of the kind of work being done at the time is a paper by computer scientists Ted Selker and Jonathan Goler. Selker and Goler are professors of computer science at MIT. Selker was also one of the ten peers who inspected the SERVE security system, and one of the six who did not call for a halt to the project.

During the time SERVE was being built Selker and Goler published their paper explaining how a secure Internet voting system would operate.208 Their system is based on numerous modules. Each module performs a necessary function in the voting process. For example, one module authenticates the voter when he or she visits the voting website. Another module checks the voter's registration, and prevents multiple voting. Separate modules present the ballot, show a confirmation page, record and store the vote, and tally the results. Each module is constructed with open source code. Each one has redundant systems. These not only act as back up, but make hacking an impossibly complex task, and help prevent the kind of overloading that could shut down an inferior system. Each module would have its own memory, so that the modules would create an Electronic Audit Trail, which could be used as a reliable source for recounts, if the results are challenged.

While SERVE had many of these features, Selker and Goler also included the most advanced election server security technology of the time; that is, Ed Gerck's system of electronic witnesses. Every module in the process, from end to end, can be monitored for secure and correct operation via an electronic witness. These witnesses can be placed on each module by political parties, public interest groups, or any one else.

As a standard of reliability for a voting process, suppose a vote is taken in a room full of people, but not too many people for everyone to see and count the raised hands. With electronic eyes on every module, the results would be as reliable as those in which all voters are in one room and can count one another's raised hands. Of course, these voters would give up privacy for reliability. But the electronic witnesses would have no memory of how a particular voter voted, because the name of the voter would be separated from the vote before the vote was cast and stored; hence, privacy and reliability.

Quite the opposite of Rubin and Mercuri, Selker and Goler wrote, "Internet voting can be safer and more reliable than voting has ever been." They were strongly opposed to the claim that paper ballots could be more reliable than electronically counted and stored ballots. Contrary to Mercuri's demand, they argued that "there should *not* be a voter verifiable paper trail."[209]

The history of voting, they write, is full of instances of problems due to primitive paper ballot systems. "In the 2000 election, [for example,] there were many reports of entire precincts worth of paper ballots [lost], as well as ballots that were found weeks later in the backs of trucks."[210] They gave their opinion that while paper balloting is vulnerable to interception, alteration, and fraud, these interferences are *not possible* with an Internet voting network using, among other things, redundant systems, cryptography, and message authentication codes (which, by the way, are also what SERVE used).

Eerie Echoes of the Past

Hall and Alvarez, like Selker and Goler, reflect the pre-SERVE cancellation confidence that existed in the US when the former were finishing their book in mid-2003. "This book is not about the technology for conducting Internet voting," wrote Hall and Alvarez. "The technology – the code to create such a system and the computers and servers to host it – is well known and has been tested numerous times."211 Writing with the SERVE project in mind, they declared, "We believe that Internet voting can be successfully implemented *now* for specific populations of voters – such as military, overseas, and disabled voters."212 Perceiving no threat to the project, and of course blind to the future, Hall and Alvarez wrote confidently that SERVE "will be in operation during the entire 2004 election cycle."213

They assumed that the SERVE experiment would go well, and optimistically predicted that this experience would "begin the process of phasing in Internet voting across the nation."214 "There is no question that [a national] Internet voting system can be constructed."215 They were so optimistic that they even outlined a 10 year transition period.216 Thus, "by the 2010 midterm elections and the 2012 presidential election, [Americans] may find themselves voting for members of Congress and the president with the click of a mouse."217

Unhappily, these jubilant self-assured declarations now seem eerily like those of the White Star Line ads, which in 1912 declared their new luxury liner, the Titanic, to be "unsinkable."218

The Cook Testimony

Unknown to Hall and Alvarez, Gordon Cook was reporting on his experiences and observations of the Internet voting debate at about the same time as they were. Gordon Cook has published online a widely read subscription newsletter about e-commerce since the early

1990s.219 One day, prior to the termination of SERVE, an old friend of Cook's, Eva Waskell, complained to him about the shrillness of anti-Internet voting zealots in the media and other forums. Eva was a journalist and computer programmer who had been investigating and reporting on electronic voting equipment since as early as 1982. Convinced that a secure and convenient system of Internet voting would make participation easier for many people, and improve the reliability of election results, she began working with Ed Gerck's team at safevote.com in 1999. But after a couple of years of trying to dispel the myths about Internet voting insecurity, Eva became very disheartened.220

The opponents of Internet voting had labeled Gerck as "just another vendor." They were trying to persuade people to dismiss him as nothing more than a guy with something to sell, like Diebold and the other DRE vendors. Even in professional conferences and hearings held by elections officials, they loudly dismissed Gerck's "witness voting system" as impossible, insecure, and a danger to democracy.

Yet Waskell told Cook that what Gerck "is doing is real. It works. It is fundamentally different than any other approach. I have read all Ed's work and the documents that support it and I fully understand at a technical level what is going on."

Cook writes, "These words from a person so dedicated were difficult for me to ignore." He began taking a closer look at the way the public dialogue was being conducted. Working independently of Hall and Alvarez, Cook became especially concerned over the lack of open-mindedness about Gerck shown by Avi Rubin, Rebecca Mercuri, and two of their colleagues, Lauren Weinstein and Peter Neumann.

Cook observed that "they have dismissed [Gerck's] work out of hand. I have talked both to them and to Gerck and have found that it is clear that what review of Gerck's work they have done has been marked by the unceasing assertion that what he was proposing was not possible. ... However, many experts, including Waskell [and Selker, whom Cook mentioned], agree with Gerck. Also more than 300,000 voters in 35 elections, reportedly, have used Gerck's system successfully."[221]

While not a computer scientist himself, Cook worried about whether these e-voting critics were acting as reasonable computer scientists, in his opinion, should act. He was disturbed by the *unscientific* method Gerck's opposition was using to smear, rather than engage, him. Cook understood that the progress of science over the past few centuries was largely due to the willingness of scientists with different opinions and hypotheses to engage one another in rational and public argument. Whether differences are over facts or theories, the reasons for affirming or denying these must be given, so that other experts can evaluate the evidence by testing it for themselves. Science, unlike religions or mystic cults, cannot, and does not, proceed by imposing sacred dogma, which cannot be questioned.

Cook stated his view that the opponents of Internet voting "are, of course, entitled to use their scholarship to advocate any positions they choose and can defend with due intellectual rigor. But they also have responsibilities. … They are expected to study, to debate, and to think. They are expected to probe and keep an open mind until independently verifiable facts move in to drive their analysis to a defensible conclusion."

With these ideals in mind, he began to email some of the critics, and to admonish them to live up to the ordinary standards of science and scholarship. He asked them to take Gerck's system seriously, to engage Gerck in a thoroughgoing debate over the issues of Internet voting as distinct from the problems of DREs, and to show why it cannot work, or admit that it can. Mercury and Neumann replied saying that they "believe they did understand what Gerck was saying and that they believed his work was simply not credible on its face."

Cook emailed back, urging them to reconsider their positions. He offered to sponsor a debate, and to use his newsletter as an unrestricted forum for all sides to air their views. He reports, "I emailed Peter Neumann and asked him out of his long knowledge of Eva and her dedication to [electronic voting integrity] to sit down with [her and Ed Gerck] and try to grasp how Gerck differed from the … DRE vendors. He politely declined." Then, writes Cook, "I contacted Rebecca Mercuri by email and told her that in my opinion Eva would not have gone to work [with] Ed if he were just 'another DRE vendor.' I pleaded with Rebecca to study Gerck's ideas with care." She said she already had, and that in her opinion, "Gerck has never supplied a strong mathematical proof."

Finally, "In December 2001 I met Avi Rubin in person at [a conference] in San Diego. I told him what I have outlined here. He declined as well."

Cook emailed Gerck to tell him that his offers to host a debate had been declined. Gerck replied sharing his disappointment with the unscientific and unreasonable way in which his work had been treated by the more vocal critics. Gerck wrote that in his experience the "whole issue of electronic-voting and Internet-voting has been addressed by Peter Neumann, Rebecca Mercuri, Avi Rubin and other critics with a complete determination to arrive at a negative answer. That any attempt undertaken will fail, since by their own definition all needed infra- structure is insecure. And that anyone who claims to the contrary is incorrect by principle. Consequently it should be no surprise that my technology fails to meet their re- quirements, if by their definition, it is impossible to do what I am in fact doing."

Summation of the Critique of the Critics

The testimony of Hall and Alvarez, along with the other evidence I have presented, has shown that prior to the SERVE shutdown, a solid consensus existed among the community of Internet voting experts that an online election could be conducted with *greater security* than a paper ballot election could ever achieve. This consensus was not simply based on theory, but experience. Republicans in Alaska, Democrats in Arizona, and Department of Defense technicians, using a variety of private contractors, had all conducted Internet voting trials in 2000 without any security slip ups. The US Congress was so confident in the technology that, at the request of the Department of Defense, it allocated up to forty million dollars to build a second and larger experimental system. Computer scientists were publishing papers on how to construct secure Internet voting systems, and forming groups to set uniform standards for Internet voting around the world.

After seeing the success of VOI, European nations began conducting successful trials. The political leadership, and the people, of Michigan were sold on the new voting technology. In late 2003, men and women in uniform had begun filling out applications to take part in the SERVE trial.

This evidence clearly shows that during the few years before the termination of SERVE, a *can-do spirit* about Internet voting informed the consensus of opinion among computer scientists working in the field of election tech-nology, and among elections experts in government, as well as among political scientists and interested citizens. For many of these folks, the closed-minded and can't-do attitude of the few vocal anti-Internet voting activists stood out in comparison to this consensus as unreasonable in the circumstances.

Such was the climate of opinion in December of 2003. That is when the members of the SERVE team – from federal, state, and county governments, DoD technicians, private company technicians, and experts from such centers of learning as MIT and CalTech – invited known anti-e-voting activists, such as Avi Rubin and others, to come in and try to improve upon the system in which they had great confidence, and called the *"Secure* Election and Registration Voting Experiment."

Rubin Takes the Lead

Avi Rubin has testified as to how he orchestrated the slaying of the SERVE project. About two years after Wolfowitz issued his halt order on January 30, 2004, Rubin published his memoir of that period in his life.222 The story focuses on two main events, one occurring in early 2003, and the other in early 2004. The first event entails his attack on the Diebold touch screen voting machines, or DREs, and the other involves his assault on SERVE.

In the Spring of 2003, Bev Harris, a little known free lance writer, discovered that Diebold had posted the supposedly secret source code for its DRE on its website without any password protection. The posting was inadvertent. Although unable to read the code, Harris suspected her find would at least embarrass the company. So she copied the code and posted it on her website. Then she sent out emails saying the joke was on Diebold.

An acquaintance of Rubin's was on one of the anti-e-voting email lists that passed along the news of the prank. He happened to mention it to Rubin in a phone conversation around the first of July. Rubin writes that he was engaged in an academic research project at the time. He was a computer science professor at The Johns Hopkins University. But when he heard the news, he dropped everything. He immediately copied the code to have on his office computer. Then he began to study it for security weaknesses. He took his two research assistants off the academic project, and put them to work on analyzing the Diebold code.

After two weeks of analyzing thousands of lines of computer hieroglyphics, Rubin and his two Johns Hopkins grad students had uncovered a variety of security vulnerabilities. Then Rubin donned his Super Sleuth costume, and let his imagination run wild. While DREs generally operate offline, he suggested that they could be programmed to be controlled remotely. Votes could be changed by a secret agent sitting in his car across the street from the polling place, and no one would ever know. Or, a "Trojan horse" code could be hidden in the operating code by a rogue programmer at the factory. A bad guy could conspire with workers at a polling place, and install the malicious code there. The Trojan horse could be activated by a secret device, such as pressing the "enter" button three times. Then the Trojan horse code would take over the vote tallying mechanism, and change the outcome to favor the candidate preferred by the conspirators. With the evil deed completed, the Trojan horse code could erase itself, and no one would ever know what happened.

Besides those vulnerabilities, the machines could be programmed to flip a vote from one candidate to another candidate. Someone posted an illustration of this on YouTube, with Homer Simpson in the voting booth going bonkers as his vote for Kerry was flipped over to the Bush column.223 (Indeed, a couple of times this was reported by voters to have actually happened in the 2004 election. But machine vendors insisted that if it did occur, it was by accident, and on machines that simply needed re-calibration.) Rubin also claimed that since the DREs made no paper record of the votes they counted, there was no way to independently verify that the tallies were true. He prescribed voting on paper ballots as the most reliable way to keep the count honest.

Once Rubin had written out his report on these, and other, undesirable characteristics of the Diebold machines, he devised a strategy for publicizing his expose. Prior to teaching, he had worked for six years at AT&T, where he fortuitously had the benefit of "media training."[224] Given this training, writes Rubin, he "sensed that [his expose] was going to be a public relations hot potato."[225]

He put his PR training to use. "From the beginning, my plan was to break the story in the New York Times. I wanted this story in the hands of a reporter I could trust to get it right, someone who was ... sensitive to the political ramifications. If the first story doesn't get it right, any misinformation it contains is likely to be repeated countless times. The reporter I trusted most was John Schwartz, who covered technical issues for the Times."[226] Rubin had provided Schwartz with technical advice in the past.

Rubin knew that the New York Times had been quite adamant in proclaiming its paper purist policy. That is, it denounced paperless electronic voting technology, including Internet voting, and proselytized for paper-based methods of voting, especially where voters directly mark their votes on paper cards that can be read by scanners.[227]

Of course, the economic interest of the Times in promoting paper-based systems over electronic technology is obvious. All newspapers felt threatened by the electronic technology emerging in the beginning of the 21st Century. Online newspapers made far less money in advertising than paper newspapers. And the Times also had numerous holdings in paper mills and other paper-based businesses.228 So the Times welcomed news that jibed with its economic interests.

Rubin offered Schwartz an exclusive on the Diebold report, in the hope that Schwartz would try to have the story printed on the front page. The date for publication was set at July 24, 2003. As agreed, the New York Times ran the story, but "not on the front page, as I had secretly hoped."229

However, Rubin's disappointment was not long lasting. He had learned from his media training that "the second day after a news release is the big day for media coverage. That's when all the stories that follow the original one appear."230 Sure enough, the next day, his local paper, the Baltimore Sun, made his report "its lead story on the front page."231 Not only that, the story was printed "above the fold," where readers could see it in vending machines. Beyond that, the following "Sunday the Sun put the story on the front page again."232

The Sun regarded Rubin's expose as really hot news, not only because it had similar material interests as the New York Times, but also because Maryland election officials had just committed over $50,000,000 to purchasing new Diebold DREs. Now the government would be forced to explain to the public why this was not a scandalous boondoggle, and a plot to guarantee the Republican Party victory in the November election, as the foes of e-voting had charged.

State election officials all across the country were suddenly thrust into the same disconcerting position. The federal government's 2002 Help America Vote Act was providing rebates for those states that bought electronic voting equipment. 2004 was a presidential election year, so hundreds of millions of tax-payer dollars were being spent on DREs as election officials prepared for the vote. On the day the New York Times broke the story, Rubin contacted "the vice president at the CNN national desk, Nancy Lane." The next morning, Rubin proudly writes, "CNN Interviewed me …"233

A man of foresight and energy, Rubin made further preparations. He informs his readers that the day before the New York Times was to run the expose, "I had prepped Adam and Yoshi," his two assistants.234 The trio spent several hours in a Johns Hopkins classroom polishing, memorizing, and rehearsing the key phrases that Rubin wanted to feed the media. He had learned from his public relations training at AT&T that the more complex a statement to the press is, the more likely they are to get it wrong when they present it to the public. To control the message, you have to keep it simple. "The main idea is to boil your information down to no more than three short, simple, and memorable messages … that will stick in the minds of readers and [TV] viewers."235 Rubin writes, "we practiced ways to work these quotes into our answers, even if they didn't directly answer the questions asked. ... I grilled them for hours." The effort paid off, and the trio was "amused and gratified" when "many of these quotes turned up verbatim in news stories over the next few weeks."236

Once the story came out, Rubin shot to stardom. His memoir is replete with detailed accounts of all his TV appearances. He writes, for example, "I was on The Today Show a couple of times and on NBC's and CBS's national evening news shows, and ... on The Daily Show with Jon Stewart."237 (His wife said he "seemed more excited about being on The Daily Show than about getting tenure."238) He also fully discusses his radio and press interviews, his speeches, and the articles he was asked to write for magazines and newspapers. He became so famous, according to his narrative, that one story on his blog, about serving as a voluntary poll worker, received "forty thousand hits," and became the subject of even more stories in the press.239

Later, Rubin was called for a meeting with members of the House of Representatives, which he notes was covered by the "NBC Nightly news."240 He became so sought after that sometimes he fell short of fulfilling his family and teaching responsibilities.241

The anti-e-voting community was electrified by the revelations in Rubin's report. Armed with that report, one anti-e-voting group in Maryland sought an injunction to try to stop the state from using the Diebold machines in the November election, or at least to compel Diebold to make its machines print a paper record of the votes.

Here was the first time that the kind of scary claims made by Rubin would be subjected to the scrutiny of reason. Indeed, Rubin was the expert witness for the petitioners.

But after examining the evidence, the court held that mere speculative allegations of a threat, or fears of harm to come, without any facts showing actual threats to the democratic process, were not reasonable grounds for granting such an injunction.242 No election fraud or other wrongs done with DREs had ever been proven. In other words, the judge formed the same opinion as Hall and Alvarez that no evidence was given to show the likelihood of any of the potential evil deeds alleged; therefore, they were not real possibilities. The petition for an injunction was denied. The decision was upheld on appeal.243

Rubin was outraged by this ruling. He had testified in the hearing that *he,* a computer science professor, *knew* what a threat these machines are to our democracy. Showing his pique, Rubin contemptuously dismissed the lawyers, the expert witnesses who testified in favor of the DREs, and the judge as more of those "technically illiterate people" found "throughout the legal system."244

Because of that experience, Rubin rejects the US legal system as a source of "truth," and says that only by funding research institutes, like the one he had just founded, can the truth be known.245 The National Science Foundation seems to have been in harmony with that opinion, because Rubin happily reports that in 2005 his foundation was "funded to the tune of $7.5 million."246

Incidentally, a similar lawsuit was brought by some anti-e-voting activists in Germany, including a group calling itself "The Chaos Computer Club." Using many of Rubin's claims, they sought to have an election overturned because of their suspicions, among other things, that the DREs may have been rigged. After giving a detailed analysis of the arguments pro and con in the case, the German Supreme Court reached a conclusion similar to that of the Maryland court: there was insufficient evidence to back up the case against the machines. The request by the petitioners "for a scrutiny of the election" was denied.247

A Twist of Fate

Some seekers of fame are favored by fortune. Rubin is surely among them. Not only did events unfold just as he had hoped they would from the day he first heard about that Diebold code, but purely by sweet coincidence another opportunity knocked on his door. Only a few days before he learned about the Diebold code on Harris's website, Rubin was invited by one of the SERVE project officials (perhaps Alvarez) to join the SERVE Peer Review Group, or SPRG. This was in May of 2003. He hesitated to accept the invitation, in part, because it might infringe on his precious time for academic research.248

But after he found out who else was on SPRG he began to see the gift he had been given. He knew the other three dissenters (Simons, Jefferson, and Wagner) from prior professional activities. He also knew that like Mercuri, Neumann, and others, they shared his anti-Internet voting philosophy.

Before any SPRG business had been conducted, Rubin had become the central celebrity of the anti-e-voting movement in the US. So prior to the first official meeting of the SPRG members, the soon-to-be dissenters formed their own communications network. When the SERVE officials presented them with a standard "nondisclosure agreement" to sign, including an agreement to issue a joint SPRG report after all the meetings were completed, they refused. Rubin writes that "our little group" insisted on the freedom to write their own report. Thus, before the first official meeting, these "unbiased" scientists were already planning "to issue our own independent report on the system, which we could release to the public."249

According to Rubin, "After some touchy negotiations," during which he may have mentioned that his new celebrity status gave him access to the press, the SERVE officials "agreed to our terms."250 However, SERVE spokesperson, Glen Flood, seems to dispute Rubin's account of what was agreed. An article in Computer World states that the four dissenters had agreed to a "joint report," and had "jumped the scheduling gun and issued an early report of their own."251

Of course, Rubin would deny that he and his little group approached their inspection of SERVE with any sort of bias; as he often mentions, "I am...a scientist."252 He also writes that the SERVE officials "had been very open, sharing every relevant piece of the SERVE design, and in the same spirit our little cadre of e-voting critics had remained completely open-minded, evaluating the system objectively and without prejudice."253 (Yes, and it was with such salivating "open-mindedness" that the "little cadre" planned from the first to write their own report!)

In any case, whatever open-mindedness Rubin started out with, it flew out the window by the end of the first meeting, which Rubin "was only able to attend by phone."254 During that meeting, reports Rubin, the SERVE team "seemed unafraid to share openly the details of the system. Those details, unfortunately, horrified me."255 First of all, the SERVE process depended on voters using a particular type of Microsoft software, called "Active X," in their personal computers, "and no security expert worth his or her salt would ever condone a system that relies on it."256 Secondly, despite the efforts of the SERVE team to anticipate and to mitigate it, a denial of service attack could still get through, insisted Rubin, and "disenfranchise thousands of voters."257

Another problem with voters using their own computers at home is "phishing."258 Voters could be lured to a phony website, posing as the SERVE website. Their vote could be wasted by casting it there, and their personal information could be captured and used by the bad guys to cast a vote on the actual SERVE website. The SERVE system could not protect voters from such phishing schemes.259

Rubin's "horror" proved to be infectious. "After the second day of review, several of us determined that if we failed to act, SERVE would almost certainly be adopted and implemented."260 That is when the four dissenters decided they had to kill the beast, and to save democracy. It was time to write their anticipated expose for the public to see. "We set at it immediately, working late into the night and continuing over the next couple of weeks, firing drafts back and forth to each other over e-mail."261

Rubin's Diebold expose had hit the news stands about six months before he and the other three started in on their SERVE expose. Rubin had learned many lessons from the earlier experience, and it sharpened his shrewdness. So he took the lead of his "little cadre." He writes, "I convinced the others to work again with John Schwartz of the New York Times."262 As before, Schwartz was given the exclusive.

Rubin notes that he and his cohorts "had hoped to manage the release of the report to the media carefully, as had happened with the Diebold report."263 Unfortunately, says Rubin, "all our best laid plans for the media release of the report fell apart. The day before our allegedly exclusive release in the Times, ... it was leaked to the press."264

Rubin blames the leak on Accenture, one of the SERVE private contractors.265 Curiously, however, the leak somehow got to Rubin's school newspaper at Johns Hopkins University, which ran the story on January 21, 2004, the very day the New York Times was to run its "exclusive."266 (Rubin does not explain why Accenture would want to see such a damning story on the front page of *his* school newspaper.)

Despite Rubin's hopes, once again Schwartz failed to get the story on the front page of the New York Times; but not to worry, the Washington Post ran it on their front page the next day.267 (It, too, has a material interest in forestalling the nation's shift to a paperless world, whether in elections, books, or newspapers.) The leak had reached the Post by the 21st, but too late to print it that day.268

As we all know, Rubin hit another PR home run. The story took Rubin on another round of celebrity appearances on TV, with more interviews by the newspapers and radio. He was called back to Congress, and invited to advise the agency that sets the standards for elections technology, the federal Elections Assistance Commission. The New York Times seized the opportunity to again advance its interests, and on January 23, 2004, published an editorial righteously demanding that "Congress should suspend the [SERVE] program."269 Exactly one week later, Wolfowitz issued his halt order, and SERVE was done for.

After SERVE's death knell had rung, David Jefferson, one of the four dissenters, told the New York Times that Rubin is "the most important figure in the United States in articulating the security problems with electronic and Internet voting."270 I agree with Jefferson on that point.

In the Aftermath

Several consequences have followed from Rubin's rise to the leadership of the anti-e-voting movement in the US. Chief among these is the fear and confusion his campaigning has caused the general public. The risk element of Internet voting has been so sensationalized that public support for it is too tepid to put pressure on lawmakers to institute new Internet voting trials. Indeed, the anti-Internet voting extremists are well organized through the efforts of richly funded foundations, like Verified Voting, the Overseas Voting Foundation, and Rubin's Accurate Voting.271 Their researchers follow the legislative processes in the states and Congress. Whenever a bill is introduced which would set up an Internet voting trial, the activists are activated, and the pressure is applied to stop the bill from becoming law. The same scare tactics that killed SERVE can be employed to kill any other like measure proposed in the states or in Congress.

Some state legislatures have been pressured into passing laws requiring paper-based systems of voting, which would make Internet voting impossible. Representative Rush Holt (D-NJ) has made numerous attempts to have a bill passed in Congress requiring paper-based voting for all federal elections. Fortunately, so far, clearer thinking minds have kept this from happening.

The primary reason that there is very little organized public support for Internet voting trials to counter this pressure is that the Rubinites have achieved so much influence over how the public understands the issue. As a result of their propaganda, the general understanding of the choice to be made is that between the convenience of voting over the Internet versus the near-certainty that hackers will hijack the election and put their puppet in office. If that were truly the choice, then no reasonable person could do otherwise than oppose Internet voting. Almost everyone will agree that a little inconvenience is not too high a price to pay for having honest elections. So long as pro-Internet voting groups are few in number, disorganized, and unable to attract the interest of the mass media, the public will not know of any alternative to the false image of Internet voting as merely a form of convenience with a high risk of being hacked.

As I have mentioned, Hall and Alvarez had envisioned, naively, enlightened political leaders carefully and scientifically increasing the numbers of elections based on Internet voting until the happy moment in 2012, when Americans "may find themselves voting for members of Congress and the president with the click of a mouse."272 Instead, elected officials all across the country have learned to avoid like the plague any mention of implementing Internet voting.

While Michigan held its primary, which included some Internet voting, in February of 2004, after Wolfowitz ordered a halt to SERVE, no Internet voting trials the size of SERVE have taken place in the U.S. A few tiny experiments have been tried since the demise of SERVE. One example is the trial in one county in Florida to enable overseas military personnel to vote via the Net. Despite the spoiler efforts of the New York Times, that went off well.273

Two small trials were held in 2009. Honolulu had a successful Internet vote for city offices.274 And, in the very hometown of the Times, the New York City School Board held elections with Internet voting, which went off without any security glitches.275

The technical issues involved with the security of Internet voting are so complex that only a small group of highly specialized experts can claim to understand them. This is what gives the extremists their leverage. They skillfully use their status as trained experts to back up their sensationalist claims, while press, broadcast media, and professional bloggers only see the attention, and hence advertising sales, they can garner from publishing such unproven claims. A headline reading "Internet Voting Can Work" would simply flop next to one that reads "Internet Voting is a Hoax." As a result of the attention they get, the extremists seem to speak for the entire profession of technical experts. In fact, however, just as they were a minority in SPRG, they are a minority within the entire profession of experts.

The Professional Consensus *After* SERVE's Demise

Although petrifying politicians, and confusing the public, Rubin's personal success at attaining fame and fortune has had very little affect on the opinions of his professional colleagues. The evidence I have presented shows that before the demise of SERVE the majority of voting technology specialists had confidence in the security of Internet voting. The shut down of SERVE did not change this landscape of opinion.

This observation is made by Michael Shamos. Shamos was also among the ten peers who inspected SERVE's hardware and software for security vulnerabilities. He was one of the six peers who did not sign on with the four dissenters. In fact, he rejected their alarmist sentiments. Long after the shut down, he told an interviewer, "I thought SERVE was a great idea." In his professional opinion, the "downside was very small."276

Shamos has a Ph.D. in computer science from Yale University. He is a computer science professor at the Carnegie Mellon University, where he teaches, among other things, classes on electronic voting technology security. Also an elections law and patent law expert, he is licensed to practice law before the United States Supreme Court, as well as numerous federal and state courts. For 20 years, from 1980-2000, he was Pennsylvania's official examiner of electronic voting systems. He was a tough examiner.

He had examined more than 100 different computerized voting systems for certification purposes, and refused to certify over half of them.277 Shamos had presented his views on the security of electronic voting technologies in a paper written for the National Institute of Science and Technology (NIST) just a few months after Wolfowitz stopped the SERVE project. In that paper he stated his observations of the post-SERVE prevailing opinion in the technical community, as well as his reasons for supporting Internet voting.278

Shamos noted that the leading anti-electronic voting website at the time, verifiedvoting.org, had posted a "resolution," which visitors were invited to sign. The resolution called for all voting to be recorded on paper ballots. This would supposedly keep touch screen machines honest, and, of course, would prevent the use of Internet voting. Shamos writes, "According to the Bureau of Labor Statistics," there "are over one million computer scientists and mathematicians in the United States... About 100 of them have signed [the] resolution ... No information is available on how many have any familiarity with the processes of [electronic] voting ... but the total number represents about 1 in 10,000, a minuscule proportion. The good news seems to be that the other 9,999 out of 10,000 have remained open-minded on the subject."[279]

Shamos's testimony makes it clear that even after all the bad press given the SERVE project, the prevailing view about Internet voting among the community of computer scientists is at least to remain "open-minded on the subject." This community view sets the standard for reasonableness among these experts. Therefore, computer scientists who have a dogmatic and closed-minded attitude on this subject fall far short of that standard of reasonableness.

E-Voting v. Paper-Based Voting Revisited

Shamos went on to explain in his NIST paper why, in his expert opinion, the few anti-e-voting computer scientists are unreasonable in their insistence upon the use of paper ballots. Experience shows, argues Shamos, like Hall, Alvarez, Selker, and Goler, that, while no system is absolutely perfect, electronic voting systems are far more secure and accurate than paper-based voting systems. Among the arguments against "paperless" electronic voting is the claim that in those systems the voter cannot verify whether his or her vote has been counted as cast, or even counted at all.

Online voting offers one remedy for this. It is, as I mentioned earlier, that after the voter votes online, a confirmation page will come up with a confirmation number. The voter can check this number on a list of counted votes posted by the election officials. In spite of this remedy, the anti-Internet voting extremists insist that only a paper ballot, seen and verified by the voter, can ever provide the confidence needed that the vote will be counted as cast.

Of course, as Shamos makes clear, this is nonsense. Once the piece of paper leaves the voter's hand, it enters into just as much of a "black box" as any vote cast online. In both polling place voting and vote by mail systems, once the ballot is turned in, or dropped in the mail box, the voter will never know what happened to it. If mailed, was it lost in delivery? Was it in one of those boxes of ballots found floating in the local river, or on the back of a truck? Was it one of those piles of uncounted ballots misplaced underneath somebody's desk in the local election official's office? Or was it subjected to unlawful activity?

Shamos describes one trick used by insiders to invalidate paper ballots that are to be counted by scanning machines. If the person who opens the envelops, or stacks the optical scan cards, does not like the vote he sees, he simply puts an extra mark on the ballot so that it looks like a double vote (aka an "over vote"). This invalidates the vote, so it is not counted. No voter will ever know whether this has happened to his or her paper ballot.

Nor are paper ballots reliable evidence for recounts. According to Shamos, studies show that as many as 20% of paper ballots are not available for recounts, because they have either gone missing, are marked incorrectly, or are illegible. Audits based on the leftover valid ballots are hardly proof of an election result.

For all forms of voting, one problem is the same. Unless all the voters are in one room, so that they can count one another's raised hands, ballots must leave the sight of the voter before they are counted. Thus, every large scale voting procedure requires that the voter has some basic level of trust in the system. People who lack this basic degree of confidence in the integrity of the process will probably not vote in that system. So, every vote cast carries with it at least a minimum of confidence and hope that it will be counted as cast. Shamos suggests that confidence in Internet voting technology can reasonably be as high as it currently is in e-commerce technology.

Shamos argues that at least since the 1990s, human experience with Internet commerce shows that online transactions are far more secure than paper-based transactions. Consider, for example, the business of foreign currency trading. In this field "two trillion dollars per day" flashes across cyber space at lightening speed with no so-called "paper trail." It is all done via electronic record keeping on systems so secure that even "insiders" cannot steal the money.

As a practicing lawyer, Shamos is in a position to observe that modern law has radically changed to keep pace with electronic commerce. Electronic signatures are regarded in law as just as valid and binding as hand written signatures on paper. In fact, he says, electronic records are now *preferred* as evidence in courts all around the world.

If there is a contract dispute, emails may be used as evidence to show how a party understood the paper contract. In cases where a bank customer offers an ATM paper receipt as proof of a transaction, courts routinely rely instead on the bank's electronic records as the definitive source of proof. Even claims to have a winning lottery ticket can be disproven by the lottery administrator's electronic records of both where and when the ticket was sold, and the winning number. In all these cases, where electronic records are shown to have been well-maintained, they are given preference over paper, which is far easier to modify or fake.

These changing practices in law and commerce present a very powerful challenge to the poorly supported theory that the most trustworthy form of voting is the paper ballot. If Shamos is right, and I think he is, then the American public has been egregiously misinformed and sorely misled by the fear-mongering rhetoric of the pro-paper anti-Internet voting extremists.

Assessing Likelihood

Shamos is unsparing, in his essay, with his criticism of these extremists. He mocks them for their unthinking faith in an "Omniscient Hacker," lurking somewhere out there in the ether of cyber space. As the Founders intended, and like Hall and Alvarez, Shamos turns to *experience* as the most reasonable guide in assessing the probabilities of future harms. Despite all the irresponsible rumor-spreading by the over active alarmists and the sensationalist media, Shamos reports that there has *never been* a verified case of electronic voting fraud in the history of the technology, whether touch screen machines or Internet voting systems. While there have been allegations, suspicions, and even lawsuits challenging the results of electronic vote tallies, all proven cases of voting fraud have only involved paper-based systems.

Shamos suggests that the demonstrated integrity of e-voting and e-commerce reasonably warrants public confidence in the technology. He dismisses as ridiculous the mystic notion that an Omniscient Hacker will *somehow* find a way to break into electronic voting systems, bypassing all the security technology already in use and proven to be effective. The absurd claim that the Omniscient Hacker may have struck, but his evil work is undetectable, appeals more to a belief in the magic of witchcraft than in the rational methods of science. And the claim that the Omniscient Hacker is just waiting for Americans to institute widespread Internet voting so that he can control an entire national election is beyond the reach of even the most childish and primitive superstition.

Authentic science uses experience to calculate probabilities. Experience shows that electronic voting technology has been tried in the US, and in countries all around the world, without fraud for more than 20 years. Based on these facts, and the experience of e-commerce, the probability of massive electronic voting fraud in the future is extremely low. Of course, the Web is a hazardous environment, and all security protections must be maintained and kept up to date, but as long as officials are vigilant, the Omniscient Hacker can be kept at bay.

No reasonable person, in Shamos's informed opinion, would reject a well-designed electronic voting system purely on the bases of an imagination run wild. He has confronted Rubin with these arguments. And Rubin understands that for Shamos, "the lack of fraud in previous electronic elections made the concerns about it unrealistic."280 But Rubin rejects this method of trying to assess likelihood from the study of what happens in actual situations. He writes, "I believe in assessing vulnerability, not past performance. Potential, not experience."281

To further illustrate his point, Rubin writes that when questioned about his DRE expose by Ohio congresswoman, Marcy Kaptur, he admitted that in his examination of the Diebold DRE code, "we had not seen even the slightest indication that the voting machines were rigged to favor one party over another. In fact, [he and his two assistants] hadn't seen any evidence of tampering at all. Our point had to do with *potential* fraud."282 It seems, then, that for Rubin's methodology, what *he* can *divine* has more reality than what can be observed as having actually happened!

A Fightless Victory

Pathetically, after the big SERVE "expose" by the four dissenters came out, there was not a peep of public protest against it by the SERVE team members. Wolfowitz had a line in his memo stating that he might reconsider his decision "if it can be shown that the integrity of the election results can be assured."283 But this invitation had no takers.

There was plenty of time to fight. Wolfowitz's memo was issued at the end of January, but the election would not be held until November. Apparently, no one on the SERVE team had either the gumption, or the media savvy, needed to quickly organize and mount a defensive action to counteract the dissenters. Not even Accenture, which had the most to lose monetarily, put up a fight to protect its interests.

As Rubin's memoirs show, Diebold and several secretaries of state fought back after his expose against them came out. They fought in the print and broadcast media, at professional meetings, and at government hearings. Their efforts paid off. Contrary to Rubin's aims, the use of DREs in the US, and around the world, is actually increasing.284 Ironically, for all the personal fame and fortune Rubin gained by his attack on DREs, he lost the war. If the SERVE team had mounted an effective campaign to put counter pressure on Wolfowitz, he might have allowed the project to proceed. Certainly fellow SPRG members like Shamos, Selker, Hall, and Alvarez knew what to say to debunk Rubin's rebels. How these folks would explain their apparent passivity is yet to be known. This absence of resistance is a major factor in explaining why the attack on SERVE was such a smashing success. The SERVE team was *right*, but they appear to have ducked the fight.

Rubin as Scholar and Scientist

Rubin laments that being a public figure comes at a price. For instance he has often been publicly accused of acting in an unscholarly manner, and he cites instances.

One example involved Britain J. Williams, a professor emeritus of computer science at Kennesaw State University in Georgia, and a consultant on voting systems. He was a frequent opponent of Rubin at professional meetings and government hearings, and criticized Rubin for, among other things, seeking "publicity."285

Also, Maryland hired an independent testing authority, RABA Technologies, to examine the state's DREs in the light of Rubin's expose. Rubin writes that their report criticized his Diebold paper as full of "attention gathering 'sound bites' [rather] than actual statements of fact."286 And, as to the specific DRE security vulnerabilities Rubin listed, the RABA study concluded that "each of these vulnerabilities has a mitigating recommendation that can be implemented."287

There were other instances Rubin mentions when he received "grief from his peers." At one professional meeting an unnamed fellow professor remarked in front of other colleagues, "I don't publish my research in the New York Times."288

But Rubin denies the charge that his Diebold expose was not handled in a scientific or scholarly manner. He explains that, in order to satisfy the scientific requirement of "peer review," he emailed the report "to some of the top computer security experts in the country;" albeit "only a few days" before the report was to be published in the New York Times.289 He received two replies. One was from Rebecca Mercuri. She advised Rubin "not to go public" with the report because of some "misconceptions or inaccuracies about election procedures," among other things.290 Her "criticism stung," writes Rubin, but he decided to go ahead and publish anyway.291

The other reply Rubin received was from Steve Bellovin, with whom Rubin had worked at AT&T. In Rubin's estimation, Bellovin is "one of the leading authorities on network security."292 Mr. Bellovin echoed some of Professor Mercuri's stinging criticisms; however, by the time Rubin received his comments "the report was already in the hands" of the Times.293 Rubin regretted that he could not have made some of the corrections suggested in his old friend's "peer review."

After the Times had run their story on Rubin's expose of the Diebold DREs, he took even further action to comply with the scientific requirement of peer review. He submitted the paper as a subject for a panel in a conference to be held at the "Claremont Resort in Berkeley."294 Rubin reports proudly that it "was accepted with high marks."295 When yet another computer scientist charged that sending out the paper "to a few 'friends' did not constitute peer review," a Rubin supporter came to his defense. The defender pointed to the paper's acceptance for the resort conference as proof of peer review.296 Apparently, if the fellas at the resort liked it, then its good science.

Whatever the critics say, Rubin cautions that peer review should be seen in proper perspective. Savvy to the politics of science, Rubin observes that the "demand for peer review is a common delaying tactic" used by special interests to avert inconvenient truths.297 He cleverly avoided having his Diebold "scientific research paper" caught in that trap.

Saving Democracy

Unfortunately, Rubin and the other three SERVE dissenters did not have time to comply with the technical requirement of peer review for their scientific research paper on the security vulnerabilities of the DoD's Internet voting system. Their sense of civic duty precluded them from tolerating any such delay. They were on the noble mission of "safeguarding a creditable democracy through fair and verifiable voting procedures."[298] Rubin insists that he and his followers have always sought to expose the faults of e-voting systems with "a single motivation: our desire to preserve the integrity of the American democratic process."[299]

It was with fidelity to this mission alone that Rubin and company took their paper to the New York Times. But their service to the nation did not stop with the delivery of that paper. While Rubin does not describe how he "prepped" his fellow SERVE dissenters to meet the press, as he described the way he prepped his two grad students, there is evidence in the record of well practiced lines. One seemingly coordinated theme concerns their main reason as to why no Internet voting trials can ever be allowed. In their view, if SERVE succeeded, it would surely become a slippery slope to catastrophe. The whole country would rush to Internet voting, and then the Omniscient Hacker would strike. Was it only co-incidence that this fear-inspiring thought was expressed to the press by each of the other three dissenters? For example, in 2004 Barbara Simons told PC World, "What gives me nightmares is that SERVE might go forward and appear to work correctly ...

then Internet voting might [become] widespread for the whole country, perhaps in the 2008 election, and that could be a serious threat to our democracy."300

The techie magazine, Wired, interviewed David Jefferson. Journalist Kim Zetter wrote, "If the experiment experiences no detectable attack, Jefferson fears it could mislead organizers to conclude falsely that the system is secure and ready for expansion. 'Just because there wasn't an attack that you detected doesn't mean there won't be one [in the future] or that there wasn't one that you didn't detect,' he said."301

David Wagner told the Huffington Post, "If I was a bad guy who knew a way to hack the election, I wouldn't attack a small-scale pilot and tip my hand; I'd wait for the voting system to be used on a large scale in an important election and then attack."302 In order to save democracy, then, no trials of Internet voting can be allowed, precisely because they might be successful!

Barbara Simons goes on to state specifically why a successful SERVE trial could lead to catastrophe. Speaking to Computer World, on behalf of the "little cadre" of SERVE dissenters, "Our great fear is that there will be a major move to Internet voting, which I personally feel is a threat to our democracy. The bottom line is we could have our president selected by [hackers in] Iran."303

Because Simons did not elaborate on this nightmarish prognostication, she leaves me, for one, with several unanswered questions. For example, what, exactly, did she fear would happen? Did she fear that US law enforcement would be unable to stop the Iranian hackers from electing someone like the Muslim cleric Ayatollah Khomeini as the President of the United States? And did she *really* think this could be done without being detected? Did she think that because there was no paper trail to audit, the country would have to tolerate the Ayatollah in the White House until the next election, or forever?

Or, was her fear that the Iranian hackers would tilt the vote in favor of either a Republican or a Democratic co-conspirator? One of the necessary implications of this Sci-Fi horror fantasy, of course, is that a president who is a puppet of Iran will then cut off all military and financial assistance to Israel. After that, the Iranian Revolutionary Guard could pounce upon Israel, drive out all the Jews, and give the country to Jihadist Palestinians.

Not much of a thought experiment is needed to expose this fear mongering as a goofy plot, not worthy of a made-for-TV movie. But the choice of "Iran" as the Ultimate Demon reveals more of the PR cleverness of the dissenters. Since Iranian leaders have often threatened to "destroy Israel," no one in the Jewish community would miss the point – i.e., Internet voting = the destruction of Israel!

Rubin does not say whether he planted this PR zinger in Simons's mind, or whether she devised it out of her own cunning. Either way, once examined from a realistic point of view, the scenario predicted becomes astonishingly improbable. In the first place, Internet voting will emerge in America on a county-by-county basis. That is, each local voting jurisdiction will make its own decisions as to what kind of Internet voting system they will use, which company they will hire, and as to when and where they will have the system set up. With over 3000 separate voting jurisdictions in the US, and each with its own secure server and secret codes, and each taking all the security precautions once taken for SERVE, the notion of a teenage hacker in Iran controlling a presidential election is as likely to happen as a Martian Invasion.

Would any *reasonable person* accept Simons's Iran fairy tale as sufficient reason to halt all trials of Internet voting?

What kind of mind would so fear this event that they would sincerely warn their friends and neighbors of its certain occurrence if Internet voting is adopted? Worse yet, what kind of country would allow its public policy discussions to be dominated by such hysterical absurdities?

What are They Really Saving?

The Rubinites agree that their "single motivation" is their "desire to preserve the integrity of the American democratic process." But, what type of "democracy" are they protecting? It is the current money dependent "democracy" of the two-party system. This is the democracy of campaign promises, us-versus-them team spirit with convention hoopla, sound bites, and clever commercials deliberately designed to by-pass the reasoning faculties of the American voter, and to try to stimulate their emotions of fear, prejudice, anger, and sporting rivalry against "the other side." In short, they are protecting our democracy of Unreason.

Examples of unreason abound in American politics today. For example, the 2009 health care reform debate had numerous instances of unreason. In the hope of gaining partisan advantage for the 2010 midterm congressional elections, leaders of the Republican Party sought to derail what they contemptuously called "Obamacare." Whatever reforms the Democrats proposed, the Republicans opposed it – no reasoning about the nation's best interests needed.

One Republican Party leader, Bill Kristol, wrote in a party organ, The Weekly Standard, that "this is no time to pull punches. Go for the kill." Also with his sights on 2010, Republican Senator Jim DeMint of South Carolina sought to rally a group of party activists with the idea that "if we're able to stop Obama on this, it will be his Waterloo. It will break him."304 These party strategists calculated correctly that the low road would lead to party victory in the 2010 mid-term elections. Republicans gained 6 seats in the Senate, and with a win of over 60 seats in the House of Representatives they became the majority in that chamber.

Elderly Medicare recipients, made to fear the loss of their health care by Republican leadership, loudly protested in "town hall meetings" that government must be kept out of the health care system. Not much reasoning is required to see that the Medicare they depend on is an instance of government *in* health care. But unreasoning fear drove them to be irrationally disruptive of the public discourse.

Also a part of the opposition was ardent anti-abortionists, who call doctors "baby killers." They screamed "socialism" when the president called for universally affordable health insurance; yet, due largely to lack of health care affordability, the US has one of the highest infant mortality rates in the industrial world. A little reasoning would have led them to the conclusion that if you really want to save the lives of babies, you should make health care more affordable to mothers without health insurance. But in the two-party system, "leadership" consists of stoking unreason for partisan gain.

Of course, the Republicans were not the only players in the health care drama to display unreason. In his campaign, candidate Obama promised to include more Americans in the health care system, and at the same time to keep down the costs to the government of health care management. But once in office, our 44th President renewed George Bush's seedy pact with the pharmaceutical corporations not to negotiate over government purchased drugs for Medicare and Medicaid; thereby letting the companies name their own prices.[305] If agency heads could negotiate the costs of drugs, hundreds of millions of dollars could be saved for these programs. While reducing the costs of drugs for Medicare and Medicaid is clearly in the national interest, Obama had political debts to repay. Pharmaceutical corporations had contributed millions of dollars to his campaign a year before. Apparently, the pressures of political debts overrode the President's rational understanding of the national interest.

In the conditions of our paper-based, and money-dependent democracy, the Contributing Class has the supreme power. It can block a "Medicare-for-all" plan in Congress, and have laws passed forcing us all to buy health insurance, and perhaps soon, life insurance. Congress is such an eager servant to the Contributing Class that although the money just isn't there for national health care, it is suddenly discovered in abundance to bailout the top corporations every time one of them fails at business, or whenever a risky investment scheme goes sour. These are the priorities of the two-party system.

The Big Money elites own every branch of government. Acting on their behalf, the Supreme Court stretched its authority further than the Court had ever gone, and in *Bush v. Gore* decided the 2000 presidential election in favor of the Court majority's party – the Republicans. In 2009 they seized the opportunity to go way beyond what the lawyers in *Citizens United* asked them to do, and they struck down several limits on campaign spending. As a result, corporations can spend more money than ever before on presidential elections.

Like they have done in the past, the corporate special interests can continue to have new laws passed to protect themselves from private law suits, so that the individuals their products injure or maim, or the families of those who have been killed, will be unable to seek redress in the courts. They can further tighten bankruptcy laws so that those small businesses which are unable to repay loans, and individuals with medical debts, won't get a "fresh start" until after the bank or medical corporation has been paid off in full, with interest and penalties. While "debtor's prison" has been abolished, people who are stuck with unwanted debts that will last far into the future certainly feel a loss of Liberty, and of the right to pursue happiness, just as if they were in prison.

The superrich bankers have already made sure that Congress passes no legal limits on the interest they can charge for credit card debts. So, as their power approaches completeness, the bankers will be free to double those rates, and to impose more fines for late payments, fees for lost card replacements, and penalties for bounced checks and for looking cross-eyed.

As the power of the wealthy corporations reaches its apogee, they will be able to further weaken unions, and demand more of workers. The rich will continue to jack up the costs of higher education, so as to control and limit who will join the growing aristocracy of wealth in our country. With the paper-based voting systems demanded by the Rubinites, the future of our democracy will be much like the past – dominated by a few self-serving superrich special interests. (Small wonder NSF awarded Rubin's foundation "to the tune of $7.5 million," to keep up the good work!)

But within the system of Internet voting that could be ours, public interest, rather than private interests, will become the top public policy priority. The people will be encouraged to exercise their rational faculties. Campaigns will become an education to the electorate. Rational discourse will rise to new heights as a cultural value; and this value, as the Founders understood, is essential for the success of a Republic.

The Most Egregious Election Injustice

As I explained in detail in the previous chapter, Internet voting, properly organized, has the potential to advance Liberty through self-government in the US further than any election reform since the ratification of the Constitution in 1788. Whereas past reforms have served specific aggrieved groups, such as disenfranchised poor white males, women, former slaves, those who were too poor to pay poll taxes, and youths, Internet voting can empower *the entire electorate* in the United States by sidelining special interest money and making elected officials wholly dependent upon the voters for their offices. This would be the largest class of people to benefit from election reform in American history.

The harm caused by the cancellation of SERVE, then, is at least as severe as any of the election injustices which led to reforms in the past; for, nearly the whole electorate has been hurt. The termination of SERVE was not only the denial to overseas voters of a convenient way to vote. The fundamental damage inflicted by killing the SERVE project was to the advancement of real democracy in America through Internet voting.

As I have shown, Internet voting can be every lover of democracy's Dream Come True, if we want it to be. Every elected office, at all levels of government, can be made to directly depend on the will of the voters. In addition, we can have secure, convenient, private, perfectly accurate, and speedy results for every election we hold. So called "political debts" will never again be owed to Fat Cats, unknown bundlers, PACs, or 527s, but only to the proper power base of American politics – the American people. Every day this reform is delayed only serves the interests of the ruling 1%, at the expense of the rest of us, the exploited 99%.

Is there a Remedy for the Harms Caused by the Four Dissenters?

Freedom of speech is not itself free. One of the costs of free speech is that some abuses must be tolerated. While falsely screaming "fire!" in a crowded theater should be punished, fooling the public into fearing the unreal should be tolerated as a hard, but enriching, lesson. Let Lincoln's words, "you can fool some of the people some of the time," stand as a reminder that freedom of speech has costs. An old saying goes, "fool me once, shame on you; fool me twice, shame on me."

In other words, democracy is a learning experience. Some lessons come at a greater cost than others. The delay in the development of Internet voting, caused by the four dissenters to the SERVE project, is one such lesson. It is up to the American people to learn from that lesson, and to not continue to let themselves be duped. The principle to be learned here is that, in public discourse, appeals to fear must be carefully scrutinized by reason before a response to the fear is permitted. Franklin D. Roosevelt understood this when he warned that "the only thing to fear is fear itself."

Conclusion

In Chapter Four I showed how an election process based on Internet voting can be organized so that the people can directly elect the president and vice president, without the intervening domination of Big Money.306 Here in Chapter Five I have shown how four computer scientists, behaving unreasonably, have shaped American public opinion into a state of baseless fear about Internet voting. That fear alone prevents the people from demanding a reform in election technology that can democratize our country beyond anything ever done here, or in any other nation. In my view, the offenders should be left to contemplate the harms they have caused without imposing any punishment. But the rest of us should learn our lesson, and not abandon our critical faculties so easily the next time demagogues appeal to fear in public discourse.

I have noted that a constitutional amendment is necessary to fully reform our presidential elections. In this book's Conclusion, coming next, I will show, among other things, how Internet voting can be implemented for all non-presidential elections, without a constitutional amendment.

Conclusion

What is to be Done?

Citizen action is required to make change in a democracy. If sufficient numbers of people want it, and are willing to work for it, Internet voting technology can open many doors to more democracy and citizen empowerment. In this Conclusion, I will suggest two items of change that can be made on the federal level, and other reforms which can be made within the states

At The Federal Level

1. Restart SERVE

The first item at the federal level is to demand that Congress restart SERVE. For those who see the value to overseas Americans of secure Internet voting this can be done by urging your senators and congresspersons to enact the needed legislation. Because the military, the Department of Defense, and overseas voter organizations have long been after Congress to provide Internet voting for Americans abroad, elected officials only need to know that their constituents favor that reform. Once the negative input from the anti-Internet voting activists is outweighed by the positive input of pro-democracy forces, Congress will act.

The four SERVE dissenters have set back the progress of democracy for all six million overseas Americans, including the three million members of the US armed forces stationed away from home. Our men and women in uniform are fighting and dying to defend our country, and in return we have denied many of them the right to vote by imposing on them cumbersome and ineffective registration and voting requirements. Internet voting can put a stop to that injustice.

Having learned our lesson, we, as a nation, should not look backward, but forward. Those who see the value to our country, and its overseas citizens, of secure Internet voting can demand that Congress mandate and fund the renewal of the 2004 SERVE project. Of course, the exact technology of the original SERVE system need not be replicated. While it was effective, electronic technology in general improves every year as smart inventors devise new techniques. Indeed, since SERVE was stopped in January of 2004 there have been hundreds of new patents issued by the United States Patent Office specifically for every aspect of online registration and secure Internet voting.307 Today there are scores of ways to combine a variety of excellent products into superb electronic registration and voting systems.

2. A Constitutional Amendment

Chapter Four ends with a proposed constitutional amendment abolishing the Electoral College, and providing for the use of electronic technology in the conduct of elections for president and vice president. Such an amendment is necessary because the Constitution's Electoral College now blocks the direct election of these two executives. This is the second item of change to be made at the federal level.

The Constitution sets out two ways by which an amendment can be passed. Article Five provides that the amendment process can be started with two thirds of both houses of Congress agreeing to a proposed amendment; or, when two thirds of the states call for a convention. After either method, three quarters of the state legislatures must vote to ratify the final proposal.

In my view, as I have mentioned, putting pressure on Congress seems to me to be far more efficient than calling for a convention. A convention would be open to an unlimited number of amendment proposals, and could easily become bogged down with endless debates, and eventual deadlock. Therefore, the amendment process should be initiated in Congress. While the amendment proposed in this book has not been handed down from atop Mount Sinai, at least it gives Congress and the public a specific target at which to aim.

Success at this second task will come with far greater difficulty than success at the first item, restoring SERVE. Our nation's current power structure is grounded in the existence of the corporate controlled two-party system. The constitutional amendment proposed here will take the control of presidential elections out of the unclean hands of those two parties, and put the control directly in the hands of the citizens.

Thus corporations will fight like the devil to prevent this amendment from becoming the law of the land. Consider how hard the health care industry fought the modest reforms proposed under the Obama administration. Multiply that by every corporate special interest in the Contributing Class. They will spend hundreds of millions of dollars on PR propaganda designed to fool and frighten the American people with scary stories instead of science. They might even enlist Avi Rubin, and his little cadre of foundations, to lead their campaign!

In addition, many party loving individuals and groups will likely oppose this amendment; especially those that receive material benefits and social status from the current system. For them, nothing is more important than pre-serving their special privileges.

Pro-Internet voting citizens will need a determined national organization to fight for more democracy, and with such an organization this fight can be won!

You will not be Alone

Politics makes strange bed fellows. Those who struggle to be free of corporate dominated government will have corporate allies. The corporations that make, sell, install, and maintain Internet voting systems are already doing all they can to persuade state governments to allow their local election officials to try Internet voting. Thus, they are preparing state officials to favor a constitutional amendment like the one proposed here, and this will make the ratification fight much easier to win.

One of the strongest selling points the corporations use is that once installed, remote Internet voting is much cheaper to operate than any system based on polling places and pieces of paper. If the voters use their own equipment, and vote from home, or any where else, the state is immediately relieved of all the costs of polling place voting. Renting space for polling places, paying poll workers, purchasing, storing, and maintaining DREs or other voting machines, plus the costs of printing and mailing voter information materials and paper ballots, are all very expensive. Voting machines can cost thousands of dollars apiece, and large voting jurisdictions must have hundreds of them. The voting machines are only used occasionally, and must be kept in secure rented storage space for the rest of the time. This way of doing things is costly and inefficient.

But the cost of installing a secure Internet voting server is, in many cases, less than one year of the costs of using polling place voting systems. And, as more counties turn to Internet voting, competition between providers will drive the cost down even further.

The corporations involved in the Internet voting process have been making their case to state and local officials for several years. The officials can do the math, they see the cost savings and are eager to enjoy such savings. But they have been intimidated by the threats of the anti-Internet voting extremists, and there have been little or no countervailing pressures coming from the public. Once a critical mass of pro-Internet voting pressure is applied to state and local authorities, they will happily adopt the new technology. The more states that are already voting online, the more states there will be that are receptive to ratifying the amendment our democracy needs.

Action in the States

Simultaneous efforts to implement Internet voting processes on a smaller scale than presidential elections can be carried on in the several states. One of the great advantages of Internet voting, as I have shown, is that if it is properly organized it can serve as the basis for nonpartisan elections. Nonpartisan elections free the office seeker to be his or her True Self. That is, each candidate can tell the electorate of his or her proposals without the pressures of party loyalty or party elites slanting those proposals to favor the party over the best interests of the state or the nation. In this Conclusion, therefore, I will offer some suggestions as to how states can conduct elections based on Internet voting, for both federal and state offices.

Our Constitution gives the states the authority to regulate all elections within their borders – including elections for the federal offices of US Senator and representatives in the House of Representatives. Election reform for these offices, both state and federal, need not require a constitutional amendment. Thus, if the citizenry wants it, state laws can be enacted to require every election within a state to be conducted online, from dog catcher to school board to the governorship, including the US Congress.

Congressional Elections

Article One, Section Four, gives the states the administrative responsibility for the "times, places, and manner of holding elections for Senators and Rep-resentatives." This is a sweeping range of authority. Its parameters have never been finally established. The "manner" clause seems to me to empower the states to make Internet voting the *manner* by which federal offices are filled. Thus there is no need for a change in the Constitution for the states to make elections to the US House and Senate Internet based.

The Constitution sets forth three requirements for these offices. Under Article One, Section Two, a representative must be at least 25 years old, seven years a citizen, and reside in the state wherein he or she is elected. Section Three of that Article requires that a senator must be at least

30 years old, nine years a citizen, and reside in the state wherein he or she is elected.

If the people of a state want to require a *written* test as one of the criteria for becoming eligible to run for offices besides the presidency, they could pressure their legislatures to enact such laws. However, a constitutional amendment might be necessary before that requirement can be imposed on candidates for the House and Senate, because it exceeds the Constitution's stated requirements. Having the amendment for democratizing presidential elections proposed in Congress, and then ratified in three-quarters of the states, is enough of an arduous task. Taking on yet another amendment would needlessly drain energy and resources necessary for success with the first one. Fortunately, an alternative to the difficult challenge of enacting another constitutional amendment is already practiced in states like California.

California Proposition 14 and Internet Voting

For much of California's history, the political parties dominated the method by which candidates were nominated and elected to office. First, to give themselves legal cover, the parties had a law enacted requiring political parties to *qualify* to run candidates. If a party filed a petition with the Secretary of State (SOS) with a sufficient number of signatures by registered voters it could qualify to place candidates on the ballot for a primary election. If the party's candidates received a sufficient number of votes in the general election, it could remain qualified for the next election. This process was designed to accommodate the two major parties. In practice, minor parties would occasionally qualify for a few election cycles, and then fail to stay qualified. Early in the 20th Century, for instance, the Socialist Party qualified as a third party in the election process, but fell by the wayside within a couple of decades. But the Democratic and Republican parties have become permanent fixtures in California politics.

Until recently, California followed a closed primary system of elections. That is, each qualified party could nominate its own candidates for office, and the state would place their names on the ballot for the primary election. The state printed separate ballots for each qualified party. The parties, and not the government, controlled whose name would be printed on the primary ballot, at the government's expense. Also, voters were limited as to which candidates they could vote for. Voters could only vote for candidates in the party which the voter had declared to be his or her party at the time of registering to vote. If a citizen declined to state a party affiliation, or declared membership in an unqualified party, then he or she was *penalized* – he or she could not vote for any primary candidate (except for the rare write-in candidates).

Clearly, this penalty was designed to put subtle pressure on people to support the qualified party system, and thereby the two-party system, when they registered to vote. "Decline to state" voters could vote for nonpartisan offices, such as judge or insurance commissioner, and on the other issues presented on the ballot, but not for candidates for partisan offices. Here was a form of blatant discrimination based solely on a person's beliefs. If a voter did not believe in one of the "qualified" parties, he or she could not vote for a partisan candidate in the primary.

By 2010, there were over *three million* California voters who could not vote for candidates to the governorship, state legislature, or the US House and Senate in the primary, because they did not want to register as a member of a "qualified" political party; that is, a party in which they did not believe. In each case, the person who did not register with such a party understood that he or she would be denied the right to vote in a qualified party's primary. But, for these folks, *remaining True to Themselves* was more important than lying about their party preference simply so that they could vote in a party primary.

In other words, just as the pressures of partisan dominated election processes can compel candidates to take positions they do not always believe in, partisan domination also pressures citizens to register as members of a political party, even though they might not fully believe in that party's policies. They were forced to be *inauthentic.*

Moral Liberation

Then in June of 2010 a majority of voters in the state passed a measure put before them by the state legislature. It was called "Proposition 14." This law expanded the *moral liberty* of Californians, and respected their First Amendment right to Be as they Believed, and to associate freely with any party, or no party. Prop 14 exploded the control the parties had over the nomination of candidates.

Now, *anyone* can qualify for a spot on the primary ballot simply by meeting the signature requirements and paying a filing fee. The state only prints one primary ballot, listing all candidates; and voting on it is open to all registered voters, no matter what party, if any, the voter had identified with when registering to vote.

Because candidates no longer have to be on a party ballot, they no longer have to tow a party line to get on the ballot. Candidates are now free to be more authentic in presenting themselves to the electorate. With the passage of Prop 14, the right to vote in primaries was immediately restored to over three million California citizens. They were no longer forced to choose between selling out their personal integrity so they could vote in some party's primary, or preserving their integrity at the cost of voting in the primaries.

Ideally, no one should be required to state their beliefs, or party affiliation (which is the same thing), just in order to register to vote. Voter registration should be based on age and citizenship alone. The rights to privacy and to the freedom of association require nonpartisan voter registration. While California still requires voters to register with a party affiliation, or "decline to state," at least now no one is limited to voting only in the primary of the party they registered with.

How Prop 14 Works

As I have said, candidates once had to be in a qualified party to have their name appear on a primary ballot. Each qualified party had its own primary ballot, printed at state expense. Often the party elites, in cahoots with the contributors of campaign money, would determine who would be the candidates for the party's primary. California law made the task of getting a name on the primary ballot relatively easy for the party's chosen candidate, and relatively more difficult for anyone else who wanted to be considered by the electorate. For example, a party outsider would be required to submit a "petition for candidacy" to the Secretary of State's office with many times more valid signatures than required of a party favorite. The outsider would also have to pay a higher filing fee. And, party elites would lavish their candidate with support in the form of advertising and supplying campaign workers; however, outsiders could see party money being spent against them, and party activists would be discouraged from working on the outsider's campaign.

Under Prop 14 the government prints only one ballot for the whole primary election, and takes control over ballot access. The parties are free to hold conventions, and to nominate candidates, but these candidates must meet the same requirements to get on the primary ballot as non-party, or independent candidates. No more special privileges for political parties. Generally, if a hopeful, with or without party affiliation, meets the signature requirements on a petition to be placed on the primary ballot, his or her name will be printed on the ballot. The filing fee is the same for everyone. This makes ballot access *nonpartisan*, and changes the nature of election politics in California.

Proposition 14 does not enact any reforms of the presidential election process; in part because this is a national election, and beyond the power of one state to reform. The presidential election is left in the hands of the two-party system. Prop 14 only applies to state offices and the US Senate and House.

Under Prop 14 there are *three* stages in the election process for these offices. The first is the signature gathering stage for those who petition for a spot on the primary ballot. The second is the primary vote for the candidates and issues on that ballot. In this vote, the candidates with the two highest votes will go on to the general election. The top two may be in no party, different parties, or both from one party. The third step is the general election, which is when the voters decide between the top two winners of the primary by a majority vote. I will briefly discuss each of these three stages.

Petition Signatures

While I have suggested a written test as a way of screening candidates for the series of elimination debates in presidential elections, the people of California have decided on signature gathering as the way hopefuls will become candidates under Prop 14. Suppose that, for example, a number of signatures equal to 1% of the registered voters in a given election year are required for a petition to have one's name placed on the primary ballot for governor in California. In 2010 that would have been about 175,000 signatures.[308]

Gathering these signatures will involve a lot of traditional political activity. The hopeful will have to personally appear before all sorts of groups and organizations within the state to convince their leadership and membership to support the hopeful's candidacy. Groups of supporters will be needed to make the hopeful's name known, and to help in the signature gathering by circulating the petition to place him or her on the primary ballot. Having a website, and being active on social networking will help. Someday electronic signatures will enable citizens to sign petitions online.

The signature gathering process does not necessarily favor folks with big bucks. As I will explain further in a moment, experience shows that quite often, hopefuls who try to buy their way into office with their own money create more resentment than support among the voters. So, candidates who have to get on the ballot by hiring businesses to gather signatures, because they had little or no popular support, and who flooded the air waves and the Internet with their name and picture, could be criticized for that in the primary debates, and risk being swiftly tossed out of the game by the voters.

This first stage opens up a great opportunity for all the people who were discouraged from seeking office by the way political parties once controlled access to the primary ballot. Members of small groups that were unhappy being in one of the major parties, and only stayed in them so they could be on a winning team, can now form new coalitions outside the two majors, and work to have their own candidate meet the requirements for placement on the ballot. Third parties need no longer worry about qualifying or staying qualified. In this respect, third parties are now on a level playing field with the two major parties.

Individual activists, who are not affiliated with any state wide or national party, can rely on their own initiative within a district to form their own "party-within-the-district," whether for state Senate, Assembly, or congressional district. Prop 14 is centered on *individual hopefuls* meeting the requirements for ballot access, and party qualification is no longer relevant. It's a game with a whole new focus on respecting individual integrity, and on facilitating individual initiative and achievement. The petition signing stage is a screening process for Prop 14 offices, just as the written test I have suggested is a way to screen presidential hopefuls. When citizens sign petitions they express their confidence in the ability of a hopeful to fulfill the duties of the office sought. Hopefuls who fail to inspire folks to sign a petition for them will be screened out of the process.

Conducting the Primary Vote

Under Prop 14, the parties have no control over the party label the candidate chooses, if any – even if the party central committee does not actually endorse the candidate![309] The candidate is free to call himself or herself "Republican," or "Democrat," "Socialist," "Green," "Independent," or any other name.

But this freedom is a two-edge sword. While voters might use the party label as a cue for voting, the freedom of candidate choice will render all party labels suspect, because they can be used deceptively. For example, a Socialist at heart, who deceptively registered as a "Republican" can, as a candidate, have himself listed as a "Republican," and attract voters who respond automatically to that cue. Consequently, debunking party labels could become a part of every campaign. Few candidates will escape the charge of deceptive labeling. One result of this is that voters will have to make more of an effort to find out what each candidate really stands for. But when several candidates for a single office are on the ballot, and party labels cannot be trusted, how is a voter to sort through them all to determine which one to vote for?310

California currently prints a useful voter information pamphlet. While the state should continue to assemble the pamphlet, to save paper and printing costs, this could be just posted on the SOS website, and emails sent out to voters advertising it. Also, debates online and on the air are probably the best way for voters to inform themselves about candidate positions. Then the voter can vote on his or her impression of the candidate *as a person*, and not have to rely on a party label or other outside information.

These debates can be broadcast online and on TV, and followed by Internet voting. The governor can be elected in a series of debates held statewide. The two US Senators can also be elected in a series of statewide debates. All the other offices that are based in particular legislative and congressional districts within the state can be filled by broadcasting the debates online, on radio, and on TV, and limiting the online voting to registered voters who live in the particular district.

Of course, once the announcement is made as to who has qualified to be on the primary ballot, the candidates will begin to campaign prior to voting day. As everyone knows, campaigns cost money. But campaigns under the Prop 14 reforms need not favor the rich. Just as in the series of elimination debates for president, the voter in elections for state offices and congressional offices will not base his or her decision on the advertising calculated to condition the voter's decision, but on his or her direct impression of each candidate, formed by watching them debate.

The General Election

Following the primary vote, the *top two* candidates for each office will then go on to the general election, and the voters will decide which one wins. Limiting the general election to the top two winners for each office in the primary is essential for a democratic political system. This way, the winner is guaranteed to win by a majority of votes.

Suppose there were three candidates in a general election. The results could be as follows: candidate "A" with 34%, "B" with 33%, and "C" with 33%. "A" would not have been elected by a majority; indeed, a super majority of 66% would have their hopes frustrated by such an outcome. The great risk with this kind of process is that the elected candidate's legitimacy with the voters could be undermined. That risk is easily avoided by the top two method.

After the primary vote, the top two candidates for each office will have time to campaign prior to the general election.311 Here again, wealth is not necessarily an advantage. As 2010 showed repeatedly, big spending does not guarantee success in an election. In the California gubernatorial contest that year, Meg Whitman spent over one hundred sixty million dollars, nearly all of it her own money. In the race for one of that state's seats in the US Senate Carly Fiorina spend over twenty-two million dollars of her own dough. Both ladies lost; Whitman lost to Jerry Brown, and Fiorina lost to Barbara Boxer.

In Connecticut, wrestling magnate Linda McMahon burned through $47 million in her unsuccessful run for a US Senate seat. And, in Florida, billionaire Senate hopeful Jeff Greene spent twenty-four million of his own dollars, and failed to win the Democratic Party primary. These facts show that the voters can be trusted to think independently of all the crafty ads (Whitman spent over $100 million on advertising, all for naught).312 So, as I have said before, spending on political speech prior to the elimination debates is not a threat to democracy, and, in accord with the First Amendment, need not be regulated nor feared.

Electronic Democracy

Once in office, legislators, whether state or federal, can be required by the voters to hold online town hall meetings. Truly democratic officials will not only invite constituent letter writing, phone calls, and emails, but will post ideas and proposals online and ask for comments. For example, a legislator can post on his or her website a plan to vote to support or oppose a pending bill. Constituents can post their comments, to which the legislator can reply. A debate over how the official should vote can be conducted. There might even be an online referendum vote on how he or she should vote. The same procedure can be followed before a legislator submits a bill for consideration by his or her legislative body.

A legislator can also invite citizen initiatives. Constituents can post proposed bills in a section on an official's website. Then interested persons can discuss its merits, or lack thereof. Perhaps a referendum can be held. If a majority supports the initiative, the official would have to submit it to his or her legislative body.

While a *national* referendum or initiative would require a constitutional amendment to have any effect, no law is needed to begin the process of requiring legislators to honor the online votes of their constituents. Voter pressure should be enough to enlist a legislator's cooperation. Any elected official who refuses to engage his or her constituents in this form of electronic democracy can be voted out of office and replaced with a truly democratic minded official.

The old maxim "politics is the art of the possible" applies here. Pro-Internet voting organizations within the states will strive to achieve what is possible to achieve within their own political systems. States will vary in the choices they make. Some may go all out for online voting.

Others may take it one step at a time. The rate of progress will vary from state to state. There will surely be experiments with different technical systems, and with the choice of companies to which contracts will be awarded to set up and operate the systems.

In this way, Internet voting will grow in each state only as its citizens are ready to have it. And, the quality of the systems used will improve as states learn from experience and as companies compete for state contracts. Competition among these companies will result in continuing cost reductions and technical improvements.313

The potential for electronically democratizing American politics and government is only limited by what the American people want for themselves. If they want a government that does it all for them, so they can stay out of politics and watch TV, surf the Net, play with e-toys, or whatever, then that is what they will have. However, our Founding Generation's spirit of seeking *Liberty through self-government* – the original American Dream – once drove them to fight, sacrifice, and sometimes die in the American Revolution. The same spirit moved the struggles for worker's rights, civil rights, and voting rights. If that spirit is still alive in our generation, then that spirit will find its way to realization through an electronic democracy based on Internet voting.314

Why Internet Voting Favors Moderation

In large part, the current gridlock in the US government is a consequence of voting technology; that is, the technology suited for polling places. With polling places away from the home, office, or other work place, a special effort must be made to find the place to vote, park the car, and often wait in line. The vote must be cast on unfamiliar machines, and in a hurry because other voters are awaiting their turn. While voters try to make the best of "doing their civic duty," the experience is neither convenient nor all that pleasant.

As practical minded people, then, the American voters must weigh the costs and benefits of voting. On balance, the cost of the trek to the polls is not justified by the benefits of voting in primaries for most voters. These folks simply do not feel the motivation needed to expend the time and energy required – they often think, "I'll endure the inconvenience in November." For these voters, civic duty is adequately satisfied by one episode of incon-venience, and two such episodes is asking too much. Thus, primary turnout is regularly less than half the turnout for general elections.

Those who do vote in primaries are people who feel more motivation than the stay-at-homes. Primary voters generally have stronger political beliefs than the non-voters. Indeed, voters with extreme views and extra-ordinary feelings of partisan fervor make up a much higher percent of the turnout in primaries than in general elections. While participation is widely regarded as a contribution to the democratic process, extreme views can have deleterious consequences for the happiness a population has with its politics and government.

The key threat of extremism, whether from the right or left, is its *inhumane tendency* to value ideological purity above the well being of actually living people. "If some people must suffer impoverishment so that the ideal of a 'free market' economy can be realized, then so be it," proclaim the extremists on the American right. "If many people must suffer under the yoke of government regulation so that the ideal of 'material equality for all' can be realized, then so be it," counter the extremists on the American left. Such highly motivated, or ideologically driven, folks tend to be the decisive factor in primary elections. Consequently, the winning candidates in primaries tend to be those who appealed to the ideological and partisan extremists.

Some concerned citizens might make the "heroic argument;" that is, that people who do not want to pay the price of voting should not vote, and democracy is better served by those who put out the effort. But, of course, these "heroes" drive their cars to work, buy their food from grocery stores, and often get their news from watching TV because reading requires too much effort. Are they really "heroes"?

Current circumstances suggest that the opposite of the heroic argument is true. That is, the inconvenience of voting is a significant cause of the gridlock and partisan bickering in our democratic government. In our times, therefore, democracy might be better served by a more convenient method of voting, which would provide the way for more moderate voices to be heard. Internet voting can make it easier for voters of moderate motivation to vote. The resulting influx of moderately motivated voters can temper the influence of the highly motivated extremists.

Convenience of voting, in my opinion, would help to move the locus of power to where it should be in a democracy; that is, to the wiser, more moderate, more humane middle of public opinion. Government by alternating between partisan extremists has proven to *not* be conducive to political happiness in America. With Internet voting, more moderate minded Americans can emerge as the center of electoral power.

Because, as history shows, average Americans are a naturally humane people who care deeply about fairness, the officials they elect will enact policies that reflect their will. Having office holders elected by the center of public opinion will also provide stability to public policy, because the humane nature of Americans is as stable as their DNA. Such stability will be further supported by Internet voting because it enables nonpartisan election processes, and because it can neutralize the power of Big Money in all US elections. With all sorts of extreme and selfish interests well tempered by moderate majorities, truly, the Golden Mean will be The Way to our political happiness.

ENDNOTES

1. Unless otherwise indicated, the term "Internet voting" will mean persons logged on to a secure website, and voting from any place via PC or cell phone.

2. **http://internetvotingforall.blogspot.com/2010/10/does-dc-fiasco-damn-internetvoting.html**

3. See, Report of the Chief Electoral Officer of Canada on the 41st general election of May 2, 2011, at **www.elections.ca**

An elections official in Russia announced that in December 2011 the Duma would begin hearings on the use of Internet voting, at least for remote areas. See **http://tinyurl.com/IVinRuski**

To implement the Estonian model, two types of hardware are needed. One: cell phones for all voters, as in Estonia. Cell phones are ubiquitous, even in the developing world. Two: secure servers in various voting districts, so that voters can log on and vote. The servers would support a voting website, PC owners could also use it. Using several different servers would insure defense against DOS attacks. Secure PINs can be issued upon biometric voter registration. Every country in the world can have honest, democratic elections based on Internet voting.

According to Tarvi Martens, the designer of the Estonian system, security and privacy are assured because each voter uses a digital signature tied specifically to his or her citizen ID card, and the vote itself is encrypted. "I can say we are more secure than Internet banking. I would guarantee it," Mr. Martens said. **http://elections2011.estonianfreepress.com/05/how-secure-is-internet-voting/? sms_ss=twitter&at_xt=4d7417107f54a6e8,0**

4. **http://www.fec.gov/press/press2009/20090608PresStat.shtml**
References for the factual statements made in this Introduction can be found in the notes to Chapter One, and other chapters.

5. **http://www.csoonline.com/article/220340/**
The_Five_Most_Shocking_Things_About_the_ChoicePoint_Data_Security_Brea ch.

6. Specifically, **http://datalossdb.org/blotter; also see,
http://www.privacyrights.org/,**
and **http://www.idtheftcenter.org**.

7.
**http://archives.cnn.com/2002/LAW/11/12/military.hacker/in
dex.html** and
**http://query.nytimes.com/gst/fullpage.html?
res=9C0CE2DC1E31F937A15752C0A96F9C8B63**.

8. **http://arstechnica.com/tech-policy/news/2009/01/uk-
hacker-gary-mckinnonsextradition-
briefly-delayed.ars;** and,
**http://www.wired.com/threatlevel/2009/07/
mckinnon/**.

9.
**http://www.nytimes.com/2006/11/02/nyregion/02veteran.htm
l?_r=1&scp=1&sq=
%20US%20Department%20of%20Veterans%20Affairs%2
02006%20computer
%20stolen%20&st=cse**.

10. **http://datalossdb.org/incidents/1922-patient-names-social-
security-numbersdates-
of-birth-and-medical-histories-of-about-3200-on-stolen-
blackberry**

11 **http://www.pcworld.com/businesscenter/article/151901/
tmobile_lost_disk_containing_data_on_17_million_customer
s.html**

12 For a list of trash cases, including LA Co, see
**http://datalossdb.org/search?breach_type%5B%5D=Disposa
l_Document**

13.
**http://www.nytimes.com/2006/09/25/technology/25link.html?
scp=1&sq=Chase
%20Card%20Services%20trash&st=cse;** and,
**http://www.foxnews.com/story/
0,2933,212739,00.html**

14.
**http://www.nytimes.com/2006/09/25/technology/25link.html?s
cp=1&sq=Chase
%20Card%20Services%20trash&st=cse** and
**http://www.foxnews.com/story/
0,2933,212739,00.html**.

15 **http://datalossdb.org/search?breach_type%5B%5D=Web& page=14**.

16. **http://www.computerworld.com/action/article.do? command=viewArticleBasic&articleId=9056004&intsrc=hm _list** and

http://datalossdb.org/incidents/877-credit-card-numbers-names-and-addressespossibly-compromised-on-hacker-safe-web-site accessed 5-1-09.

17 **"The Internet Is Infected,"** broadcast on 3-5-09. **http://www.cbsnews.com/video/watch/?id=4908267n** accessed 5-1-09.

18 **http://www.seattlepi.com/local/404885_filesharing06.html** accessed 5-1-09.

19 See the Web Accessibility Initiative (WAI), at **http://www.w3.org/WAI/**.

20 **http://www.govtechblogs.com/lohrmann_on_infrastructure/2 009/05/honolulusinternet-vote-worked.php;** and, **http://www.nytimes.com/2009/03/15/nyregion/ 15voting.html?scp=10&sq=New%20York%20City%20Scho ol%20Board %20Internet%20voting&st=cse**

21. In 2010, the District of Columbia invited the public to test its experimental Internet voting website. The system was incompetently constructed by novice programmers, and within a few hours a University of Michigan computer science professor broke into the server, changed votes, and installed the school's football fight song. Later, Internet voting opponents tried to make hay of the incident, but many questions concerning the causes of the system's security failure remain unanswered. For more on this, see their over-blown claims, and my comments, at **http://voices.washingtonpost.com/local-opinions/2010/10/ in_dcs_web_voting_test_the_hac.html**

22. Two anti-Internet voting sites that specialize in following state legislation are **VoterAction.org** and **Verified Voting.org**.

23 **http://www.nytimes.com/2009/01/20/us/politics/20minnesota. html?fta=y**, and

http://thecaucus.blogs.nytimes.com/2009/04/07/the-minnesota-senatesaga/?scp=2&sq=Minnesota%20Senate%20Race%20&st=cse.

24 http://www.pewcenteronthestates.org/uploadedFiles/NTTV_Report_Web.pdf.

25. Cf. Kevin Coleman, http://fpc.state.gov/documents/organization/22714.pdf.

26. http://www.notablesoftware.com/Press/JDunbar.html (accessed 11-5-10).

27 http://www.roa.org/site/Search?query=internet+voting&inc=10&x=11&y=8.

28 http://www.roa.org/site/PageServer?pagename=law_review_0759

29 http://www.roa.org/site/DocServer/0711_officer.pdf?docID=4101.

30 DoD Report, pages 10-11, http://www.servesecurityreport.org/DoDMay2007.pdf. RE: the similar security measures taken for the 2000 online primary vote in Arizona see Mohen, Joe and Glidden, Julia. (2001) 'The Case for Internet Voting,' Communications of the ACM, 44:1, p72-85. (Made available to me from one of the authors at: http://www.21cconsultancy.com).

31 "A Security Analysis of the Secure Electronic Registration and Voting Experiment (SERVE)," January 21, 2004; hereinafter, "Analysis." Dr. David Jefferson, Dr. Aviel D. Rubin, Dr. Barbara Simons, Dr. David Wagner, page 2. http://www.servesecurityreport.org/paper.pdf.

32 Analysis, page 2.

33 DoD Report, p 11, http://www.servesecurityreport.org/DoDMay2007.pdf; and, http://www.nytimes.com/2004/02/06/us/the-2004-campaign-voting-online-ballotscanceled-for-americans-overseas.html?scp=1&sq=Online%20Voting%20Canceled%20for%20Americans%20Overseas&st=cse

34 http://www.nytimes.com/2007/05/18/washington/18wolfowitz.html.

35 Analysis, page 21.

36 Analysis, page 7.

37 Analysis, page 7.

38 Analysis, page 8.

39 Analysis, page 14.

40 Analysis, page 9.

41 http://www.newsweek.com/id/167581

42 http://www.nytimes.com/2010/01/20/technology/20cyber.html?ref=technology;
http://www.nytimes.com/2010/02/22/technology/22cyber.html;and,
http://www.nytimes.com/2010/02/19/technology/19china.html

43 Analysis, page 15.

44 Analysis, page 15.

45 Analysis, page 14.

46 http://www.brennancenter.org/content/resource/truthaboutvoterfraud/,page 31 f. For an example of innuendo, rather than fact, see http://www.effwa.org/files/pdf/VIP_Recommendation_3.pdf.

47 Analysis, page 16.

48 Analysis, page 16.

49 http://tinyurl.com/NonPartPol

50 Analysis, page 16 f.

51 Analysis, page 17.

52 Analysis, pages 17-18.

53 http://www.wired.com/politics/security/magazine/15-09/ff_estonia

54 http://tinyurl.com/IVinRuski

55 Analysis, page18.

56 Analysis, page 14.

57 Analysis, page 14.

58 Analysis, page 19.

59 Analysis, page 19.

60 Analysis, page 19.

61 http://www.wired.com/politics/security/news/2004/01/62041

62
http://losangeles.fbi.gov/dojpressrel/pressrel08/la041608usa.
htm;and, http://www.computerworld.com/s/article/9129054/
Botnet_ringleader_gets_four_years_in_prison_for_stealing_
data_from_PCs
63 DoD Report,
http://www.servesecurityreport.org/DoDMay2007.pdf. All
quotes in this paragraph are from page 10.
64 DoD Report, page 11.
65 DoD Report, page 11.
66 DoD Report, page 11.
67 DoD Report, pages 19-20.
68 DoD Report, page 27.
69 DoD Report, page 6, repeated at page 28, italics added.
70. DoD Report, page 28.
71. DoD Report, page 28. One computer scientist with experience
in building successful Internet voting systems, Ed Gerck, has
criticized the SERVE team for omitting a very effective security
device. He calls it the "electronic witness." This is a device that
can be added to each module in a server to monitor its
operations. The electronic witness would be programmed to
follow a specific operation in a module, to be sure it operated
according to its specified code. If any bad code was
surreptitiously inserted in a module, the witness would detect it
and alert election officials.

The witnesses can verify that ballots have only been issued to
a voter after his or her registration was checked and verified. (As
we have seen, a secure registration system will assure that there
is only one vote per registered voter.) Next, the witness can
verify that each voted ballot was sent as marked by the voter;
that is, that no ballots have been tampered with after the voter
has marked them. The witness can verify that each vote has been
stored in the electronic ballot box exactly as voted, and not
changed in the course of being stored. Lastly, the witness can
verify that only these verified votes have been counted for the
final tally.

The electronic witnesses would not read nor record the names
of voters, nor how they voted. Their only function is to observe
that voting procedures have been followed according to code.

Every qualified stakeholder in an election, such as political
parties, can add their own electronic witnesses to check the

integrity of the server for an Internet voting system. If an insider, such as a politically zealous contractor, or some personnel in an election official's office, was foolish enough to try and alter the system by slipping in some tricky code, the electronic witnesses would catch it and alert the stakeholders before the election begins. As a check against Democratic and Republican witnesses, third parties can pool their resources and add witnesses of their own. All the witnesses would be able to see and record that a server's "ballot box," or storage memory, is empty before it is sealed and the election starts.

Witnesses can be added which would record any unauthorized activity during the election. For example, suppose someone with access to stored data tries to take an unauthorized peek at the votes, or at who had voted. The witness would record this intrusion, and alert security officers right away. Just the threat of being caught and punished would deter all but the most foolish insider improprieties. For more information go to **http://safevote.com**.

72. *The Life of John Marshall: Politician, Diplomatist Statesman 1789-1801.* By Albert Jeremiah Beveridge (1916, reprinted by Beard Books, Washington D.C.), page 410. See Google Books, at **http://tinyurl.com/MarshallBio**

73 Thomas Jefferson in a letter to Francis Hopkinson, 1789. Posted at **http://etext.virginia.edu/jefferson/quotations/jeff0800.htm**

74 Letter to Jonathan Jackson (2 October 1789), cited at **http://en.wikiquote.org/wiki/John_Adams**

75 *The Federalist Papers*. Mentor Books, New York. 1961 Introduction by Clinton Rossiter. While also posted at **http://avalon.law.yale.edu/subject_menus/ fed.asp** , all quotes are from the book.

76 Ibid, No. 15, page 111.

77 Ibid, No. 51, page 322.

78 Ibid, No. 10, page 79.

79 Ibid, No. 51, page 323.

80 Ibid, No. 14, page 99.

81 Ibid, No. 51, page 322.

82 Ibid, No. 10, page 77.

83 Ibid, No. 15, page 110.

84 Ibid, No. 10, page 81.

85 Ibid, No. 10, page 81.

86 Ibid, No. 10, page 81.

87 Ibid, No. 10, page 82.

88 Ibid, No. 45, page 289.

89 Ibid, No. 51, page 322.

90 Ibid, No. 81, page 484. Assessing how well the Supreme Court has fulfilled this expectation is not a matter for this book.

91 Ibid, No. 10, page 84

92 All quotes are taken from the copy of Washington's 1796 Farewell Address, posted at **http://avalon.law.yale.edu/18th_century/washing.asp**

93 The language of the Twelfth Amendment will be quoted, unless otherwise specified.

94 *The Federalist Papers,* id., page 377. Madison's "Notes on the Debates in the Federal Convention" are also posted at **http://avalon.law.yale.edu/subject_menus/debcont.asp**.

95 Hamilton wrote that Electors were envisioned by the Framers as a "small number of persons, selected by their fellow-citizens ..." Also, "the people should operate in the choice of [Electors, who then would be] men chosen by the people." *The Federalist Papers*, ibid, No. 68, page 412.

Jay anticipated that the president would "be chosen by select bodies of electors to be deputed by the people for that express purpose." Ibid, No. 64, page 390.

Madison writes, "The Senate will be elected absolutely and exclusively by the State legislatures." But his anticipation as to how those legislatures will function in presidential elections is more qualified. He allows for the possibility of the popular election of Electors, at least in some states, when he writes that the state legislatures "will, perhaps, in most cases, of themselves [vote for the president]." Ibid, No. 45, page 291.

96 *The Federalist Papers,* id., No. 68, page 412.

97 Sometimes called the Connecticut Compromise, **http://en.wikipedia.org/wiki/Connecticut_Compromise**.

98 See Article One, Section Two, which gives the numbers of representatives for each of the original states, and add two to reach the number of Electors for each state.

99 *The Federalist Papers,* id., No. 64, at 391.

100 Ibid. No. 64, page 391.

101 Ibid, No. 68, page 412.

102 No. 26, page 412.

103 This proposal, and the discussion of it, occurred on July 17, 1787. See

http://avalon.law.yale.edu/18th_century/debates_717.asp

104 *The Federalist Papers,* ibid, page 73.

105 See **http://www.archives.gov/federal-register/electoral-college/laws.html** and

http://en.wikipedia.org/wiki/Faithless_elector.

106 For an alternative to the deceptive practice of "framing," see my book *Progressive Logic*.

107 For more information on 527s, see

http://www.opensecrets.org/527s/527cmtes.php and

http://www.irs.gov/charities/political/index.html.

The discussion in this section primarily concerns *contributions* made to candidates, PACs, and parties. Of course, campaign *expenditures* have also been increasing since the passage of the FECA. Congress attempted to limit those expenditures in that Act, but the Supreme Court struck down that part of the law in *Buckley v. Valeo*, 96 S. Ct. 612 (1976), saying that they were unjustifiable restrictions on political speech. Following that precedent, the section of the McCain-Feingold law limiting expenditures on political advertising by independent groups, including 527s, corporations, and unions, was declared unconstitutional by the Supreme Court in *Citizens United v FEC* 130 S. Ct. 876 (2009). One consequence of this new ruling may be that independent expenditures will sky-rocket, because it gives independent persons and groups more control over how their money is spent. Why give away your money to a candidate's campaign organization or a political party, when under *Citizens United* you can make and broadcast your own political commercials that say exactly what you want them to say?

108 See

http://www.fec.gov/DisclosureSearch/mapApp.do?cand_id=P80003338, accessed 7-9-09.

109 See

http://www.whitehouseforsale.org/bundlingproposal.cfm, accessed 7-9-09.

110 See

http://www.citizen.org/pressroom/release.cfm?ID=2482

111 See, Obama:
http://www.opensecrets.org/pres08/contrib.php?cycle=2008 &cid=N00009638
McCain:
http://www.opensecrets.org/pres08/contrib.php? id=N00006424&cycle2=2008&goButt2.x=8&goButt2.y=9
112 See
http://www.opensecrets.org/pres08/bundlers.php?id=N00009 638,
accessed 7-9-09.
113 See
http://www.cleanupwashington.org/documents/FECBundlin g.pdf
114 For an excellent recounting of Obama's early years in politics, and the formation of his political character, see "Making It: How Chicago Shaped Obama," by Ryan Lizza **http://www.newyorker.com/reporting/2008/07/21/080721fa_f act_lizza? printable=true** .
115 The discussion of Obama's political career draws heavily from the New York Times, and other cited sources. See, "Loyal Network Backs Obama After His Help," **http://www.nytimes.com/2007/10/01/us/politics/01obama.htm l**, naming early bundlers. New York Times finds at least 326 bundlers, **http://www.nytimes.com/2008/07/11/us/politics/11bundlers.ht ml**; 181 names at **http://thecaucus.blogs.nytimes.com/2008/07/10/** ; and, with amounts, "Meet Obama's Bundlers," **http://www.chicagobusiness.com/cgi-bin/news.pl?id=30705** . Also, Cf. "Big Donors, Too, Have Seats at Obama Fund-Raising Table," **http://www.nytimes.com/2008/08/06/us/politics/06bundlers.ht ml**, "about two thirds of his bundlers are concentrated in four major industries…" Further, "An Obama Patron and Friend Until an Indictment" [Tony Rezko], **http://www.nytimes.com/2007/06/14/us/politics/14rezko.html** ;"Obama Donor Received a State Grant," **http://www.latimes.com/news/nationworld/nation/la-nakillerspin27apr27,0,6789688.**

story and, "After 2000 Loss, Obama Built Donor Network From Roots Up,"
http://www.nytimes.com/2007/04/03/us/politics/03obama.htm l?scp=1&sq=After %202000%20Loss,%20Obama%20Built%20Donor%20Net work%20From%20Roots%20Up&st=cse.
116 See "Even With Campaign Finance Law, Money Talks Louder Than Ever,"
http://query.nytimes.com/gst/fullpage.html? res=9C01EFDC133CF93BA35752C1A9629C8B63
117 See
http://www.politico.com/news/stories/1108/15564.html, accessed 7-9-09.
118 See
http://www.fec.gov/DisclosureSearch/mapApp.do?cand_id= P80003338,
accessed 2-20-09.
119 See
http://www.cfinst.org/pr/prRelease.aspx?ReleaseID=216, accessed 7-9-09.
120 *The Audacity of Hope*, page 130 ff, esp. pages 136-138.
121 Ibid, page 131.
122 See
http://www.nytimes.com/2008/07/10/washington/10fisa.html
123 See **http://www.greenchange.org/article.php?id=2897**re: FISA, and his vote for corporate immunity. RE: his policy to preserve insurance company dominance over the single payer alternate, vote tallies in favor of single payer have been removed from MyBarack.com and Change.gov, as of 2-14-09, but see
http://www.barackobama.com/factcheck/2008/01/05/ fact_check_obama_consistent_in.php (Obama never promised a single payer system).
124 See
http://www3.signonsandiego.com/stories/2009/jan/27/175470 84957- analysis-obama-and-technology/?zIndex=43703 .
125 See
http://www.cfinst.org/pr/prRelease.aspx?ReleaseID=216, accessed 7-9-09.

126 See
http://thecaucus.blogs.nytimes.com/2009/01/13/obama-to-selectgenachowski- to-lead-fcc/;
http://www.opensecrets.org/news/2009/05/big-donors-bundlers-amongobam.html; and,
http://news.muckety.com/2009/07/10/more-obama-bundlers-named-toambassador-jobs/17881 .
127 *The Audacity of Hope*, id., page 136f.
128 This was a nine-month, $3.5 million investigation on presidential campaign fund raising in 1996.
http://www.nytimes.com/1998/03/06/us/campaign-inquiry-stays-partisan-to-theend.html?scp=4&sq=Thompson+Committee+Report&st=nyt and **http://www.senate.gov/artandhistory/history/resources/pdf/Investigations.pdf**.
129 **http://www.census.gov/Press-Release/www/releases/archives/education/004214.html**, accessed 8-7-09.
130 For a detailed list see:
http://www.thegreenpapers.com/P08/candidates.phtml, accessed 8-7-09.
131 Of course, under Article Two, Congress sets such dates by law as it sees fit. My dates are merely illustrative.
132 This list follows the discussion of Clinton Rossiter in *The American Presidency* (The Johns Hopkins University Press, 1987).
133 This is a very rigorous standard. It requires that at least 80% of the questions be answered correctly. An alternative standard would be to pass the top 20% of the people in each test taking group. In my view, the states should be free to experiment with their approaches to testing.
134 **http://www.youtube.com/watch?v=w8rg9c4pUrg**, accessed 8-7-09.
135 RE: gaffes in presidential debates, cf.
http://news.nationalgeographic.com/news/2004/10/1008_041008_presidential_debate.html,
http://www.drudge.com/news/121881/corps-engineers-chopping-down-thousands, and
http://www.allhatnocattle.net/reagan quotes.html, accessed 8-7-09.

136 **http://www.youtube.com/watch?v=0rXmuhWrlj4&feature=c hannel,** accessed 8-7-09.

137 **http://www.youtube.com/watch?v=EpGH02DtIws,** accessed 8-7-09.

138 In February 11, 2010 the Washington Post reported that "more than seven in 10 Americans [are] now saying she is unqualified" **http://www.washingtonpost.com/wp-dyn/content/article/2010/02/10/ AR2010021004708.html** Then reporting on a poll taken October 25-28, 2010, the Washington Post states, "67 percent of all registered voters ... see her as not qualified to hold the office" **http://voices.washingtonpost.com/behind-thenumbers/ 2010/10/most_still_doubt_palins_presid.html**

139 See, Benjamin R. Barber, *Strong Democracy: Participatory Politics for a New Age* (University of California Press, 2004), page 293, note 49, quoting A. H. M. Jones's *Athenian Democracy*.

140 See **http://factcheck.org** and **http://politifact.com**

141 This division of the states into four regions is consistent with the Constitutional intention that the states be the central unit in the presidential election process. Each state was to have its own Electoral College. The State Selection Debates simply democratize that original intention, making all the voters in the state its new Electoral College. The Regional Run Offs keep the focus on the states, as the organizing units. One result of this division might be that one region, for example the West, has a few percent less in population than, say, the North East. But this difference creates no unfairness under the principle of the Equal Protection of the Law. Our federal system necessarily tolerates some differences in the states, in part because the United States began with different size units. The first Electoral College had 3 members for the smallest states, and 12 for Virginia, with 10 for Massachusetts and Pennsylvania. That's a 25% difference between Rhode Island and Virginia! The tiny difference in population size between the West and the North East can be justified as a continuation of the original Great Compromise, upon which the US is grounded.

While the Constitution requires proportional equality among congressional districts, the focus there is on the individual voters, and not the state involvement in presidential elections.

142 In the years when the incumbent president has served two terms and is not eligible to take office again, under the 22nd Amendment, the nominating debates will be between the vice president and one challenger. That challenger will be determined by holding two one-hour debates between the two winners of the Regional Run-Offs, one hour on domestic issues, the other on foreign affairs. These debates can be held on one Tuesday evening in the first week of October. If neither president nor vice president will be available for office, the two Regional Run-Off winners will face off in the December Presidential Election Debates.

143 That intention was *not* rejected, but merely by-passed, by the 12th Amendment requirement of separate lists of votes for president and vice president. The original intention that the Electors be the ones who choose both presidential and vice presidential prospects was clearly affirmed by the 12th Amendment.

144 These parts of the Constitution establish the Electoral College; hence, this new Amendment would abolish the Electoral College. The last sentence of the Twelfth Amendment, "But no person constitutionally ineligible to the office of President shall be eligible to that of Vice-President of the United States," would be covered by the first clause of the second sentence in the new Amendment.

145 *The Federalist Papers*. Mentor Books, New York. 1961 Introduction by Clinton Rossiter. No. 37, at page 231.

146 Ibid, No. 37, page 231.

147 Ibid, No. 15, page 110.

148 Ibid, No. 49, page 317.

149 "SERVE," is the acronym for the Secure Electronic Registration and Voting Experiment.

150 David Wagner stated in an interview just after the SERVE expose came out, "We were hired to evaluate the Serve Internet voting system, and to recommend repairs we thought were needed to make the system secure …" "Security experts nix Internet voting plan," by R. Colin Johnson. EE Times. January 23, 2004
http://www.eetimes.com/story/OEG20040123S0036.

151 "Four members of a team looking into the Internet voting idea became so alarmed at the prospect that they jumped the

scheduling gun and issued an early report of their own."
"Paperless E-voting Is a Threat," by Dan Gillmor. Computer World. February 9, 2004
http://www.computerworld.com/s/article/89910/Paperless_E _voting_Is_a_Threat.

152 The biological explanation for the claim that the reasonable person standard is a natural standard for humans to use to assess human behavior is given in my essay, "Respect and Empathy as Method in the Social Science Writings of Michael Polanyi." 35 Tradition & Discovery 8, 2008; and at,

http://www.missouriwestern.edu/orgs/polanyi/TAD%20WE B%20ARCHIVE/TAD35-1/TAD35-1-fnl-pg8-32-pdf.pdf, and cf. **http://ssrn.com/author=1053589**

Also see my book, *Progressive Logic*.

153 *Point, Click, and Vote: The Future of Internet Voting.* Thad Hall and R. Michael Alvarez Brookings Institute, Washington, D.C. 2004.

154 Ibid, pages 26-27.

155 Ibid, page 137.

156 Ibid, page 10.

157 Ibid, page 138.

158 See The Case for Internet Voting, by Joe Mohen and Julia Glidden, in Communications of the ACM, Volume 44 Issue 1, Jan. 2001 **http://portal.acm.org/citation.cfm?id=357511**.

159 RE: VOI, ibid, page 138; and as to SERVE, pages 146, 166.

160 Ibid, pages 136, 166.

161 Ibid, page 16. But see note 1 therein, regarding Roy Altman's prescient 1988 essay.

162 Ibid, page 17.

163 Ibid, page 18.

164
http://en.wikipedia.org/wiki/Bill_Jones_(California_politicia n)

165 Hall and Alvarez, ibid, pages 18-19.

166 See Hall and Alvarez, ibid, pages 99-100, for quotes from the report.

167 Ibid, page 19 passim.

168 Ibid, page 21 and 100. The authors emphasize that the report does not discourage Internet voting, but cautions that its implementation proceed with due care.

169 http://govinfo.library.unt.edu/npr/whoweare/historyofnpr.ht
ml

170 Hall and Alvarez, id., pages 22-23, passim.

171 Ibid, page 27.

172 Ibid, page 146.

173 Ibid, page 27.

174 Hall and Alvarez list the participants for the California group
at their note 6, page 175; and, those in the IPI group, at note 11,
page 175.

175 Ibid, page 24.

176 Ibid, page 24.

177 Ibid, page 24.

178 Ibid, page 25.

179 Ibid, page 25.

180 Ibid, page 25.

181 Ibid, page 24-25.

182 Ibid, page 26-30.

183 Ibid, page 26.

184 Ibid, page 92.

185 Ibid, page 10, 11.

186 *The Federalist Papers*, id., No. 52, at page 327.

187 Hall and Alvarez, id., page 92 passim.

188 Ibid, page 155.

189 Ibid, page 10.

190 Ibid, page 25.

191 Ibid, page 90.

192 Ibid, page 111.

193 Ibid, page 93, and the discussion in Chapter Five and its
notes.

194 Ibid, page 25.

195 Ibid, page 145, cf. 27-28.

196 Ibid, pages 146 and 166.

197 Ibid, page 145.

198 "Since 2000, Estonia has conducted two national elections in
which all voters could use Internet voting." Hall and Alvarez,
"Internet Voting in Comparative Perspective: The Case of
Estonia," at
http://www.vote.caltech.edu/drupal/http:/%252Fjournals.ca
mbridge.org/

download.php%3Ffile%3D/PSC/PSC42_03/S1049096509090
787a.pdf
%2526code%3Da7d6c94a510f95608eb4aa14d4bda045.

199 http://www.cwhonors.org/about/

200 http://www.cwhonors.org/search/his_4a_detail.asp?id=5121

201 http://www.cwhonors.org/search/his_4a.asp?
search=&cat=i&year=2005&Submit2=Search&offset=0

202 "Michigan's Online Ballot Spurs New Strategies for
Democrats," by Katharine Q. Seelye. New York Times. January
10, 2004. http://www.nytimes.com/
2004/01/10/politics/campaigns/10MICH.html

203 Ibid.

204 Ibid.

205 http://www.ivta.org/,accessed 10-17-09.

206 http://www.eac.gov/

207 *Secure Electronic Voting*, Dimitris Gritzalis, ed. (Boston,
Kulwer 2003), [n 42, p186], esp. see Chapter 11, by Ed Gerck.

208 "The SAVE System: Secure Architecture for Voting
Electronically," by Ted Selker and Jonathan Goler. January 4,
2004 http://vote.caltech.edu/drupal/files/
working_paper/vtp_wp12.pdf

209 Ibid, emphasis added.

210 Ibid.

211 Hall and Alvarez, *Point, Click, and Vote*, id., page 15.

212 Ibid, page 66.

213 Ibid, page 67.

214 Ibid, page 168.

215 Ibid, page 15.

216 Ibid, page 153, 165.

217 Ibid, page 170.

218 http://www.historyonthenet.com/Titanic/unsinkable.htm

219 http://www.cookreport.com/

220 See "Voting Editorial," by Gordon Cook. ND 2004
http://www.cookreport.com/votingeditorial.shtml . Also
archived at:
http://www.webcitation.org/query?url=http%3A%2F%2Fw
ww.cookreport.com%2Fvotingeditorial.shtml&date=2009-
12-11. All the quotes in this section are from this article.

221 Ibid, Cook.

William J. Kelleher, Ph.D.

222 *Brave New Ballot.* Avi Rubin. Morgan Road Books, NY. 2006.

223 **http://www.youtube.com/watch?v=1aBaX9GPSaQ&eurl=htt p%3A%2F %2Ftechnorati%2Ecom%2Fvideos%2Fyoutube%2Ecom% 252Fwatch%253Fv %253D1aBaX9GPSaQ&feature=player_embedded**

224 Rubin, id., page 41.

225 Ibid, page 28.

226 Ibid, page 28.

227 "Electronic voting machines that do not produce a paper record of every vote cast cannot be trusted." The Times urged passage of the Holt bill, which would require a paper record in all federal elections. The bill "would help prod election officials toward the best of the currently available technologies: optical-scan voting. … By 2014, machines that produce paper trails would have to be replaced by ones in which voters directly record their votes on paper — the best system of all." "How to Trust Electronic Voting." New York Times. June 21, 2009 **http://www.nytimes.com/2009/06/22/opinion/22mon2.html**.

228 "… the Times Company has equity interests in two other Canadian newsprint mills [besides Spruce Falls, which it is selling] as well as a partnership interest in Madison Paper Industries in Maine …" "Kimberly and Times Co. Selling Paper Mill," by Leslie Wayne. New York Times. June 30, 1990 **http://www.nytimes.com/1990/06/30/business/kimberly-and-times-co-sellingpaper-mill.html**

229 Rubin, id., page 40.

230 Ibid, page 45.

231 Ibid, page 45.

232 Ibid, page 45.

233 Ibid, page 30.

234 Ibid, page 41.

235 Ibid, page 41.

236 Ibid, page 41.

237 Ibid, page 107.

238 Ibid, page 234.

239 Ibid, page 104.

346

240 Ibid, page 46.

241 Ibid, page 115, cf. 113.

242 Ibid, page 159.

243 Ibid, page 160.

244 See ibid, 146-160, esp.149; and, judge could not understand issues, at 148-149.

245 Ibid, page 267; lawyers do not seek truth, at 157-158.

246 Ibid, page 246.

247 See "Paperless Electronic Election Upheld by German Supreme Court," by William J. Kelleher, Ph.D. Op Ed News. September 7, 2009
http://www.opednews.com/articles/1/PAPERLESS-ELECTRONIC-ELECT-by-William-J-Kellehe-090907-39.html

248 Rubin, id., page 162.

249 Ibid, page 165.

250 Ibid, page 164.

251 .See note 6, above.

252 Rubin, id., page 158; "research scientist" at 80.

253 Ibid, page 169.

254 Ibid, page 165.

255 Ibid, page 165.

256 Ibid, page 166.

257 Ibid, page 166.

258 Ibid, page 167.

259 But neither can banks prevent people from spending their money foolishly. That is not the responsibility of the banks, but of its customers. Of course, as discussed in Chapter One, except for the DOS attack, none of the above was the responsibility of SERVE, but of the users of the PCs.

260 Rubin, id., page 170.

261 Ibid, page 170.

262 Ibid, page 171.

263 Ibid, page 170.

264 Ibid, page 171.

265 Ibid, page 171.

266 "Security Experts Urge U.S. to Abandon Internet Voting Plan." January 21, 2004
http://www.jhu.edu/news_info/news/home04/jan04/vote.html
and archived at

http://www.webcitation.org/5mJxcPVeF.
267 Rubin, id., page 171.
268 "Pentagon's Online Voting Program Deemed Too Risky," by
Dan Keating. Washington Post. January 22, 2004
http://www.washingtonpost.com/ac2/wp-dyn/
A36875-2004Jan21
269. Suspending all critical judgment, and disregarding the other
six experts and the entire SERVE team, as well as the
community of experts in the country, the Times shamelessly
parroted Rubin's report: "The report makes it clear that the
possibilities for compromising the secrecy of the ballot, voting
multiple times and carrying out vote theft on a large scale would
be limited only by the imagination and skill of would-be
saboteurs. Viruses could be written that would lodge on
voters' computers and change their votes. Internet service
providers, or even foreign governments that control network
access, could interfere with votes before they reached their
destination.... a single hacker, working alone, might be
able to use an online voting system to steal a presidential
election. The authors of this week's report concede that there is
no way of knowing how likely it is that the Pentagon's voting
system would be compromised. What is clear, however, is that
until the vulnerabilities they identified are eliminated, the risks
are too great." "The Perils of Online Voting." New York Times.
January 23, 2004
http://www.nytimes.com/2004/01/23/opinion/23FRI1.html.
270. "Who Hacked the Voting System? The Teacher," by John
Schwartz. New York Times. May 3, 2004
http://www.nytimes.com/2004/05/03/technology/03vote.html
271 http://accurate-voting.org. Also see Dill on the Accurate-
Verified Voting Nexus, at
http://verify.stanford.edu/dill/accurate-essay.html. To see
how closely these opponents follow state and federal activities
related to Internet voting, see
http://www.verifiedvoting.org.
272 Hall and Alvarez, id., page 170.
273 As late as September of 2008, the New York Times published
an editorial condemning the efforts of election officials in
Okaloosa, Florida to reinstate a modified version of the SERVE

system for their UOCAVA voters. Never missing an opportunity to prop up the paper based culture, upon which their business depends, the Times writes, "The words 'Florida' and 'Internet voting,' taken together, should send a chill down everyone's spine. ... Internet voting is fraught with problems, including the possibility that a hacker could break in and alter the results."

Upon what evidence does the Times base its claim for this alleged "possibility"?

Here is their answer:

"In 2004, a group of academics reviewed an Internet voting system that the Pentagon was considering. The system was scrapped after the group identified numerous security flaws. There was a very real possibility, the professors warned, that the system could be used to steal votes." The Times disingenuously omits the fact that only four out of ten members of "the group" criticized SERVE.

Then comes the old "slippery slope" fear producer, as the distinguished New York Times takes a trick from Rubin's PR trick bag:

"The issue here goes beyond a single county. If the Okaloosa experiment goes forward, other counties around the country may decide to implement their own programs, with just as little public scrutiny and debate."

To ease the trepidation of the New York Times Editorial Board (and to preserve the market for paper) "Florida's secretary of state should deny Oskaloosa's request, and Congress should ban Internet voting in federal elections until a reliable and fully tested system is developed."

Of course, "a reliable and fully tested system" will never be developed if every trial is shot down before it is tried, as the Times would have it.

"A Bad Experiment in Voting." New York Times. September 5, 2008

http://www.nytimes.com/2008/09/05/opinion/05fri2.html

Continuing to feel threatened by electronic technology, the New York Times started out the 2010 New Year with a blast at any states which may be considering the use of Internet voting to empower overseas voters. "Internet voting is in its infancy, and still far too unreliable ..."

"Internet Voting, Still in Beta." Editorial. New York Times.
January 28, 2010
274 "Voting has ended in what is being touted as America's first
all-digital election, and city officials say it has been a success."
"Honolulu holds historic Internet vote." May 23, 2009
http://www.usatoday.com/news/politics/2009-05-23-Internet-election_N.htm
275 "New York City will conduct what election officials are
billing as the first exclusively online public election in the
United States. … The city's Department of Education is
conducting an experiment in participatory democracy. Nearly a
million public school parents will be able to cast advisory votes
for members of their community education councils. … The
parents can vote on a secure Web site from home, from schools,
from libraries — any place with Internet access…" "Parent
Voting for School Councils Is Moving Online," by Sam Roberts.
New York Times. March 15, 2009
**http://www.nytimes.com/2009/03/15/nyregion/15voting.html?
scp=3&sq=new
%20york%20city%20school%20board%20elections&st=cse**
    My search of the Net one year later turned up no reports of the
Omniscient Hacker taking over the vote, nor were any other
problems with the process reported.
276 "Election '08: Vote by TiVo," by Keith Axline. Wired.
October14, 2006
**http://www.wired.com/science/discoveries/news/2006/11/7211
3?currentPage=1**
277 See Shamos's resume at,
**http://euro.ecom.cmu.edu/people/faculty/mshamos/
resshort.htm, and the paper cited below.**
278 "Paper v. Electronic Voting Records – An Assessment," by
Michael Ian Shamos
**http://vote.nist.gov/threats/papers/paper_v_electronic_recor
ds.pdf**
279 The Rubinites did not deny these numbers in their "rebuttal,"
at
**http://www.verifiedvoting.org/downloads/shamos-
rebuttal.pdf**
280 Rubin, id., page 156.
281 Ibid, page 156.

282 Ibid, page 42, italics in original.
283 "Pentagon Drops Web Voting Plans for Military Personnel," by Todd R. Weiss. Computer World. February 9, 2004
http://www.computerworld.com/s/article/89950/ Pentagon_Drops_Web_Voting_Plans_for_Military_Personn el
284 See Shamos, "Paper v. Electronic Voting Records," id.
285 Rubin, id., page 57.
286 Ibid, page 143.
287 Ibid, page 142.
288 Ibid, page 113-114.
289 Ibid, page 25.
290 Ibid, page 25.
291 Ibid, page 25.
292 Ibid, page 26.
293 Ibid, page 26.
294 Ibid, page 52.
295 Ibid, page 52.
296 Ibid, page 52.
297 Ibid, page 52.
298 Ibid, page 46.
299 Ibid, page 266.
300 "Online Voting Plan Draws Concern," by Joris Evers. PC World. January 21, 2004.
http://www.pcworld.com/article/114398/online_voting_plan_ draws_concern.html
301 "Risky E-Vote System to Expand," by Kim Zetter. Wired. January 26, 2004
http://www.wired.com/politics/security/news/2004/01/62041
302 "An Interview with David Wagner," by Kirsten Anderson. Huffington Post. September 12, 2007.
http://www.huffingtonpost.com/kirsten-anderson/an-interview-with-davidw_b_64063.html
303 "Pentagon Drops Web Voting Plans for Military Personnel," by Todd R. Weiss. Computer World. February 9, 2004.
http://www.computerworld.com/s/article/89950/ Pentagon_Drops_Web_Voting_Plans_for_Military_Personn el [Brackets in the original article.]

304 "Kristol: Kill It, and Start Over," by William Kristol. Weekly Standard. July 20, 2009 **http://www.weeklystandard.com/weblogs/TWSFP/2009/07/ kristol_kill_it_and_start_over.asp;** "Obama rips GOP in health care forum." CNN. July 23, 2009 **http://www.cnn.com/2009/POLITICS/07/23/obama.health.ca re/index.html;** and, "Fighting Health Care Overhaul, and Proud of It," by Katharine Q. Seelye. New York Times. August 30, 2009 **http://www.nytimes.com/2009/08/31/us/politics/31demint.ht ml**

305. **http://www.politifact.com/truth-o- meter/promises/obameter/promise/73/allowmedicare- to-negotiate-for-cheaper-drug-price/;** President Obama on You Tube, February 4, 2011, "We still don't do that …" **http://pharmacycheckerblog.com/obama-interview-shows- americans-highlyconcerned- about-drug-prices-drug-importation-mentioned-as-potential- solution**

306. See Note 162, supra.

307. See **http://www.patentstorm.us/** Patent Storm is a free service offering full-text U.S. patents and patent applications from the U.S. Patent Office. My search for "Internet voting" yielded over 6000 items, including hundreds of new patents directly related to improved processes and security technology for voter registration and voting.

308. Assuming there were about 17,500,000 registered voters in that election year, this is 1%. The same number could be used for US Senate contests. Of course, other formulas can be applied, and the required number of signatures can be adjusted for districts. Each state, of course, can write its own laws for signature requirements.

309. Unfortunately, the proposition does not specify that those who qualify to have their names placed on the primary ballot are free to declare any party affiliation, or no party affiliation, as they please. The old law requiring that the affiliation stated on the ballot be the same as the one used by the candidate at the time of voter registration is still in effect. Some states have nonpartisan voter registration, and that is what California should do to further purify itself from the pollution of partisanship.

310. This goes back to the question I raised as to whether primary election ballots ought to be wholly nonpartisan, and state no party labels. An argument against this is that party labels give voters important information about the policies of the candidates. On the other hand, this information is so minimal that the usefulness of a label can be doubted. In my view, having no labels is better. Labels can fool the voter into thinking that he or she has information about the candidate's policies. But in fact the label only misleads people into making assumptions, which may not be true. Online research is so easy that voters are better served by a ballot that requires them to dig for information, rather than have it spoon fed to them.

311. California election law is in a transitionary period. Currently, the state is in the absurd position of holding its non-presidential primary election in June, and then having the general election in November. Thus, the top two candidates must wait 5 long months until the decisive votes are cast. Since federal law requires that federal elections be held in November, California would better serve candidates and voters by moving its Prop 14 primary to late September, leaving the top two candidates just a few weeks in which to campaign.

312. RE: Meg Whitman see
http://www.reuters.com/article/idUSTRE6A25HX20101103
RE: Carly Fiorina see
http://articles.latimes.com/2010/dec/03/local/la-me-1203-senate-20101203
RE: Jeff Greene see
http://content.usatoday.com/communities/onpolitics/post/201 0/08/kendrick-meekwins-democratic-senate-primary-in-florida--/1
RE: Linda McMahon see
http://www.politicsdaily.com/2010/11/03/connecticut-senate-blumenthal-takesdown-onetime-wrestling-ceo/

313. The US has around 3000 elections jurisdictions. Each will make its own decisions as to if, when, and from which company it will buy its secure Internet voting servers. Some jurisdictions could have several servers. With all of these different locations, different companies, and different codes and procedures a denial of service attack (DoS) that could have any widespread effect would be technically impossible.

INDEX

G
Gentlemen 119
Golden Gloves Boxing Tournament 188
Goler, Jonathan 261
Google 70
Gordon Cook 264
Gravel, Mike 260
Great Compromise 115, 153

H
Hacking 21f
Hall, Thad 241
Hamilton, Alexander 97, 102, 112, 124, 235
Hanna, Mark 158
HAVA 17, 274
Hawaii 7
Holt, Rush 282
Hostile environment 21

I
Internet Policy Institute study 244
Internet voting 7 passim, growth state by state 325, favors moderation 326
Internet Voting Technology Alliance" (IVTA) 260
Iowa 152, 154

J
Jackson, Andrew 147, 155, 192
Jay, John 97, 112, 116, 121
Jefferson, David 248, 281, 296
Jefferson, Thomas 36, 96, 108
Jones, Bill 245
Justice Jackson 144

R

RABA Technologies 293
Ray v. Blair 144
Reason 94, 101, 122
Reason v. Emotion in the Internet Voting Debate 236
Reasonable Person Standard 237, 239
Regional Run-Offs 213, four regions 214
Representative government 99
Republic 99
Republican Party 148
Restart SERVE 306
Rove, Karl 179, Bush's brain 178
Rubin, Avi 248, 270, peer review 293
Russia 8, 79

S

Scary stuff 50
screening the candidates 196
Security, degrees of 15, e-commerce grade 57
Self-government 128
Self-government through Reason 235
Selker, Ted 261
SERVE 35, 45, audits 47, itself secure 54, 236
Shamos, Michael 284, paper-based voting systems 286
Omniscient Hacker 289
Shay's Rebellion 125
Simons, Barbara 248, on Iran 296
Simpson, Homer 66, 271
Soft money 161
South Carolina 41
Spoofing 68, 77
SPRIG 49, 277
Spyware 59
State Selection Debates 206
SUGGESTED AMENDMENT 232

W
W3C 32
Wagner, David 249, 296
Washington DC 8, 39
Washington state 8, 74
Washington, George 104
West Virginia 7, 91
Wilson, James 126
Wilson, Pete 245
Wolfowitz, Paul 50, 84, 236
Wright, Capt. 44

Y
You will not be Alone 310
Youth 140, and draft 129

ABOUT THE AUTHOR

Dr. Kelleher was born in Chicago, in 1946. He earned a Ph.D. in political science at the University of California, Santa Barbara, in 1984. His BA and MA were earned at San Francisco State University. He has taught such subjects as American Politics and Citizenship in the Los Angeles area for over 20 years.

His first book, *The New Election Game*, was published in 1987. Inspired by R. Buckminster Fuller's idea of voting by telephone, Dr. Kelleher showed how US elections could be organized around telephone voting. Of course, this was before the "PC Revolution." The organization suggested in *The New Election Game* has been adapted to facilitate the new technology.

Dr. Kelleher's second book, *Progressive Logic*, shows how the political reforms advocated by Progressives throughout American history are expressions of "the natural order of values." This order of values is a part of human evolution. Largely because the human brain evolved in community, all normal humans have a natural sense of caring about their own kind. While humans naturally value human life as precious, social conditioning can override this natural tendency. However, if the natural order of values is articulated as a set of principles, which this work does, self-destructive social conditioning can be reversed through education.

www.ingramcontent.com/pod-product-compliance
Lightning Source LLC
Chambersburg PA
CBHW071402050326
40689CB00010B/1722